BY AGNES CARR VAUGHAN

Zenobia of Palmyra

Those Mysterious Etruscans

Bury Me in Ravenna

The House of the Double Axe

The Genesis of Human Offspring

Akka, Dwarf of Syracuse

Within the Walls

Evenings in a Greek Bazaar

Lucian Goes A-Voyaging

Madness in Greek Thought and Custom

ZENOBIA OF PALMYRA

ZENOBIA
OF PALMYRA

AGNES CARR VAUGHAN

PROFESSOR EMERITUS OF CLASSICAL LANGUAGES
AND LITERATURES, SMITH COLLEGE

ILLUSTRATED WITH PHOTOGRAPHS

DOUBLEDAY & COMPANY, INC.
GARDEN CITY, NEW YORK
1967

TO

My Good Friend

CLARA W. CRANE

With Thanks and Appreciation

Contents

ix

Illustrations

Foreword

Zenobia, the remarkable Queen of ancient Palmyra, who lived in the third century of our era, has been the subject of modern romance, of Arabic drama, and of at least one learned monograph. So far as I know, however, no attempt has been made to present Zenobia to the public in her rightful character, that of an individual determined to free her country from spreading imperialism.

Zenobia's chief opponent in this historic struggle, which involved Europe and the Near East, was Aurelian, the Emperor of Rome. Some of the significance of the conflict lies in the fact that a woman has pitted herself against a man at a period in the world's history when women were not highly regarded. Zenobia does not come off with flying colors, for history has given her one black mark, which, though in my opinion unjustified, still remains written beside her name.

We know much about Aurelian, little about Zenobia. And so, since there are in the evidence many gaps and controversies, I have used my imagination liberally where facts have failed (as they do fail often for Zenobia, though far less often for Aurelian). My use of my imagination to fill the gaps in historical sources is, I am convinced, justified. The historian Gibbon would approve, I believe, for he holds that, in the same set of circumstances, most of us, whether ancients or moderns, would react in much the same way.

In my search for circumstances, for the factual material for this book, I have received help from many people. The Board of Trustees of Smith College awarded me a Sophia Smith fellowship for two years. The American School of Classical Studies at Athens, the American School of Oriental Research in Jerusalem, the French Institute in Beirut, and the American Academy in Rome have greatly assisted me. The individuals to whom I am grateful are almost too numerous to mention. Among those connected with the School in Athens are Dr. Virginia Grace; Director and Mrs. Robinson; Professors Stillwell, Thompson, and Vanderpool; Mrs. Philippides; Dr. and Mrs. Frank Walton, and Miss Eurydike Demetriakopoulou of the Gennadeion; and La Signora Longobardi, the librarian of the Academy in Rome, who supplied me with a much-needed topographical map and an invaluable pamphlet.

In Jerusalem, Professor Dahlberg of Smith College made room for me to go with him and his family to Petra in his already crowded station wagon; Professor Campbell and Monsignor Skehan advised me about photographs; Mr. Edmond Christo of the Semiramis Hotel in Damascus managed my trip to Palmyra; Mrs. Sophia Sassy steered me through the Damascus Museum and arranged my appointment with Mr. Adnam Bounni, the busy director of the Museum, who gave me a full two hours of his valuable time and has since sent me photographs.

My thanks would not be complete without mentioning my typists, Barbara E. Doten and Katheryn M. Baker, for their patience and excellent work, Mr. Howard Rickert, the librarian of the George Bruce Branch of the New York Public Library for his continued interest in my writings, and the helpful librarians of the Union Theological Seminary.

Finally, I wish to thank Mr. Jack Bernard of Doubleday and Company for his help in disentangling a knotty problem, and my Editor, Mrs. Isabelle Taylor, who can always be relied upon to detect and suggest a remedy for the slightest flaw.

New York City
January 1966

BOOK ONE

ZENOBIA AND ODENATH

"Where through the sand
of morning-land
The camel bears the spice."
ANONYMOUS

I

Tadmor in the Wilderness

Thousands of years ago, in an arid waste south of the great Asiatic river Euphrates, there appeared through the sand one day a trickle of water. Time passed; the trickle became a flow; more water bubbled up, merged with the trickle, and spread out into a pool. Seeds drifted through the warm desert air and were wafted earthward. Nourished by the life-giving waters, the seeds grew into stately palm trees, to provide shade for a green oasis in the Syrian wilderness.

Creatures came to the oasis, winged, four-footed, and human, to escape the burning desert sun and to cool their parched throats in the bubbling springs. Nomads, driving their herds through the desert, feared at first the strange odor of the water. And what they drank, when they risked drinking it, left a strange taste in the mouth. Obviously a god dwelt below; if not propitiated, he might work evil.

It may easily have come about that one day a group of nomads built a small temple near the welling pool and invited the god to cherish it. Soon some of them forsook their wandering life and built shelters for themselves near the god's house. Millennia may have passed before the god acquired a name, but the place where the palm trees grew became known in Arabic tradition as Thadamora, a village of mud-walled huts in the Syrian Desert, where the Sun-god rises early and floods the land with his warmth. In this

3

region, about the seventh millennium B.C., or even earlier, many social anthropologists believe an important event occurred, the first deliberate human planting of seeds in the history of the world. From this achievement the Aramaic Thadamora that Biblical tradition calls Tadmor in the Wilderness must ultimately have profited.

For soon the desert peoples learned that seeds, planted, watered, and tended, would produce other seeds. These, ground between stones, mixed with water, and baked in ash, would sustain a man. Shortly afterward, as history counts time, another forward step was taken. Tadmor, the oasis, which lay in almost the center of the desert, grew into a watering-place for caravans of men and camels and donkeys. Wealth came, and cupidity, and together they brought into collision two human beings, a man and a woman, whose lives became so tangled that disaster followed. For these were no common mortals: one was Aurelian, the Emperor of Rome; the other, his arch enemy, the fabulously beautiful Zenobia, Queen of Palmyra, as Tadmor came to be known. Their century, the third of our own era, is noted for having been one of the most troubled, and most troublesome, in history. And from Aurelian's point of view, Zenobia was largely to blame. He was determined to remove her.

Long before these two were born, caravans were coming to Tadmor all the way from India and the Far East. Their road lay along the Persian Gulf, through southern Persia, and then across some six hundred miles of arid desert to the banks of the Euphrates; and they paused only where an oasis offered water and brief shelter. Many of them, both men and beasts, unable to endure the parching sun, left their bones to dry in the hot sand. Those who reached Tadmor in their westward journey found palm trees, with small round dates so bright that when the sunlight fell on them, they seemed gilded.

The dates, if ripe, they plucked and ate. But most would have refused to taste the strange water until thirst drove them. Doubtless, in those early days, they did not know that the taste they feared in the water was due to the sulphur which encouraged the palm trees to grow and produce the fruit they ate without fear.

4

Historically, ancient Syria and its desert comprised modern Syria, most of Israel and Jordan, and parts of northern Arabia. Mesopotamia, as a scholar who knew his Greek called the region between the Tigris and the Euphrates (for it means literally between rivers), is included in modern Iraq. And some believe that in the southern part of Mesopotamia, rather than in Egypt, the cradle of civilization lay. Here in the Tigris-Euphrates valley two peoples came early into contact, the mysterious Sumerians and the Aramaeans, who spoke a kindred Semitic tongue and who may have come from Syria.

We know little about the Sumerians. We know that ancient Nippur in the Tigris-Euphrates valley was the chief seat of their cult. We know that their language was distantly related to the Semitic tongues. And some scholars think that Sumer is the Biblical Eden. But we do not know when these Semitic-speaking peoples first came into contact with each other. Nor do we know which of them came to the green, palm-shaded oasis south of the Euphrates and gave to the oasis that first name, Thadamora.

The name Thadamora long persisted on Arab tongues, and is still found in some remote districts. The history of these early days in Syria is hard to follow, since over the years the name Thadamora, or Tadmor, as some said, became confused in tradition with that of another place called Tamar. No one knows when Tadmor actually became a settlement, but we do know that the first mention of the oasis appears on an Assyrian tablet of the second millennium B.C. The tablet, which comes from Cappadocia, is a contract signed by two witnesses, one of them from Tadmor. A century later, the name Tadmor occurs on an Akkadian tablet from a small place on the Euphrates. Apparently the men of Tadmor were not confined to their oasis, but were becoming known elsewhere.

The first half of this second millennium B.C. brought significant advances in the civilization of the whole region. Under Hammurabi, the wise ruler of Babylon, southern Mesopotamia became progressive, cosmopolitan, and sophisticated. In religion, it is true, polytheism and worship of the powers of nature still prevailed. But

5

in many fields great advances were made, especially in linguistics, mathematics, and the study of history.

In these advances Tadmor must have shared, for by 1100 B.C. she had become strong enough to attract the attention of the Assyrian king, Tiglath-Pilezer I. He formed a camel corps and went to northern Syria to attack the Aramaeans. Tadmor was one of their settlements, but whether Tiglath-Pilezer demolished the oasis city, as he did others, we do not know. The language he would have found spoken in Tadmor was Aramaic. Though Arabic later superseded it in common speech, Aramaic continued to be used in formal writing, even in Zenobia's day.

The name, Tadmor in the Wilderness, occurs once in the second book of the Chronicles and again, in the same wording, in the First Book of the Kings: "And Solomon built Tadmor in the Wilderness." (Recent excavations near the spring Efca show that a temple once stood there.)

We know that the city existed at the time of Tiglath-Pilezer. Therefore Solomon, who lived a century or so later, could not have "built Tadmor." The Biblical account is often taken to mean that Solomon may have rebuilt a primitive temple of some sort that had been erected to the nameless god of the strangely smelling waters. Solomon was a passionate follower of Yahweh, who would have "no other gods" before him, and he might well have rebuilt the temple and dedicated it to his own deity. Such forced transfers of allegiance often occurred in the ancient world.

Many scholars prefer another interpretation, that Solomon had nothing to do with Tadmor, but that he built Tamar. Whether Solomon built Tadmor or not, he must have heard that the oasis settlement, because of its strategic situation in the desert, one hundred and twenty-five miles from both the Euphrates and the eastern Mediterranean, had become the favorite stopping-place for the caravan trade.

Tadmor's Aramaean people could not have established themselves without a struggle, even if the city went unscathed by

Tiglath-Pilezer and untouched by Solomon. The caravan trade was too important. Damascus and Antioch both wanted a share in the prosperity the trade brought to the Tigris-Euphrates valley.

Damascus, which enjoys the reputation of being the oldest city in the world that has been continuously inhabited, was also an oasis. Her people are said to have owed their prosperity to their early discovery of the famed Ship of the Desert, the single-humped camel. This amazing creature could march three or even four days' journey without water. The discovery transformed desert travel and helped to speed up the growing civilizations of the whole region. Damascus was not slow to take advantage of her discovery. She filled her camels with water, mounted raiding-parties on them, and sent them out into the desert to loot the donkey-riders and bring home their loads.

When Tiglath-Pilezer attacked the Syrian cities, Damascus escaped capture and pillage, as possibly Tadmor did; she seems to have been so strong that the Assyrian king did not even attack her.

We hear little more of Damascus until the fourth century B.C., when Alexander the Great with his dream of brotherhood swept the whole East together and attempted to create a single political entity. Then, only two years before Alexander's death in 323 B.C., Damascus fell before his advance and Antioch took her place as the most significant city of Syria; and held it until her growing wealth aroused her neighbors' jealousy.

In Alexander's brief day of glory, the early oasis temple was not the only one in Palmyra. Other temples to other gods demanded their share of attention. To these temples, on feast-days, members of the desert caravans brought their gifts from faraway places. Local people brought what they had: barley, vegetables, olive oil, and the date wine the temple gods were not above enjoying in the company of their grateful worshippers. Clearly, Palmyra, in the time of Alexander, had become the center of a thriving agriculture.

After Alexander's death, two of his former generals divided Syria: Seleucus ruled the northern part; Ptolemy, the southern.

Since Palmyra and Damascus were in the north, this division gave Seleucus the caravan trade. Soon he assumed the royal title, and became in 305 B.C. the founder of the Seleucid Empire, with full control of Mesopotamia. During the following century Syria was torn by five successive wars, as various Eastern powers attempted to seize the camel routes.

Meanwhile, on the western coast of Italy, there had been growing up a city, known to the Etruscans as Ruma, but to other peoples of the Italian peninsula as Rome. When Alexander's widespread empire fell apart, Rome stepped in to pick up the scattered pieces, sort them out, and fit them together. In other parts of the world she repeated the process. Gradually there came into being the powerful Roman Empire.

According to the Roman writer, Pliny the Elder, when Rome became interested in putting together the pieces of Alexander's empire, Tadmor, which during the brief Greek occupation had been renamed Palmyra, tried to steer a middle course between the Romans and the vast new empire of the Parthians. The rivals were well-matched, and both were ambitious to control the world.

Since neither great power could make headway against the other, they found it expedient to declare Palmyra a neutral city where caravans might halt without fear of being molested by either Roman or Parthian raiders. In spite of this agreement, the Emperor Tiberius during the first century of our era succeeded in adding Palmyra to the Roman Empire. The Romans used the name, Palmyra, established during the Greek occupation, but the Syrians, tenacious of older custom, kept, as they still keep, the older name. Even today they talk with pride of the days when Thadamora, or Tadmor, was the rich and luxurious city of the Fertile Crescent and men called her the Bride of the Desert.

There in Tadmor now become Palmyra, lived, not in Solomon's time, but long afterward, the Emperor Aurelian's trouble-maker, Queen Zenobia, one of the most accomplished and perhaps one of the most maligned heroines of antiquity. Her Roman biographer,

8

Trebellius Pollio, wrote of her a century later that she "claimed to be of the family of the Cleopatras and the Ptolemies." And Pollio does not deny that, like Cleopatra, Septimia Zenobia—the name by which the Romans knew her—was ambitious.

We do not really know who Zenobia was. We know that she belongs to the Christian era, and that she lived in what historians call the "terrible third century of social disaster," but we do not know where or when she was born. History tells us that in her day the struggle between East and West, which began even before the Trojan War, was still vigorously alive. Whoever controlled the Bosphorus, today the Dardanelles, held the key to the riches of the East. That this was true, both Zenobia and Aurelian knew. But Zenobia, who was well-versed in history, must also have known that to possess the key, she would have to follow the example of Alexander and gain control of the Fertile Crescent with its wealthy caravan cities. And so, after her husband, King Odenath, was assassinated—some accuse her of complicity in this assassination—Zenobia entered the age-old struggle between the East and the West.

We know that Zenobia's native tongue was Aramaic (she used a dialect of Aramaic in her famous letter to Aurelian), but that she used Arabic or Greek in conversation. We know from inscriptions that her name was Bath-Zabbai, or Zabaina. That she was of Arabic descent is now taken for granted, but who her parents were, if they were not Nabataean Arabs, we do not know.

Palmyra seems to have regarded Zenobia as a *peregrina*, a foreigner. To a Roman of those days *peregrina* generally meant a person born in a district that was not his own, though perhaps only a few miles away. Pollio, who refers to Zenobia as a *peregrina*, may have intended his readers to understand merely that she was not a native of Palmyra. He ignores the rather obscure tradition that gives her a father in Palmyra whose name was Antiochus.

Some historians think it possible, even probable, that Zenobia's ancestors were indeed the freedom-loving Nabataean Arabs, who appeared in the Fertile Crescent in the seventh century B.C., drove

9

the Edomites out of their stronghold (Syria's rose-red Petra), and remained masters of the whole region for five hundred years.

Unfortunately we know nothing of Bath-Zabbai's early life. Romantic novelists have supplied us with details, interesting in themselves, but with little or nothing to support them. When she first appears in history, she is Septimia Zenobia, the second wife of Odenath, the King of Palmyra, and the mother of three sons, Vaballath, Herennianus, and Timolaus. Until recently, we have known little more.

A few years ago, however, Professor Seyrig of Princeton University advanced good reasons for regarding Zenobia as a third wife and the mother of three of Odenath's five sons. His eldest son, Herodian (assassinated with his father and so presumably his heir) was the child of his first wife. The second wife died, probably in childbirth with the second son—Professor Seyrig does not elaborate. The last three sons are Zenobia's.

Pollio tells us that after Odenath's death Zenobia "held the imperial power in the name of her sons, Herennianus and Timolaus, ruling longer than could be endured from one of the female sex." This statement of Pollio's is disputed, since no coins were struck, or at least none have been recorded, bearing the portrait and the name of either boy, and coins do exist for her surviving son, Vaballath, as the boy-king of Palmyra. Professor Seyrig thinks the two younger sons may have died in childhood.

After her husband's death, Zenobia's name was on every Roman lip; no one knew whether the whispered tales were true that she herself had caused her husband and her stepson to be assassinated and had then either proclaimed her son king and herself his regent or had seized the throne for herself. The whispers grew louder when Aurelian, who in 270 became the Emperor of Rome, finally marched against Palmyra, determined to oust "that woman" from the throne, though the act cost him his own. Rome supported Aurelian; but at first, throughout the Fertile Crescent of Arabia and far into the desert itself, the odds were not on Aurelian but on his opponent, Zenobia, the gallant Queen of Tadmor-Palmyra, who hoped to wrest the East free of Roman domination, unite the cities of the Fertile Crescent, seize the caravan trade, and hold it for her son, her Vaballath. Surely to Zenobia's ears no music could have been sweeter than the tinkle of a camel's bell.

II

The Fertile Crescent

The Fertile Crescent is that narrow strip of land which partially encloses the Tigris-Euphrates valley and the desert where Tadmor-Palmyra lies. Separated from the Mediterranean Sea by the Lebanese Mountains, this narrow strip, only fifteen to twenty miles wide, begins at a point parallel to the southeast corner of the Mediterranean, skirts the Lebanon and the foothills of the Taurus Range, and ends at the Persian Gulf near the site of ancient Ur. It has covered a distance of almost a thousand miles.

The importance of this semicircle that fringes the Arabian Desert, or to be more exact, its northern part, the Syrian Desert, can scarcely be over-estimated. For centuries it has caught and held the rainfall from the mountains behind. And in these same mountains are the sources of the life-giving waters of Syria's two great rivers, the Tigris and the Euphrates. Largely because of the water-supply, many scholars now regard this region of the world, rather than that of the Nile, as the cradle of civilization.

We should not be surprised, then, to hear that as far back in history as our knowledge goes, men have fought each other for possession of the Fertile Crescent. For, as in Egypt, when the Nile overflowed its banks and nourished the land, so in Syria when the twin rivers overflowed, the desert bloomed. But when the waters withdrew, men had to seek their food in the Fertile Crescent, or in the relatively few oases that had gradually sucked up enough water to sustain vegetation.

To this fertile region, anthropologists have traced the origin of a fertility-cult that in time spread westward and northward and exerted a powerful influence upon later religious beliefs. The chief deities who were the objects of early cult-practice here were a god and a goddess, to whom tradition later ascribed a son.

The fertility-god, known in the Aramaic tongue as Bel, but often identified with the Phoenician Baal, was also as might be expected in a desert country, a weather deity. He was believed to die with the vegetation; and only if invoked with the proper ritual would he reappear, bringing with him water from the skies or gushing from the earth. To the dwellers in Tadmor, the strange smell emanating from their pool would have been adequate proof that its water was of supernatural origin. Nor could the pool ever have lost its early reputation, for in Zenobia's day its guardian was an official of high standing.

Syrian art sometimes represents the cult-image of the god Baal with horns. One hand brandishes an axe or club, the other a curiously forked object that O. G. Crawford in his recent book, *The Eye Goddess,* thinks may be "lightning or the branch of a tree." Thrust into the god's belt is another weapon; it seems to be a dagger. He wears his hair long. Its curled ends escape from a tall conical cap. Hair and beard frame his face. His torso is bare, but the lower part of his body is clothed in a kind of kilt. He needs his weapons, because by the third century he had become a caravan-god.

The cult-image of the fertility-goddess has "staring eyes," and eyebrows that meet over the bridge of a somewhat flattened nose. She is usually pictured wearing a necklace to protect herself against evil. Primitive man, one must remember, made his deities in his own likeness and dressed them accordingly. Since he himself needed protection, he assumed that his deity did, too.

Staring eyes, owlish faces, and the so-called breast-knobs, so characteristic of fertility-deities, have appeared on pots of the third and second millennia throughout the Aegean world, and further west as well. Their appearance in such widely separated places, but not in the Nile region, has led Crawford to trace them to the Fertile Crescent, where life seemed to the early peoples there to depend upon the whim of fertility-gods.

As time passed, the goddess, who was variously named, was depicted as fully human. To her worshippers in Minoan Crete, she was the Snake Goddess, and Minoan artists represented her in the current dress of the period, with bared bosom and flounced skirt.

The ancient Eye Goddess has survived in the charm that an eastern taxi driver often suspends from his mirror. The charm our Syrian driver had was a blue crescent with a glass eye. Blue beads decorate some charms.

To the Fertile Crescent scholars have also traced the origin of a widespread belief that man's first home was in a garden, where the earth produced all he needed to support life bountifully. Tradition knows several such gardens. The Semites called theirs Eden. It lay somewhere to the north. From this garden two rivers sprang. They flowed through a desert or through an oasis, no one was quite sure which. The Babylonians knew of a place their ancestors had called the Garden of the Gods. They thought it lay somewhere to the east, perhaps near the Persian Gulf, perhaps beyond Babylon; and it also had two rivers.

The Semites always added that in their garden two trees grew. One was the "tree of the knowledge of good and evil"; the other was the "tree of life." Both had possessed a wonderful magic: they could endow with wisdom and with endless life any one who tasted their fruits. Two people lived in the garden, a man named Adam and a woman named Eve. Their god, Yahweh, had put them there to till the ground. One day the man tasted the fruit of the tree of knowledge, and straightway looked upon the woman with eyes of desire. For this, both were forced to leave their blissful garden, and a flaming sword barred their return.

It might well be that these tales of so-called gardens sprang from the activities of the Akkad kings of northern Babylonia who lived in the third millennium B.C. Before the Akkad kings came into power, the Tigris and the Euphrates had annually converted the desert into a rich and fertile plain where herds could graze and food could grow. But during the dry season the plain again became barren. The Akkad kings, by honey-combing the plain with a network of irrigation canals, transformed it into the most fertile country of the ancient world. Herodotus, the Greek historian who lived in the fifth century B.C., reports that the plain produced two hundred, occasionally three hundred, times as much grain as was grown anywhere else in the ancient world.

The legendary Garden of Eden and the Babylonian Garden of the Gods may, then, have been the region of the Near East that geographers and historians call the Fertile Crescent.

Christianity came early to the Fertile Crescent; and its teachings may have appealed to Zenobia. So far as we know, however, none of our early sources indicate that she ever became a convert. But if we can rely upon the statement of Bishop Terzi, whose date I have been unable to discover, Zenobia may in later years have embraced the new faith. In her youth the writings of a countryman of hers, the satirist, Lucian, who lived in nearby Samosata, may have had greater appeal for her. According to one story, dogs attacked and killed Lucian because he had scoffed at the old myths of Greece and at the claims of the new Christian religion that had begun to make rapid headway in Syria.

In one of his essays, Lucian writes that a certain Peregrinus, who was imprisoned for his faith, became a Cynic when he discovered that the founder of the new religion had been crucified. One day at Olympia, just after the Games of 165, Peregrinus burned himself to death, as modern Burmese monks have done, except that Peregrinus acted from disillusionment, not in support of a principle.

Lucian's writings were popular in the educated circles of Rome, and though no literary records have survived from Palmyra, his books are likely to have been read in the cultivated society of

Zenobia's day. If Zenobia herself had read him, his cynical yet witty attitude toward life might have kept her from taking seriously the ethical teaching of Christianity.

Toward the close of the second millennium, the Fertile Crescent and the plain of the Tigris-Euphrates valley changed hands. The Akkad kings, who had reclaimed the valley with their network of canals, lost their empire to the celebrated Hammurabi of Babylon. Soon this astute monarch had made Babylon the political and intellectual center, not only of the desert peoples, but of all western Asia.

Before Hammurabi's day, many caravan owners and travelers seem to have preferred long journeys through the waterless desert to the more risky travel by ship over unknown seas. Yet, though the swift riding-camel could cover great distances without water, he could not be used efficiently for carrying heavy loads. For this a slower camel had been used, and he needed water. The Akkad canals that Hammurabi now controlled made it possible to use the slower beast.

Travel across the desert soon increased to the point where the local sheiks could no longer attack the caravans and expect to rob them with impunity. And much of this orderly transition from a ruder day must be attributed to Hammurabi's success in regulating the political and commercial life of the period. Business conventions had already come into being; criminal and civil law had been systematized, and binding clauses introduced into contracts. These were written in Sumerian, said to have been the oldest legal language in the history of the ancient world.

Hammurabi's famous code of laws was also written in the Sumerian language. His method was to collect all the existing laws from every corner of his empire and arrange them systematically. Where necessary, he improved them. Finally he combined them into the first legal corpus known to history, and had them engraved on a stone column eight feet high.

Before 1901, when Susa, the ancient capital of Persia, was excavated, and the column found—it had been carried off by invaders—the modern world had known little of these early laws that had so strongly influenced later centuries. It is salutary, at the least, for those of us who think of our world as advanced and sophisticated to hear that the legal essence of codes and contracts, drawn up thousands of years ago in lands we are too apt to think of as backward, remained relatively unchanged until Roman law penetrated the Near East, and that it anticipated many of the provisions we consider as representing human liberalism today.

The inscribed stone column found at Susa contains the only fairly complete text of Hammurabi's laws. Some of its gaps, apparently caused by wanton defacement, can be filled in by fragments found at Nippur, Nineveh, and elsewhere, but the text as a whole is incomplete. Hammurabi himself, in bas-relief, heads the text inscribed on the stone column. His shaven upper lip proclaims him a man of the desert. He stands in a prayerful attitude before the throne of the seated Sun-god, who is about to give him the new laws. Probably the bas-relief was intended to remind the Semitic Babylonians of the Biblical legend that on Mt. Sinai the leader of the fleeing Israelites had received the laws from Yahweh. Now a new Moses had arisen.

Justice for the widow, the orphan, and all unfortunates might be considered the central core of Hammurabi's laws. The position of a woman was as high as in Egypt. Women engaged in business on their own account; they were employed as professional scribes. Breasted thinks they may have attended a special school to fit them for their work.

Here, toward the end of the second millennium B.C. is the expression of a civilized concept of the position of women in society. It is with something of a shock that we realize how far recent times could fall away from Hammurabi's standards when we read in the Napoleonic code that *"Woman is given to man to bear children; she is therefore his property, as the tree is the gardener's."*

Napoleon wrote thus in the early eighteenth century. And not until March, 1965, did France catch up with Hammurabi, and change the Napoleonic law. Now a Frenchwoman can hold her own property, as George Sand could not, bank her own money in her own name, and at last have something to say about her own destiny and that of her children. True, she has for some time had the vote, but legally little else. She is at last a first class citizen, as Zenobia in the third century felt herself to be.

Hammurabi belonged to the West Semitic dynasty of Babylonia. He is one of the most illustrious figures of all who shaped the world which Zenobia, centuries later, was to inherit after her husband's assassination, and then lose to Aurelian, the Emperor of Rome. But what we want to know at present is not whether Hammurabi was the first to codify the existing laws of his Babylonian Empire, but whether the changes he made in the second millennium B.C. affected Zenobia's married life in the third century of the Christian era.

Theoretically, in the ancient Arabic and Semitic worlds, marriage was a form of purchase; a girl was the property of her father, or if her father was dead, of her oldest brother, and he could sell her to a husband for whatever price the two men agreed upon. In Hammurabi's code, marriage became a legal contract between man and wife. As far as we know, it was monogamous, as it was in later Greece and in the Roman Empire, but it does not appear to have been a legal contract between man and wife. Palmyra, we know, was in Zenobia's time a part of the Roman Empire. It is likely, then, that when at the age of fourteen or fifteen, she became Odenath's wife, she was the sole mistress of his establishment.

Whether Zenobia's marriage was solemnized in Roman or in Nabataean fashion, we may be sure that incense played its part, and incense had to be brought in by caravan to the Fertile Crescent. True frankincense was available in large quantities only in southern Arabia and in the "balsam land of Punt," and so its use became gradually restricted to the worship of the gods. According to Herodotus, in Babylon the priests of Baal made a yearly offering of incense to him. When his worship spread to Palmyra, as it did before the Roman conquest in the first century B.C. incense must have become a profitable item in the caravan trade, not only for Palmyra, but for all the desert cities that the Fertile Crescent nourished.

In Palmyra alone there were at least sixty gods who demanded incense, and throughout the Roman Empire the demand must have been enormous. Funeral rites, private worship, and public sacrifices needed incense. In public sacrifices the priest sprinkled incense over the victim's head and mixed it with the blood before casting it on the flames over which the animal was roasted.

It is said that Alexander, a Greek, every morning of his life, greeted the rising sun by throwing handfuls of incense on his private altar. Once in his youth he was rebuked for extravagance; it cost so much to bring the precious incense from Arabia.

The reason for offering incense to one's deity, and especially to the Sun-god, is easily understood. Primitive man feared that the failure of the sun to appear in the sky might be that he was angered. He must be propitiated with something pleasing to him.

Gradually, as the centuries passed and the balance of power shifted from one country to another, with new trading-centers along the "King's Highway," the culture and wealth of the Fertile Crescent became concentrated in northern Syria. The two cities that at first benefited most from the flourishing caravan trade were Aleppo and Damascus. They vied with each other in the beauty and magnificence of their buildings, and in the high standard of living they maintained.

Their only rival was Ur, at the far eastern end of the Crescent. Ur is said to have surpassed Damascus in beauty and in splendor. Like Tadmor, she commanded a strategic situation. She was near the junction of the Tigris and the Euphrates rivers. She was close to the sea, too, and that helped to make her a convenient center for both export and import trade, possibly more convenient than Tadmor.

Beyond what we read in the Old Testament, we know little of Ur except that her empire once extended as far as the Lebanese Mountains. Excavations have shown that the site of the city of Ur has been occupied from extreme antiquity, possibly even before the middle of the sixteenth century B.C., which is usually given as Abraham's day. Some historians prefer the middle of the fifteenth century. In whichever century it was, Abraham persuaded his people to abandon their native city. Historians tell us that this move was merely a part of the migrations that were occurring at that period.

In 1927 Sir Leonard Woolley led an expedition into southern Mesopotamia, where earlier excavations had unearthed some ruins of the long-dead city. Beneath the debris Woolley discovered the Royal Tomb.

A steep ramp led down to the burial chambers. Inside one chamber lay, dressed in full regalia, the body of a royal personage. He was surrounded by precious objects, here a gold harp, there an inlaid gaming-board or a gold drinking cup. In another chamber Woolley found sixty bodies. Men and women lay in "orderly rows": helmeted soldiers, musicians with their harps, ladies wearing fragile head-dresses. Woolley thinks they had walked down the ramp, taken a drug, perhaps hashish, and composed themselves for death. Doubtless they expected to awaken in another world and resume their interrupted lives.

A small tightly rolled object near the skeleton of a woman proved to be a head-band with a silver clasp that, protected by its owner's robe, had not corroded. She had been late for the ceremony, Woolley surmises, and had slipped the roll into her pocket, thinking she would put it on later. Perhaps she had no time, or in her nervousness, she forgot.

Nothing to compare with this Royal Tomb of Ur have archaeologists found anywhere else in the Fertile Crescent. The thousands of business contracts that have been found and deciphered prove how extensive Ur's commerce was. Doubtless her merchants crossed and recrossed the desert, visiting other centers of business activity and making alliances with them.

Such was the world into which Zenobia was born. As we think of all these ancient cities, Aleppo, Antioch, Damascus, Palmyra, Petra, and Ur, and reflect upon the centuries of trial and error that went into their making, and the disasters to which each succumbed, we wonder where and how they made their mistakes. A recent writer has put the blame for Palmyra's fall and eventual disappearance upon her greed. But, if this is the sole cause of her ruin, then the blame rests equally well upon all the cities of the Fertile Crescent, and upon Rome. For Rome exceeded them all in greed.

Ambition is a better word. And this, as Zenobia's biographer tells us, was the dominant force throughout her brief career as the Queen of Palmyra. Pollio says she fought for her sons' rights. Whether she fought for their rights, or for the rights of her surviving son Vaballath, she knew that she would have to convince the cities of the Fertile Crescent that union under her leadership would be to their advantage. But to persuade them of this, she needed an outlet on the sea, and that meant enticing away from Rome all the cities between Palmyra in Syria and Chalcedon on the distant Bosphorus. There is some evidence that Zenobia had urged Odenath to adopt this course of action. His steadfast loyalty to Rome, however, led him to war against the Empire's bitterest enemy in the East, Sapor I, the King of the Sassanid Persians.

III

Palmyra, Bride of the Desert

"A white skeleton of a town, standing knee-deep in the blown sand." This was the impression Zenobia's city made upon Gertrude Bell when in 1900 she first visited Palmyra. "And beyond all, the desert, sand and white stretches of salt, and sand again, with the dust clouds whirling over it, and the Euphrates five days away. Except Petra, Palmyra is the loveliest thing I have seen in this country."

White in her loveliness Palmyra may have been sixty-six years ago, but today she wears not white but honey-beige: her temples, her pillared colonnades, and her triumphal archway all wear the warm glow of the Parthenon on the Acropolis in Athens.

Whatever her color, Palmyra may still claim to be the Bride of the Desert. The title recalls the days of her glowing youth, when the desert made her its own. Though despoiled century after century, she has not lost her grandeur, nor has she reverted to her primitive station as Tadmor in the Wilderness. She is Palmyra, the city of Odenath, King of Kings, and of Zenobia, his Queen.

Modern Palmyra, a growing city of some five thousand people, with a new museum where modern finds are being housed, lies within sight of her storied ancestress. Little known until the middle of the eighteenth century, ancient Palmyra slept quietly in the desert. Then the drawings of the English artist, Robert Wood, brought

22

her ruins to world attention. English merchants who lived in Aleppo had already visited the ruins far out in the Syrian Desert, and their enthusiastic reports of sun-warmed columns and crumbling temple walls half buried in the sand had stirred Wood's imagination. As soon as he had the opportunity, with Sir William Dawkins, an archaeologist and geologist, and a caravan of two hundred or so mounted on camels and horses, he went to the pillared city that men in the bazaars of Aleppo and Damascus were talking about.

The drawings in Wood's book, published in 1753, two years after he had returned to England, aroused interest throughout the world. Soon the inscriptions he had copied led to the discovery of a key to the Palmyrene alphabet. Eager scholars rushed to Palmyra to study. In Russia, friends of Catherine the Great christened St. Petersburg, her capital, the "Palmyra of the North," and compared Catherine herself to Zenobia, as formerly they had compared her to the Assyrian Empress, Semiramis.

Robert Wood and his caravan approached Palmyra through the City of the Dead, or Valley of the Tombs. Wood describes the valley as a "flat waste, as far as the eye could reach, without any object which showed life or motion." To his artist's eye, the first glimpse of Palmyra's Grand Colonnade, some thirty feet wide and outlined with its lofty Corinthian pillars, "mixed with so little wall or solid building, afforded a breath-taking sight."

Travelers who, before Gertrude Bell, had braved the nomads and other perils of the desert to visit the ruins of Palmyra, speak of an Arab village inside the ancient temple of Bel. Actually, these Arab villagers—Wood and Dawkins had also seen them—were living within the courtyard that enclosed the temple. This temple, on the sixth day of April, in 32 B.C., a wealthy citizen of Palmyra had dedicated to the god Bel and his two associates, Yarhibol and Aglibol. We know the date from an inscribed statue the donor's sons erected in their father's honor. The present entrance, where visitors buy their tickets, leads into the walled courtyard, or sanctuary, which the Arabs thought a secure place in which to build their mud village. In 1929, the squatters were evicted and the entire sanctuary

23

declared government property. Many of the squatters found homes in the nearby town.

The nineteenth century saw travelers flocking to Palmyra, eager to see the ruins of the city where the beautiful Zenobia had once been Queen. One of these travelers was John Fuller. At the head of a large caravan, in 1818, he had crossed the desert on horseback from Damascus to Palmyra, a distance of some two hundred miles. The Arab sheik whom he had engaged to take his party to Palmyra told him, when he protested against an unexpected doubling of the original charge, that if he had brought a letter of introduction from the "King's daughter," he would have taken him to Palmyra free of expense.

The "King's daughter," Fuller discovered, was Lady Hester Stanhope, who eight years before had made history by being the first woman to risk the desert journey to Palmyra. Fuller also learned of a belief, which was common at that time among the Arabs, that many English people visit Palmyra because they consider it the region they themselves originally came from. This belief is interesting; it reflects the ancient tradition that man's first home was in the Fertile Crescent.

Fuller's route from Damascus to Palmyra required seven days' travel. Perhaps he felt rewarded when at the end he passed through a defile and saw ahead the "magnificent ruins of Palmyra." He paused at the sulphur springs, where his horses drank thirstily the warm brackish water that bubbled up among stunted date trees. From the springs to the enormous courtyard that surrounded the temple of Bel, he reports the distance as about half a mile. Like his predecessors, Fuller found that the squatter village occupied only a small part of the courtyard.

The traveler Addison describes the Arab village as follows:

"Through a narrow street of dilapidated mud houses, we were conducted into a large court, and received . . . by an Arab lady, adorned with amber necklaces and bracelets, and having her head surrounded with a band of gold coins strung together. She appeared about six feet high, and as strong as a lion. We were shown up a staircase to the mud terrace . . . into a square room with an earthen floor, a large mat, and a jar of water; and spreading down our carpets and coverlids, we soon lost the remembrance of our fatigue in sleep."

The head-band of the tall Arab lady does not seem to have reminded Addison of a great snail-shaped jewel that Pollio says Zenobia wore suspended from her helmet. Zenobia was not six feet tall, but she was above the normal stature of the Arab women of her day.

Like his predecessors, Addison in 1838 had arrived in Palmyra with the usual complement of baggage animals, dromedaries, and their keepers. He had had trouble with his own dromedary, because the wayward beast would always spring up before his rider had time to mount. To restrain such temperamental creatures, the Arabs would tie a thigh and shin together. This kept the knee from opening and, supposedly, the dromedary from rising. Addison's animal, however, would frequently outwit his keeper by getting up and walking off on three legs.

The Arab sheik of the district, with a large escort, had accompanied Addison and his party. Like his men, the sheik wore ostrich plumes on his head. Unlike his men, he remained on his horse; they kept leaping on and off, running alongside, singing wild songs, and brandishing their long spears.

Lady Hester Stanhope, the niece of Sir William Pitt, the Prime Minister of England, had amazed the Arabs by entering Palmyra dressed like a wealthy Arab sheik and astride a horse! Badly shaken by an unfortunate love affair and depressed by her uncle's death, Lady Hester had decided to leave England. When on February 10, 1810, she and her small party boarded the frigate detailed to escort a convoy bound for Gibraltar, Lady Hester's life as an Englishwoman ended.

From Gibraltar, Lady Hester went to Malta. In May Michael Bruce arrived, a rich, handsome young Englishman some eleven years younger than Lady Hester. Within a few weeks she had become his mistress. She was then in her early thirties. Since England had not yet reached the Victorian era, Lady Hester, a talented, charming, and proud lady, was not inhibited by Victorian niceties.

After idyllic weeks spent in Malta, the party, now grown to large proportions, as additional servants and bodyguards were needed, cruised the Greek islands and finally reached Athens. Here Lord Byron joined them. In October, the party quitted Athens for Constantinople, leaving Byron behind.

Determined to be the first woman to cross the desert to Palmyra, Lady Hester and the rest of her party set out for their goal. Lady Hester had not only outfitted herself as a wealthy Arab sheik; she had forced her outraged companion, Mrs. Fry, also to wear male attire. Confident that a woman on horseback and dressed as a male Bedouin would be considered "little less than a Prophet," Lady Hester made her way to Palmyra, where she expected to be hailed as another Zenobia. She was not disappointed.

The party was not quite so large as Robert Wood's; there were only seventy camels, "loaded with provisions, with water and with presents for the Arabs." Lady Hester rode at the head of the procession. With her were Michael, Dr. Meryon, Mrs. Fry, a dozen sheiks, and an armed escort. All the Europeans were dressed as male Bedouins. Photographs of Lady Hester show her wearing a red cloth jacket and wide trousers embroidered in gold.

When the impressive caravan arrived, the whole population turned out to greet "the daughter of the English King." Many of the lofty, honey-colored pillars on either side of the Grand Colonnade had now been specially decorated for the occasion with lightly clad dancing-girls, each holding a garland of flowers. The projecting consoles the girls stood on were about ten feet from the ground. On these consoles had once stood the statues of wealthy merchants or bankers, which the grateful citizens of Palmyra had erected in their honor.

The final act of the festivities the Arabs had arranged to celebrate the well-heralded arrival of their important visitor took place at the great triple archway through which Lady Hester would pass to reach the sanctuary of Bel. Here the most beautiful of the living statues, clad in a diaphanous robe, floated down from her stand, removed Lady Hester's turban, and replaced it with her garland of flowers. The other girls then floated down—Lady Hester's letters do not describe the mechanism—and all danced for their visitor. Last of all, an official solemnly conferred upon the "King's daughter," the Freedom of the Desert.

Escorted by the entire village, Lady Hester then entered the sanctuary of Bel and was taken to her hut in the northwest angle of the courtyard. Some accounts of her visit assert that her hut was actually inside the ruins of the temple itself.

In a letter written afterward to a friend, Lady Hester joyously remarks: "I have been crowned Queen of the Desert, under the triumphal arch at Palmyra."

One of the entertainments provided for Lady Hester during the few days she remained in Palmyra was a sham battle between wild, shrieking Bedouins and a caravan trying to enter the closed gate of the caravansery. No doubt similar encounters took place after Palmyra became the regular halting-place for the caravans. Located in the center of the desert, with Bedouin encampments all around her, Tadmor, long after she became wealthy Palmyra, must often have been under just such an attack.

Pliny has handed down the first detailed account of Palmyra. Its situation is remarkable, he writes, its soil rich, and its streams pleasant. He warns his readers, however, that because of the sandy desert which surrounds the oasis city, a visitor may feel that he is cut off from the world. As indeed to most tourists Palmyra still seems to be, for caravans are no longer seen there, and even in these days of rapid transit travelers must make their arrangements in advance, otherwise they may find themselves stranded in the desert. If one is lucky and not nervous, one can arrange for a seat in a small two-engined plane that twice a week flies between Damascus and Palmyra.

There is no airport at Palmyra, but the gravelly desert sand makes a satisfactory tarmac. When I reached Damascus—by service-taxi from Beirut—I learned that a seat would be available for the following day. To see the wonderful oasis city from the air was what I had hoped for. We started, a plane-load of French tourists and I, not in the small plane, but in a large craft that had come from Beirut on a chartered flight. Halfway to Palmyra, an engine began to fail. Ignominiously, we turned tail and limped back to Damascus.

Two days later, I started again in another of those useful service-taxis in which you can book a seat. In Athens I had heard that it was advisable to book the whole front seat, but not until I changed cars at Homs did I appreciate the advantage.

At Homs—Emesa in Zenobia's day, and the scene of Odenath's murder—the front seat in the second car was already pre-empted, and so I was wedged into the back seat with two well-nourished Arab men. Both wore the usual voluminous robes and white flowing headgear. For a while my companions ignored me, as was proper, since I was only a foreign woman traveling alone. Finally their curiosity overcame them, and they flung questions at me—in Arabic, which I could neither understand nor speak.

During the few moments I was in Homs, I saw nothing to remind me of the luxurious Emesa that Zenobia and Odenath had known. And, since I was unable to communicate with my companions, I had no way of finding out whether they had ever heard of the part Emesa had played when Zenobia had had to relinquish her northern campaign and retreat before Aurelian's advance. We had now covered, in about two hours, half the distance from Damascus to Palmyra. My companions gave up trying to make me understand Arabic and went to sleep. The man in the front seat had already gone to sleep. Fortunately, our driver stayed awake.

I had better luck, when after four days at the Hotel Zenobia, I left Palmyra by air. The small plane picked up its dozen or so passengers, waiting at the desert's fringe, flew us low over the triumphal archway where Lady Hester had been crowned, over part of the Grand Colonnade and the gigantic tower-tombs in the City of the Dead, then headed south over the golden sands of the desert toward Damascus.

To be leaving Palmyra by air was not quite the same that entering would have been: to see those marvelous ruins become clearer and clearer instead of fading into the horizon would have been a thrilling experience. But if I had flown in, I should have missed Emesa with its reminders of Zenobia's desperate attempt to check Aurelian.

Zenobia seems not to have known how jealous Emesa had become of Palmyra's growing wealth. By the first century B.C., Palmyra had become rich enough through her caravan trade to arouse not only the jealousy of Emesa but the cupidity of Rome. But when Rome tried to conquer Syria and seize her trade, she clashed with the growing empire of Parthia, and never, even though in 64 B.C. Syria became a Roman province, did Rome succeed in brushing Parthia aside. Eventually the Emperor Augustus compromised with Parthia, and Palmyra reaped the benefit.

Since most of our information about Parthia comes from Greek and Roman writers who were hostile, or at least not friendly, to that troublesome part of the world Rome was steadily adding to her eastern possessions, we tend to think of the Parthians as barbarians who, though "slightly veneered with Hellenic culture, were ruled by cruel, avaricious kings." Whatever Rome had heard about the Parthians, she must have been stunned when in 53 B.C. the news came that the Parthians had defeated an army of Roman legionaries and captured and beheaded its commander, the consul Crassus.

It is recorded that at a performance of the *Bacchae* of Euripides, the actors had used as stage property the consul's severed head. Notwithstanding this gruesome act, the production of a Greek play by "barbarians" as early as 53 B.C. argues a certain degree of culture. This, under the circumstances, neither Greek nor Roman writers could be expected to appreciate.

In spite of the constant bickering between Rome and Parthia, the safest caravan route continued to run through the oasis city. By Zenobia's day, the route had become in Palmyra one of the finest avenues of any city in Roman Syria. This superb avenue, lined with its more than three hundred and seventy-five Corinthian columns, most of them at least sixty feet high, must have astounded the ancient world. Today, less than half of the avenue's handsome columns are still standing, but enough are left to justify the name by which it is generally known, the Grand Colonnade of Palmyra. Many columns still have their consoles, but all have lost their statues.

Since the greater part of the Grand Colonnade was built before 200, to Odenath and Zenobia it would have been a familiar sight. One cannot but wonder whether so spirited a creature as Zenobia walked here in modest Oriental fashion a step or so behind her Odenath, or whether, with head erect and unveiled, she walked at his side, as Hammurabi's Code might have preferred. Women in Palmyra, we know from sculpture, always had their heads covered, but they did not wear veils, except on rare occasions.

Colonnades were a characteristic feature of Greco-Syrian cities, but none of them, not even the celebrated one in Jerash, are as spectacular as the Grand Colonnade. Unfortunately, since not all the columns have been found, we are at a loss to know where the avenue began and where it ended. Its two sharp turns, one at the monumental tetrapylon, now being restored, and the other at the archway where Lady Hester was crowned, have led scholars to presume that the caravans, originally at least, ended their long journey at the temple of the god who had protected them from the perils of the desert.

There were many gods in Palmyra, as we know; but by the time the colonnade was built, the chief deity had come to be the god Bel, whose temple outshone all others. But the god Bel was really a usurper, as we shall see later, who had taken over the modest temple of earlier days and altered it to suit his convenience. To reach the new temple, the caravans had to make certain changes in their road through the city. Gradually this would become the established route, and columns set up on either side would soon turn the route into a splendid avenue.

From far places Palmyra's caravans came, from the mouth of the Nile, where the Fertile Crescent began, from the Persian Gulf, and from India and the Orient, bringing beautiful objects wrought in ivory, gold, or silver, spices, ointments, incense, whatever the East had that the West needed or desired.

The most essential need of a caravan city such as Palmyra was, is a caravansery, or overnight camping ground. Since the ground must accommodate loaded donkeys, camels with bulging panniers, drivers and guards and travelers, who have no other means of transport, the space reserved must be extensive. One such space, originally surrounded by high walls, lies near the tetrapylon, which may have been the entrance gate to Palmyra's caravansery.

At first, such a large place in a caravan city may have served only as a huge uncovered market, where haggling over merchandise, so dear to the Oriental heart, sharpened a man's appetite and perhaps haunted his dreams by night. As caravans grew in number, and transactions became more involved, something more than mere space would be required. Soon the ancient equivalent of the modern motel would arise, where man and beast might find accommodation and protection. In ancient days, the caravan routes that crossed and recrossed the deserts were as definitely marked out as are the great trucking routes of today. Along these routes the caravan-chief and his drivers could stop in caravanseries as well equipped to meet their needs as is the motel.

In one important respect the ancient caravansery differed from the modern motel. There were shrines and temples, either in the caravansery or near by, where men of every faith might go to offer thanks for their safe arrival. For the perils of the desert were many, and many were the whitened bones a man could see as he passed, and oftener than not a flock of vultures intent on their feast.

Palmyra's caravansery, according to Rostovtzeff, was a great walled "rectangle containing interesting interior porticoes and a fine and monumental entrance." Whether this was actually a building or merely a walled-off space is not clear. Rostovtzeff bases his identification upon the "general plan," and on the numerous inscriptions that have been found there, some of which sing the praise of worthy caravan leaders and lay stress on "their able, disinterested, and devoted service to the merchants and the city."

The arrival of a caravan at its headquarters might be compared to the coming of a modern circus to a country town. People would gather to watch the long procession of loaded donkeys and grunting camels pass through the pillared colonnade. Excitement would mount when the time came for the camels to kneel and yield their loads before being led off to their tethering-grounds. Merchants, camel-drivers, and travelers could then attend to more personal affairs, perform their ablutions, bring their thank-offerings to the proper temple, and retire to take their pleasure in the brothels.

In the London *Illustrated News* (January 23, 1965), there appeared a photograph by the Irish artist, Derek Hill, of a "long forgotten Caravanserai on Marco Polo's road." Known as the caravansery of Robert Sharaf, it is now presented to the public in a series of astonishing photographs (hitherto forbidden).

The caravansery, in shape roughly that of a "smaller Oxford College," dates from early in the twelfth century. It is surrounded by walls some twenty feet high, ornamented with carved stucco of a "warm honey colour." Its two courtyards lie one behind the other, and the entrance is through three massive arches, also richly decorated. This caravansery was not built in desert country, but in a great grassy plain, burnt brown by the sun when Derek Hill visited it.

Each courtyard has two rooms or "house mosques." Scooped-out places in each courtyard may have been wells or pools for watering camels. If the great caravansery in Palmyra bore any resemblance to the Robert Sharaf, it is a thousand pities that Nature, aided by man, has wreaked such destruction that it requires an immense effort of the imagination to reconstruct it as it must have appeared to Odenath, Zenobia, and to their enemies.

From the inscriptions we learn that the Arab merchants of Palmyra who financed the caravans piped in water to supplement the sulphur springs and reclaimed much of the desert to accommodate their growing population. They established offices in the East and in the West, sent ships into Parthian ports and into Roman ports, lent and borrowed money to increase their caravan trade. The inscriptions tell of caravans traveling between Babylon and small Parthian cities, but say nothing of commerce with the Syrian cities of the Roman Empire. The omission, Rostovtzeff suggests, may imply that, since journeys to and from Parthia were risky, they were worthy of record, while those under Roman protection were safe and need not be mentioned.

Many of these inscriptions speak of establishments set up by the merchants of Palmyra in various Parthian cities that became almost independent political bodies, with their own temples, storehouses, and caravanseries. One inscription found near a filled-in well in the desert south of Palmyra eulogizes a certain public-spirited citizen whose generosity was praised in "letters of the god Hadrian." Seven statues were erected in this citizen's honor: the four in Palmyra and three beyond the city limits. The merchants were organized into companies, each with its own president. Companies such as these were unknown in the Roman Empire, but were common in Babylonia, where merchants banded together for profit and for protection.

Early in the second century the Emperor Trajan reversed the wise policy of compromise with Parthia that his predecessor Augustus had made, and turned from diplomatic negotiation and treaties to strategy and to conquest. Trajan may have thought that even if others had failed to conquer Parthia, he would be able to subdue her and open the way to build an empire equal to the one Alexander the Great had built—and lost.

At first, Trajan had some success. He detached Mesopotamia from Parthia and annexed her as a Roman province. An arch excavated at Doura, not far from Palmyra and the nearest crossing-point over the Euphrates, has an inscription indicating that Trajan seized Doura to use as a military base.

Trajan's conquests boded no good to Palmyra; if they succeeded, her usefulness as a buffer state between Rome and Parthia would end, and she would sink to the status of a Roman provincial town.

33

Luckily for Palmyra, Trajan died before he was able to mount an effective campaign against Parthia.

Hadrian, Trajan's successor, reverted to the earlier policy of Augustus. When he restored Mesopotamia and Doura to the Parthians, Palmyra's merchants ceased to worry. Under Hadrian's rule and that of his immediate successors, Palmyra enjoyed her longest period of peace and prosperity. Doura now furnished the caravans with wine, bread, vegetables, beasts of burden, and whatever else they needed. In return, she levied taxes upon all caravans that used her facilities. And so by the close of the second century Doura on the Euphrates had become almost as rich as Palmyra.

During the summer of 199, the Emperor Septimius Severus concluded what historians call the First Parthian War. For Palmyra, the most important result was that Septimius granted her colonial status. This meant that Palmyra would enjoy a measure of freedom she had not known for centuries. Her unique position as the only true caravan city of the Fertile Crescent soon became fully established. Married, in very truth, as she now was to the desert, if she were deprived of that support by either Rome or Parthia, acting separately or jointly, Palmyra could not live.

In Palmyra's main square a "theatre-like building" that was excavated some years ago has been thought to be a Greek theater. Rostovtzeff prefers to regard it as a kind of ancient town-hall, where business relating to the caravans was transacted: honors voted, religious ceremonies decided upon, perhaps held, even sacrifices performed. He bases this interpretation of the building's use upon what we know of the uses to which auditoriums were put in the "non-Greek regions of Syria."

The few private houses that have been excavated had palatial rooms opening on courts with mosaic floors similar to those in wealthy houses in Antioch; they tell us much of the life that was lived in the Palmyra of Zenobia's day. As for the poor, they lived as best they could in mud huts, or on the doorsteps of the rich. Smaller houses, of course, existed somewhere.

While Palmyra was still a Roman colony, people traveled freely between the East and the West. Merchants and soldiers often spent years in Egypt and in Italy; they even went as far west as Britain. Many families became members of the Roman aristocracy, as Odenath's family did. Such families, doubtless wealthy caravan owners, probably lived in these fine houses, furnished in semi-Oriental style, their couches and floors covered with thick rugs, their plates and cups studded with precious stones. Their sculptures show women in embroidered gowns and heavy jewelry; men in wide-flowing trousers and embroidered robes. A pleasant, luxurious life, far more complex than appears on the surface, as every life must be when men of diverse nationalities rub shoulders.

In the Palmyra and nearby Doura of Zenobia's day, though Aramaic was the written language and Arabic was commonly used in speech, both Greek and Latin could have been heard. There is some evidence that young boys of noble Palmyrene families began to study Greek at an early age. An attractive tomb statue represents a Palmyrene boy holding in his hands a notebook apparently made of wooden tablets. On one tablet are written the last letters of the Greek alphabet. Zenobia herself was an excellent linguist, proficient in five languages, Aramaic, Arabic, Egyptian, Greek, and Latin. She is said to have regarded Greek as second only to her native Aramaic.

Near the monumental tetrapylon that may mark the entrance to Palmyra's caravansery stand two columns that are taller than the rest. One supported a statue of Zenobia, the other that of Odenath. The inscription on the first (in Arabic and in Greek) reads some-what as follows: "This is the statue of Septimia Bat-Zabbai (the Greek reads Zenobia), our most illustrious and pious Queen. The excellent Septimii Zabdas, general-in-chief, and Zabda, military governor of Tadmor, have raised it to their Lady. . . ." The occasion may have been Zenobia's conquest of Lower Egypt in 271.

The same two officials were responsible for Odenath's statue; both statues were dedicated in the same year, after Odenath's assassination. Surely these inscriptions have some bearing upon the unsolved problem of Zenobia's complicity in her husband's murder.

If these statues were in place today and could look down upon the ruins of the Great Colonnade, the caravansery, and the nearby theater, they would see a heartening sight. Day after day Arab village boys of every age, books (a few sheets of paper sewed together) in their hands, pace slowly up and down or sprawl over the worn stone seats of the theater, learning their lessons. These boys have nowhere else to study. In the mud hovels of the village where many live, and even in the more pretentious houses, they have no privacy. And so they walk, hour after hour, where in the once luxurious city the boy with the wooden tablets lived and studied his Greek.

Avid for education, these boys will rush up to you, one question on their lips: "You speak English? This word, pronounce, please." Older boys imitate their elders, and ask another inevitable question—but only of a woman with ringless hand—"You have husband?" Many will walk along with you, to try out their English or teach you Arabic.

In the museum at Baalbek, there is a statue from Palmyra of an unusually attractive boy. Richly dressed, he stands with hands lightly folded and one trousered knee slightly advanced, giving him an easy pose. His short hair is curled close to his well-shaped head. His face is pear-shaped, and his deep-set eyes seem to look out sadly upon the world. We should be glad to accept him as Vaballath, the boy-king of Palmyra, but unfortunately there is not the slightest resemblance to the coin, struck in Antioch, that bears the head of Zenobia's son.

The sculpture of Palmyra, of which these two statues seem typical examples, has been called the "Hellenized offspring of Aramaean and Anatolian art." Scarcely any painting has survived, but of the hundreds of statues, busts, and bas-reliefs that we have, not one of them seems to owe anything to Greek influence. The treatment of the heads and bodies shows the minute rendering of details typical of eastern art. This occurs not only in sculpture, but in pictorial representations of dress and of furniture.

For painting, we must turn to Doura, since similar gay frescoes must also have decorated Palmyra's houses and temples. A few still exist in Palmyra, but to see them we must go either to the museums or to Palmyra's City of the Dead.

As the Bride of the Desert, we should expect Palmyra to have been not only a mixture of East and West, but far more Eastern than Western, certainly in almost all external aspects. Internally, however, the situation may have been slightly different. Zenobia, as we know, was an educated woman, but she was not the only one. Pollio suggests that she had all her sons instructed in Latin because she herself was not so well acquainted with that tongue.

Public education under the Roman Empire, which attempted to train both the mind and the body, followed, especially in the Hellenized cities of the East, the lines laid down in the philosophical schools of Athens, but this was a privilege reserved for free-born youths. The handsome boy with the notebook and the attractive boy in Baalbek may have studied Greek with tutors trained in such schools.

Palmyra, then, must have been neither Greco-Roman nor entirely Greco-Syrian, but as polyglot and as diverse as many a city in the United States. As a city with one overwhelming interest, the caravan trade, Palmyra should have been unified. But the caravans came from peoples who had their own gods, unlike the Greek Zeus or the Roman Jupiter or the Hebrew Yahweh. These gods the caravans brought with them to Palmyra, and to them they soon erected temples. Into only a few of these temples could Zenobia have entered, even to offer sacrifice, for, though she was a Queen, she was after all a woman. And where religion was concerned, Palmyra demanded segregation.

IV

The Caravan Gods of Palmyra

The wealth of Palmyra and of her royal family, King Odenath, Queen Zenobia, and the young Princes, had been built upon the caravan trade. And since the shortest route between East and West ran through the oasis city, there seemed in those early years no likelihood that Zenobia would ever cease to enjoy the tinkle of a camel's bell.

One ever-present danger, though, lay uppermost in men's minds. Should their caravan gods forsake them, they were doomed. The people of the Fertile Crescent had long known that their lives depended upon the good will of their fertility-gods, and they had cultivated them assiduously. But for some years now the priests of the god Bel had been demanding a greater share of the sacrificial meat, insisting that Bel was both a fertility-god and a caravan god. It was all very confusing, yet no one, not even Odenath nor Zenobia, dared gainsay a priest of the powerful god Bel.

In Lady Hester's day, Bel and his associates, Yarhibol and Aglibol, who formed the Divine Triad of Palmyra, had long since fled from the city, and with them had gone the caravans and all the prosperity they had brought. No one in that squalid mud village could have visualized the anger of Bel if he could have seen Lady Hester desecrate with her female foot the sacred threshold of his temple. Over that threshold not even Zenobia would have stepped, so deep-seated and irrational has always been the fear of that strange creature, a woman. Into the women's temples Zenobia could have gone, and there were many in Palmyra, but the Divine Triad was composed of male deities, and they would have had none of her, nor of Lady Hester either.

The best known modern example of the exclusion of women from all-male religious establishments is Mt. Athos in Greece. From these monasteries once even hens were barred. Perhaps even the enlightened Hammurabi would not have allowed his temples to be so defiled. The feeling still persists, however, in some localities; women are permitted to enter churches, but their heads must be covered and they must sit apart from the men, sometimes behind latticework. An ancient proverb runs that Satan waits at a church-door for a woman with uncovered head. Then he tries to enter with her, his feet entangled in her hair.

This age-old attitude of the human male toward the female springs from the primitive fear that a man of Neanderthal days must have felt the first time he saw his woman with a small, helpless creature at her side.

In Palmyra, the temples the women might enter were equipped with theaters. These were not theaters in the modern sense of the word, buildings or auditoriums where plays are performed or spectacles presented. They seem to have been special chambers set apart in the temples for some kind of ritual. What the ritual was we do not know, since no reference to the rite occurs in the inscriptions from Palmyra that have been so far deciphered. Perhaps, as in Eleusis in Greece, some mystery was divulged that was forbidden to men.

The deities the women worshipped in these temples were goddesses, and since a woman's life was not complete unless she had produced sons, we may hazard a guess that prayers for sons were included in the ritual. The goddesses were not the mighty caravan gods the men prayed to; still, many a woman, waiting for her man to return from a perilous desert trip, must have begged her goddess to intercede with a caravan god to bring him safely home.

39

Here, too, in these segregated temples the women may have offered gifts to placate the spirits of those who had left this world and, instead of enjoying their new life, were filled with resentment because of something that had not been carried out in the prescribed fashion, sacrificial meat underdone or overdone, or less wine than a bibulous forefather was accustomed to. There could be many reasons, real or fancied, for placating angry spirits who might otherwise bring diseases, famines, or other misfortunes. In those far-off days, to avert anger even at the cost of giving up her own life often fell to a woman's lot.

The temple of Bel and his male associates had no so-called theater. Nor has any theater been found in other temples to male deities. Neither in Palmyra, nor in Doura on the Euphrates, where scholars often turn for additional information about Palmyra, have they found any sign of a theater. Further excavations in both places may shed more light upon the problem. Until then, however, we must rest content with the assumption that temples with theaters were for women.

Perhaps Zenobia had in her palace what we would call today a chapel, with a private "theater."

The discovery of a ruined stone bench, originally semi-circular, at the spot where Palmyra's colonnaded avenue makes its second turn to reach the temple of Bel has led to the suggestion that this short stretch of roadway may have served as a kind of Via Sacra, with seats provided for spectators. Here, on days when the caravans were coming in, excited people might gather to watch the long processions: camels and donkeys loaded with presents for the temple, slaves leading the animals shortly to be sacrificed as thank-offerings to the gods and to provide roasted flesh for the city. Nor would there be any lack of merchants come to buy jewels or costly incense, hawkers shouting their wares, and fine ladies searching for stout slaves to carry their litters. And as usual there would be the inevitable thief slipping along through the crowd.

And here Zenobia would be free to come, if she wished, not alone certainly, but attended by her eunuchs, her ladies-in-waiting, and her guards.

If the sacrifices were performed inside the temple, as some scholars believe, the spectators could have watched only the preliminaries. But one can still see the remains of a paved ramp that passed under the temple portico into the courtyard, and up this ramp the sacrificial animals could easily have been led straight to the altar in front of the temple proper. No swine, but camels, bulls, and rams, all male, would have been the chosen victims.

There before the temple the faithful would gather to watch the priests kill and flay the animals, burn selected portions to the god, and roast the remainder for the feast to follow. We hope that some of that nourishing meat reached the wives and children waiting patiently for their share.

Near the altar there was a pool—sulphur water was piped in—where before the sacrifice the priests probably purified themselves, their animals, and their utensils. Only then could they approach the altar and conduct a sacrifice without incurring the anger of the very god they wished to please.

Though women must have been excluded from the sacrifices in honor of Bel and his associates, there is some evidence that they participated in the religious processions. A bas-relief from the temple of Bel shows a ritual procession that is transporting the gods to their places of worship. The relief also shows the sacrificial animals and a number of veiled women. On one bas-relief from Doura there are faint lines which scholars have interpreted as possibly attempts to portray musical instruments. Though no one, so far as I know, has identified the instruments, it is not too far-fetched to assume that when the citizens of Doura or of Palmyra assembled to honor their gods, music, perhaps singing, and dancing would play a part.

We are on firmer ground when we examine the sculptured representations of Palmyrene gods. They are almost invariably shown as warriors, fully armed, mounted on horses or on camels, ready at all times to protect their people against attack.

The Divine Triad, Bel and Yarhibol and Aglibol, the prototypes, as it were, of the *djinns* so prominent in the *Arabian Nights,* could be called upon at need. The numerous inscriptions that have been found dedicated to the Triad, petitioning one, sometimes all three, show the strong hold these powerful deities had upon the imaginations of the desert people.

When Robert Wood and Sir William Dawkins visited the ruined temple of Bel they saw niches in the walls with inscriptions carved beneath them to identify the gods who had once been seated there. For seated gods, and generally gods seated in niches, are as characteristic of Semitic temples as gods on pedestals are of Greek and Roman temples. In the temple of Bel, the niche is a cupola where the Roman Jupiter, who has superseded Bel, is portrayed in the center with the twelve signs of the Zodiac grouped around him.

The temple of Bel, according to some inscriptions that Professor Seyrig found while excavating there, was begun in the first century B.C., then rebuilt on a larger scale during the following century.

Rostovtzeff feels that the temple of Bel may also have served as a fort where people could take refuge against sudden attacks by the Bedouins of the desert, as in the early days of the United States people fled to the fortified garrison to escape the scalp-hunting Indians.

In the course of time, the temple to the god Bel became Palmyra's official sanctuary. No one really knows the god's origin. Some scholars think that he was an indigenous deity; others that, since in sculpture and in painting he appears in Parthian dress, he may have come from Babylon, when the Parthians conquered that city. Bel's two associates may have come with him, or they may have come later. They may also have been local deities whose cult became absorbed in that of the Babylonian Bel.

There is also some confusion about the functions of Bel's two associates. They are generally thought to have been gods of the sun and the moon, respectively—Aglibol is portrayed with horns— who afterward came to be caravan gods. This would be a natural transition in a desert country where caravans rely upon sun and moon and stars to guide them on their way through the endless sands that shift with every gust of wind.

Erected near the site of the rude hut-shrine built in earlier days to house the god who lived in the pool, the temple of Bel, Yarhibol, and Aglibol must have resembled its humble predecessor as little as Bel himself resembled the ancient water-god of Tadmor. But since there is some evidence that Bel was originally a fertility-god, and since water is essential to growth, the god's worshippers could easily have made the proper connection.

When the temple was rebuilt in the second century, the inner sanctuary, or holy of holies, retained its original three unequal divisions, which may have symbolized the inequality of the three gods. Columns with gilt-bronze capitals once enclosed the sanctuary, but we are told that long ago the Arabs stripped off the bronze, leaving the stone cores exposed to the weather.

In the fifth century the temple was consecrated to Christian use. In the twelfth it became a mosque and remained so until 1929, when the government declared it an historical monument. But for Zenobia and Odenath, the temple of Bel and his associates, Yarhibol and Aglibol, was the temple of the Divine Triad.

M. l'Abbé Jean Starcky suggests that Bol may have been the name of an indigenous god, who was confused, as time passed, with the well known Baal, into whose fiery belly Phoenician parents were required to toss an infant child that the god might be fed. Bol, or Baal, also according to Starcky, seems to have survived in the Greco-Roman god, Adonis, whose name is interpreted as protector, or savior.

In Roman times, the Syrian soldiers thought of the Divine Triad as their warrior gods who protected them when they fought under the Roman eagles. Today in Greece, some peasant soldiers believe that the Virgin Mary precedes them into battle, and that without her they cannot succeed.

The notion of a Divine Triad is not, of course, peculiar to the peoples of the Fertile Crescent, though it may have originated there. It exists in such historical religions as those of India and of Egypt, with the difference that in these faiths one member of the so-called Trinity is feminine. The Christian Trinity, on the other hand, is closer to the ancient Divine Triad in that it is composed of three masculine elements: Father, Son, and Spirit. Here the Virgin has no place. She belongs in the Holy Family, also three in number, but she is not one of the Trinity.

Babylonia was not the only country whose gods were represented at Palmyra. Since caravans came in from all parts of the known world—and Alexander's conquests had reached as far as India—the gods of these strange countries also came to the Fertile Crescent, and temples were erected in their honor.

The powerful couple, Hadad and Atargatis, came from Anatolia; from Phoenicia came Eshmun (equivalent to Asclepius, the Greek god of medicine who in Rome became Aesculapius) about whom we know little, and Astarte, the eastern counterpart of Aphrodite, the great goddess of fertility. The recently discovered marble plaque, which aroused such interest when Syrian newspapers hinted that it might represent Zenobia, has now, in the opinion of Mr. Adnam Bounni, the director of the Damascus Museum, turned out to be an artist's conception of Astarte. Bounni, while excavating in Palmyra a few years ago, found the first of the three pieces into which the plaque had been broken. During successive excavations the other two pieces appeared. Visitors to the museum may now see in bas-relief a seated woman who rests her right foot upon the prostrate body of a male figure. Bounni interprets the figure as symbolizing the Euphrates in bondage to the goddess Astarte.

Astarte appears several times in the Old Testament as Ashtoreth, a Semitic goddess. She personifies the female element as Baal personifies the male. Since she is a nature goddess, the attributes of fertility and reproduction belong to her. Robertson Smith feels that Astarte was originally a sheep goddess, and so she may well have been, for in the eyes of nomad peoples the welfare of their flocks was all-important.

The best representation of the Anatolian couple, Hadad and

Atargatis, is a bas-relief found in the ruins of a temple in Doura. Though the temple was sacred to Atargatis alone, the bas-relief shows the goddess and her husband seated side by side in their shrine. Here Hadad is the inferior. The sculptor has indicated his inferiority by representing him in smaller proportions than the opulent figure of his divine consort. Columns rise on either side of the couple. Hadad's sacred animal, the bull, adorns his column; the lion, sacred to Atargatis, is symbolized by a great head with lolling tongue that forms the armrest of her chair. Both deities are richly dressed. Each wears a crown, and Atargatis has gold earrings. Hadad holds a thunderbolt; Atargatis, what seem to be flowers.

This divine couple often appears in Syrian art, Hadad invariably overshadowed by his consort. There seems to be little doubt that Atargatis represented to her Syrian worshippers the Great Goddess who is so prevalent in early cultures where the magical ability of the female predominates over that of the male.

The caravan deities, Arsu and Azizu, each had a temple in Palmyra. On Syrian coins and reliefs, Arsu appears as a young soldier in military dress, either astride a camel or standing beside his beast and holding him by his rope. Since the camel is his holy emblem, his *alter ego*, he himself is sometimes depicted as a camel.

Azizu, who is young and handsome, is generally shown on horseback. He may belong to the group of mounted caravan deities whom the Syrians worshipped and whose cult Syrian soldiers and merchants carried into other countries.

But Arzu and Azizu were not merely caravan gods; they were also thought to be acolytes of the sun. In religious processions, Arzu is the Morning Star who precedes the Sun; Azizu, the Evening Star who follows the Sun. They are the guiding lights of those who travel the desert from dawn to dark, for whose kind and merciful protection caravans offer up their daily prayers. And when the caravans reach their destinations, it is to the temples of their gods that the leaders hasten, to offer thankful sacrifices for their safe arrival. Nothing else so epitomizes the risks involved in ancient desert

45

travel as the numerous representations in the art of the Near East of the caravan gods.

Thousands of inscriptions cut upon rocks and upon gates and temple walls bear witness to the gratitude daily expressed by all who ventured out upon the desert's arid waste and returned safely home. And for him who failed to return there was always the hope that if those he left behind brought to his empty tomb the food and drink he needed, Hadad or some other caravan god might, when the proper time came, escort him to the After World.

In Jerash there is a temple that Rostovtzeff thinks may once have been Hadad's home. To this quiet retreat Hadad may have withdrawn in awe of his wife's greatness, as did many another male deity of Syria and Asia Minor. For here, suggests Rostovtzeff, the "great Goddess, the incarnation of the Eternal Female, dominated over the masculine in the sphere of religion, if not also in the sphere of everyday life."

From Arabia came her Sun-deity who was believed to be a goddess, contrary to the belief held in most countries that the sun is masculine. From Arabia came also the wise goddess Allat, the counterpart of the Greek Athene, who in Petra was the moon-goddess. Arabia also contributed an interesting god who was the opposite of the Greek Dionysus, a kindly god who, like his people, abstained from wine.

Though the temple of Bel was the official sanctuary of Palmyra, and though Palmyra became the home of numerous lesser deities, there was another temple, somewhat more modest, that was equally important. This was the sanctuary of the god Baalshamin, whose name means Master of the Skies. Starcky explains the anomaly of two supreme gods in one place at the same time by suggesting that each represents the folk-memory of an over-all deity, El, creator of the earth. Starcky also points out that El appears as a suffix in such proper names as Raphael or Rabbel.

The god Baalshamin, according to Starcky, is not peculiar to Palmyra, for his cult was familiar throughout Syria. With his Aramaean worshippers, he came to Syria during the second millennium and remained there with them. The many epithets that appear in dedications to him testify to his spiritual growth; he is *good, compassionate,* and *eternal.* Other deities, when represented with him, often share his epithets. Sometimes he is the nameless god, either alone or in a triad, as may be seen in a bas-relief now in the Louvre.

Though, as Starcky points out, traces of polytheism are still evident in the cult of the nameless god, enlightened persons in Palmyra, such as Zenobia, who had the advantage of associating with the philosopher Longinus or with the so-called heretical Bishop Paul of Antioch may have reached the intellectual stage of regarding the three as a unity and thus have become receptive to the Christian point of view when the new religion became established in the Fertile Crescent.

Since no texts from Palmyra have survived from which to learn something about the ritualistic tendance of the caravan gods, we must fall back upon the dedications and the monuments. From these we learn that Syrian worshippers came to their temples, as the Greeks and the Romans did, and that to the statues of their deities they addressed their petitions and their prayers.

There is some evidence that in Palmyra and in Doura the worship of betyls also existed. A betyl was a stone that was more or less associated with a divinity, a miraculous stone, as it were. The veneration of betyls was common among Arabs, and has survived in the well known Aladdin's Lamp. The most famous betyl of antiquity is the holy stone preserved at Delphi, which the god Kronos swallowed, under the impression that it was his last-born son.

During the excavation of Palmyra an interesting tessera was discovered: a triple shrine on a pedestal. In each shrine there is a sacred stone. Starcky suggests that the red pavilion on the bas-relief from the temple of Bel that is carried on the back of a camel may have contained a sacred stone. He has come to this conclusion because the relief was found on the cella (holy of holies) wall of the temple. The position of the relief and the introduction of a camel also suggest to Starcky that the deity who is being honored is a caravan god.

47

Palmyra needed to honor her caravan gods. Her commercial growth, built upon her caravan trade, had not only made the other cities of the Fertile Crescent envious; it had caused the new Persian king, Sapor, to cast greedy eyes upon the whole of Roman Syria. Soon Sapor began to style himself King of Kings, which meant that he aspired to world dominion. And in all Syria only one man was strong enough to oppose him. That man was Odenath, who also called himself King of Kings. But not until Sapor captured and grossly mistreated an Emperor of Rome did a clash between Odenath and Sapor become as inevitable as the later clash between Aurelian and Zenobia.

V

Odenath, King of Kings

Palmyra awoke with the dawn, that spring morning in 263. Early
as it was, the smoke of altar fires was already drifting over the city;
the priests had spoken with their gods, then had announced to King
Odenath that his attack upon Sapor would be successful. Shortly
afterward, an observer in Palmyra might have seen a caravan heading eastward through the Grand Colonnade, on its way to the salt
flats and the desert beyond. But, instead of camels with bulging
panniers, there were sleek riding-camels, each with an armed man
on its back.

Sad-faced women and eager-eyed, excited children lined either
side of the broad colonnade. Beside the great columns that loomed
high overhead, the women, many with babies in their arms, looked
small and insignificant. Now and then a woman glanced over her
shoulder out toward the sand dunes where the high tower-tombs
stood, then brought her eyes slowly back to rest once more upon
the lines of mounted and marching men swinging steadily toward
the East. Somewhere out in the desert, as all Palmyra knew, Sapor
and his Sassanid Persians lay in wait.

Roman cavalry and infantry, Arabs mounted on swift camels,
Palmyra's noted archers, trained to shoot in Parthian fashion, half-
naked men carrying on their backs the long scaling-ladders, donkeys
attached to siege-engines—all the armament men needed to fight the

49

dreaded Persian was passing before the eyes of the women and children waiting in the Grand Colonnade. At the head of the long caravan rode Odenath, King of Kings, in his war-chariot. Behind him came Zenobia, his Queen, astride her favorite Nubian horse. Encased in shining chain armor, this husband and wife team, said to have been the first in history, were setting forth to punish Sapor for his atrocious treatment, three years before, of Valerian, the Emperor of Rome.

According to the biographers, the custom of that early period in the history of the East seems to have been for a chief of state to take with him to war his immediate family, perhaps even all his relatives. Sapor is said to have brought along his wives, his concubines, his children, and all their numerous attendants.

Odenath had with him, besides Zenobia, his eldest son, Herodian, presumably his heir, and, according to Pollio, two of his three younger sons. Also with Odenath was Maeonius, his cousin or his nephew—the exact relationship is disputed—who, on this occasion at least, had been entrusted with a command of his own. No mention is made of Vaballath. If Professor Seyrig's figures are accepted, Vaballath may have been about six years old, yet for some reason he seems not to have accompanied his parents and his two younger brothers.

Odenath's path to glory began that spring morning when, erect in his chariot, he drove out through Palmyra's wide-flung gates and took the desert road across to the Euphrates. The King of Palmyra was a formidable opponent for anyone to meet. Vopiscus, his biographer, tells us that from early boyhood Odenath had been trained to hunt lions, leopards, bears, and other wild animals in the distant forests, that he had learned to endure the dangers of the chase, and that he had often clashed with the desert nomads. Zenobia, who, according to Pollio, was an even more daring hunter than her husband, seems to have been equally daring in warfare.

For neither Maeonius nor Herodian has their biographer, Pollio, a single good word. He characterizes Maeonius as a "filthy fellow," *spurcissimus* in the Latin text, and intimates that he is devoured by envy of the young heir to the throne, Herodian.

As for Herodian, Pollio says frankly that during the campaign against Sapor the young princeling showed clearly that he could not measure up to his distinguished forefathers. Effeminate and Oriental in his tastes, Herodian took his comfort in "embroidered tents and pavilions made from cloth of gold."

To understand Odenath's quarrel with Sapor and its final outcome, we must turn the clock of history back a few years to watch the political situation of the Roman Empire in the East, in which Palmyra for two centuries or so had played an increasingly important part.

By this time, however, the whole vast Empire was rapidly disintegrating. For some years the legionaries, who were being recruited more and more from distant provinces, had been making and unmaking emperors at will. Far to the west, the half-savage Britons were rebelling against their Roman conquerors; the Goths were everywhere; along the Euphrates local wars were constantly breaking out; and throughout Syria anarchy reigned. The desert sheiks had regained their boldness and were attacking the caravans. And the legionaries had no time to cope with the situation. They were far too busy murdering their commanders, who were often their emperors, and setting up new ones.

The Parthian Empire was in equally bad shape. In the early part of the third century, the Parthian king had been strong enough to refuse a daughter in marriage to a Roman emperor. A short time later, that same king found himself at the mercy of a Sassanid king who claimed to have inherited the ancient Persian Empire, and who had taken upon himself the task of restoring it to its former glory. By 230, the Sassanid Empire had vanquished the Parthians and had become a threat to Rome's eastern possessions, including Syria. The Sassanids had developed terrifying new siege-engines, and city walls crumbled before them. Soon the Sassanids began to covet Palmyra and her caravan trade.

Finally, Palmyra's first families banded together to save their city.

Of these families, Odenath's was the most distinguished. At the turn of the century, Odenath's grandfather, some accounts say his father, received from the reigning Emperor, Septimius Severus, a native of Africa and the first of his countrymen to become Emperor, the full rights and privileges of Roman citizenship. In acknowledgement, or for political reasons, Odenath I had added the Imperial name to his own. He became Septimius Odenath. Apparently the honor was hereditary, for our Odenath kept the same name, and, according to her biographer, Zenobia after her marriage became Septimia Zenobia.

Septimius Severus, after the death of his first wife, married Julia, called Domna, who was a daughter of the high priest of the Sun-god's temple in Emesa. Domna's sister, also named Julia but called Maesa, had two daughters, on each of whom she also bestowed the name Julia. History distinguishes between these second-generation Julias by calling one Soaemias and the other Mamaea. All four Julias were educated women, adept each in her turn at manipulating the political situation to her own advantage. It may well be that later on Zenobia looked back upon the Julias as shining examples of what women could achieve in public life. These ladies, however, were not to be blindly emulated.

A bi-lingual inscription in Aramaic and in Greek, carved in 251 on the base of a statue—now lost—refers to the father of Odenath, or perhaps to his brother, as Senator and Exarch of Palmyra. This title may correspond to the older expression, Ras of Tadmor. At least one recent authority interprets the title as meaning that the "free city" which the Emperor Hadrian had created had now become an Arab principate, though still subject to Rome.

The statue had been set up on one of the columns of the Grand Colonnade. On a nearby column stood the statue of Odenath himself. Its inscription reads that in April 258 the goldsmiths' guild presented the statue to honor Septimius Odenath, "our monarch, of consular rank." Some historians think that the title was bestowed upon Odenath by the ill-fated Valerian, the army officer who succeeded his murdered predecessor and became Emperor of Rome in

253. Mommsen disagrees with this interpretation; he thinks Odenath was now acting as an independent lieutenant of the "Emperor for the East." However the title is interpreted, the inscription should indicate that by 258 Odenath was regarded in Palmyra as being in full control of the city.

Odenath's biographer states that he possessed the vigor and the astute qualities of the old Arab stock from which he sprang, and that in his young wife, Zenobia, he found strong support for his decision to uphold the Roman Empire in the East, even though it might lead to a clash with Sapor. Had it not been for his courageous leadership at that period, the Empire might have collapsed sooner than it did. Naturally, Odenath has his detractors, as Zenobia has; they accuse him of keeping a wary eye upon the course of events, motivated by a secret desire to increase his own power.

Under Odenath's administration, though civil war was devastating the rest of Syria, Palmyra began slowly to recover her former place in the East. In Rome, Arab merchants from Palmyra had built temples to their own god Bel, and to other deities their people honored. For Palmyra, by Odenath's day, was not only a true caravan city; she was also an important center for most of the financial operations of the Roman Empire. And with Palmyra's growing importance, the power of her leading family, the Julii Aurelii Septimii with which Odenath was associated, also increased. Of this increase, Sapor was well aware, even if it had escaped the attention of Rome.

In 242, Sapor invaded Syria, intending to detach Antioch from Rome. At this time he was unsuccessful, and in 249 Rome and Persia concluded a temporary peace. But since in Antioch pro-Persian sentiment continued to grow, Odenath and Zenobia knew they had not seen the last of Sapor.

Sapor returned in 253, the same year that the Roman troops took matters into their own hands, murdered their commander, the reigning Emperor, and proclaimed their leader, Valerian, the new monarch. Valerian, of senatorial rank, was acceptable to the Senate, and so the Empire enjoyed a few years of comparative peace. But the tide of fortune that swept Valerian into power was an ebb tide, for more trouble was brewing everywhere. Sapor had captured and burned Antioch. And when he left Antioch, he took with him a large number of technical experts as captives. Since Antioch had become an important center for the Christian faith, Sapor also struck a blow against the new religion by capturing Bishop Demetrianus and taking him off to his capital, Ctesiphon, in Persia.

In Palmyra, Odenath had quickly announced his allegiance to Valerian, who had gone at once to Antioch to begin rebuilding the devastated city. But Odenath's confidence in Valerian was shaken when he heard that he had chosen his weak and effeminate son, Gallienus, as his heir and co-ruler, and that the joint authority was to take effect immediately.

The Persians continued their attacks upon Syria. In 256, the presumed year of Vaballath's birth, Sapor captured Doura, and Zenobia and Odenath must have feared that Palmyra would be next on the Persian list. On her Euphrates side Doura's ruler had thought he was safe, and in this he proved to be right. But he had not sufficiently strengthened his walls on the desert side, and they crumbled under Sapor's siege-engines.

We do not know whether Odenath strengthened Palmyra's walls or not. Perhaps he trusted to the loyalty of the Roman garrison that had been stationed in Palmyra for well over a hundred years, ever since Hadrian's day. Many of the soldiers had married Palmyrene women, for Hadrian had rescinded the old law against international marriages.

Meanwhile Sapor marched into Mesopotamia and laid siege to Edessa, which belonged to the Roman Empire. And so in the summer of 260 Valerian left his son Gallienus in charge of the West and hurried by forced marches to Edessa. For ten years a terrible plague—some have thought it small-pox—had been raging through the Empire, killing daily in Rome some five thousand people. Because of this, Valerian's army was so reduced and the survivors so weak that he soon despaired of being able to relieve Edessa, and proposed entering into negotiations with Sapor. Sapor requested a personal interview. Trusting to his enemy's good faith, Valerian set out with a small number of soldiers for Edessa. At the gates of the city, Sapor, by a "perfidious ruse," captured Valerian and later displayed him, loaded with chains, to the citizens of Edessa.

Cries of rage and apprehension burst out all over the Empire. Letters and messages came to Sapor warning him not to boast of his victory over a Roman Emperor.

"The Romans are never more dangerous than when they are defeated," one letter ran.

From Palmyra, Odenath had also sent a letter to Sapor. With the letter he sent a train of camels loaded with exotic gifts.

"Who is this Odenath?" Sapor demanded, "that he dares to write a letter to me? Hurl his gifts into the sea."

In his letter Odenath had reminded Sapor that even the Goths, who had sacked and burned Rome, were later conquered and became the servants rather than the masters of Rome. This must have infuriated Sapor. The biographer who reports the content of Odenath's letter adds that Sapor sent back word to Odenath to come to "his lord" and fall prostrate before "our throne, with his hands bound behind his back." Otherwise "swift destruction" would be visited upon him and his country.

Odenath met Sapor, not flat on his face, but magnificently upright in his war-chariot with Zenobia beside him and an armed force at his back. The preceding exchange of letters may, of course, never have taken place, but until they have been proved forgeries, they may be taken at their face value. We know, however, that, regardless of all the protests, Sapor kept his royal captive in chains. Robed in purple, weighted down with fetters, Valerian was exposed to the shouts and jeers of the Persians. When Sapor made ready to mount his horse, he placed his booted foot upon Valerian's back. Crushed by constant exposure and humiliation, Valerian, who was over seventy, finally collapsed and died. Sapor had him flayed, his skin stuffed with straw, and presented him to Edessa's temples as a lasting memorial to Persia's triumph over Rome.

Gibbon questions the accuracy of this story, but it fits into what we know of the character and habits of early eastern monarchs. Today, there are still people who question the atrocities of the Second World War.

A relief near Persepolis shows Valerian kneeling before Sapor.

"I knew my father was mortal," Gallienus, now sole Emperor, is reported to have said, when the horrifying news was brought to him.

Though doubtless shocked by Sapor's treatment of an Emperor, the Christian communities of Rome and other communities of the Empire could not have greatly mourned Valerian's death. They had endured Sapor's earlier capture of Bishop Demetrianus in Antioch; it was, if an outrage, an outrage due rather to political than to religious motives, and it had left most of the Christians to worship in comparative peace. But Valerian had tried to hold the tottering Empire together by banning all public worship except that of the Emperor—Emperor-worship had been, of course, for some years an integral part of the state religion.

The community was stirred to its depths. The weak recanted; the strong suffered death. In Rome, St. Lawrence was burned to death; in Carthage, just two years before Sapor captured Valerian, the illustrious St. Cyprian was beheaded, the first African bishop to become a martyr. It is not surprising, then, that the Christians did not greatly mourn Valerian's death.

Gallienus, too busy in the West to pay attention to the East, left Odenath to his own devices. During earlier years, Odenath had been able to maintain friendly relations with both Rome and Parthia, but the Sassanid Persians were bent upon complete political and commercial control of the East. Some historians think it was at this time that Odenath took advantage of the new Emperor's negligence, proclaimed himself King of Palmyra, and offered his services as an ally to Gallienus.

We do not know precisely where Odenath and Zenobia first made contact with Sapor and his entourage, for he seems to have retreated steadily before their advance. Emesa, hearing of Sapor's retreat, succumbed almost at once to Odenath, and this helped greatly in re-establishing the unity of the Empire. When the actual encounter did take place, perhaps near the Euphrates, Sapor fled, leaving his wives, his concubines, and his children to the mercy of the conqueror. And Odenath gave all of them, including their "riches and jewels," to his profligate son Herodian. The reason for his generous act was, according to Pollio, that Zenobia had always treated Herodian in a "step-mother way." This made "Herodian all the more dear to his father."

Zenobia's alleged attitude toward her stepson may, if the allegation is true, provide us with a clue to the unusual marital relationship between Odenath and his wife that Pollio later dwells upon at some length.

In this early encounter between Odenath and Sapor, neither had won the first round. Sapor had lost his women, perhaps his children, who now seem to disappear from history; but he still had his capital city, Ctesiphon. Odenath had won back for the Roman Empire all the lost territory except Ctesiphon, and for the moment he seems to have been content to return with Zenobia and his forces to Palmyra.

According to some authorities, Odenath may now have begun to overplay his hand; they think he may have visualized a powerful Palmyrene Empire in the East. But to accomplish this, he would need Roman legions. With their help he could trounce Persia so severely that she would never be able to recover.

Gallienus, playing his own hand, soon entrusted Odenath with the supreme command over the East, including the legions stationed there. In 263 Odenath and Zenobia set out again, this time to attack Ctesiphon itself and clear the way for caravans dispatched to the Persian Gulf. An inscription dated 266 indicates that, though Odenath did not capture Ctesiphon, he did open the route to the caravans.

And he did indeed press on far enough to conquer the outskirts of the city. His withdrawal at that moment has seemed to some strategists a mistake for which Zenobia was later to pay the cost. Others do not blame Odenath, but the fearful plague that was still raging in 264, and that did not begin to recede until a year later.

57

The plague had been disastrous for Valerian, and might at this time have proved equally disastrous for Odenath, had he gone on to the conquest of the city itself.

Rostovtzeff reminds us that during Odenath's frequent absences from Palmyra a certain Worod, or Vorodes, had charge of the entire population. The full name of this official was Julius Aurelius Septimius Worod; it is half Persian and half Roman. Yet Vorodes was a member of the Palmyrene aristocracy, and as such, a suitable person to entrust the city to.

Rostovtzeff also reminds us that Vorodes enjoyed a title that was equivalent to both of Odenath's. To a Roman, Vorodes' title meant both governor and judge; to a Persian it meant a military office. This ambiguity made it difficult, later on, to define accurately just where Vorodes' authority ended and Zenobia's began. Odenath's title, *consularis*, which was definitely Roman, was conferred upon him during his lifetime. His eastern title, King of Kings, appears on an inscription dated 271, the year Zenobia sent Zabdas to Egypt. These titles of Odenath's, Rostovtzeff feels, stress the "two-sided character of Palmyra . . . the double face . . . she always showed, eastern on one side, Roman on the other." In 264, about the middle of the war against Sapor, Odenath had received another title; the Roman Senate elevated him to the rank of an Augustus, and voted him a triumphal procession in Rome. Zenobia must then have become an Augusta.

When Gallienus approved this action of the Senate, say the historians, he performed the only act of his reign that met with universal praise; and it may well be that when Odenath's triumph took place, the whole city turned out, to exult over his trophies and his prisoners. Among the prisoners were Sapor's wives and concubines. Though no ancient historian has described for us the pageantry of Odenath's procession, we hope he rode in that gorgeous war-chariot of his that figured a few years later in the Emperor Aurelian's spectacular parade through the streets of Rome.

If Pollio's statement can be trusted that Odenath presented Sapor's wives and concubines to his son, then the ladies must either have been lent for the occasion or given afterward to Herodian. Unfortunately, we have no evidence on either side. We do know, however, that the ladies were displayed in Rome, probably wearing, as was the custom, their jewels and other fine ornaments.

The splendid victories Odenath and Zenobia gained "laid the foundation of their fame and power," Gibbon writes. But we do not know whether Zenobia accompanied Odenath through all these years of combat. There is no evidence, for example, that she was with her royal husband when in that fatal year 267 or 268, he went to Emesa in Syria.

Though Odenath seems to have been almost constantly involved in warfare, he did not neglect Palmyra. By the middle of the third century he had erected many public buildings, had added more columns to the Grand Colonnade, and was in the process of setting up additional stone burial towers to accommodate those who had died in defense of the Empire, when affairs of state took him to Emesa. Herodian, his son and heir, accompanied him.

As the population of Palmyra grew, Odenath had reclaimed desert land and added it to the city. Soon villages sprang up and wealthy people began to build villas for summer living. Always mindful of their enemies, Odenath and Zenobia kept their army in trim. Restless young men they trained to use the bow and mounted them upon swift horses that they might have plenty of archers on hand to supplement the Roman cavalry based in Palmyra.

By this time Palmyra's trade was in excellent condition. Her merchants sent caravans everywhere, to Spain, to Gaul, to Dacia, though Dacia had not yet fully recovered from the fearful massacre the Emperor Trajan had earlier inflicted upon the whole country. In Rome the Arab merchants continued to build temples to their own deities and to bring to them the same gifts they had been accustomed to present when in their faraway homes. And Rome seldom interfered, so long as they paid their taxes.

Odenath seems to have had leisure for his favorite sport, hunting. One day while he was in Emesa, with Herodian, his kinsman Maeonius, their beaters, and other huntsmen, Odenath went out into the nearby forest to hunt wild animals. Upon such occasions, when the beaters had flushed a quarry, the honor of the first throw belonged to the monarch.

This time the first animal to dash out was a lion. Maeonius, either through excitement or through intention, hurled his spear first. Astonished by this breach of manners, but not yet insulted, the King merely chided his impetuous young relative. But Maeonius hurled his second spear. Enraged, Odenath ordered Maeonius off his horse and taken at once into custody. Whether both spears missed and the lion escaped, has not seemed important for history to have recorded. As for Maeonius, imprisonment, it seems, could have been borne, but to be publicly unhorsed, even by his King, was an ignominy no man could endure. Perhaps it was also an ignominy no King should have inflicted.

Soon afterward, in the midst of a gay birthday celebration, Maeonius and a band of companions assassinated King Odenath. Pollio states that they also killed Herodian and that Odenath's army, when they heard of their monarch's death, saluted Maeonius as Emperor. This does not agree with the report of the careful historian Zonaras, who says that Maeonius was struck down immediately after the murder.

At this point our knowledge of Odenath, King of Kings, comes to an abrupt end. We know that the period which closes with his death was one of great disturbance throughout the whole Empire; so many usurpers had sprung up that Pollio wrote the biographies of thirty persons whom he called Pretenders to the Imperial throne and that he included Zenobia. We also know that modern scholarship has reduced the number to eighteen, with Odenath a dubious nineteenth, since the assassin's dagger has made it forever impossible to know what his real intentions were.

The question of Zenobia's involvement in her husband's murder has long been a subject of controversy, but so far it has not been solved. Nor has anyone drawn attention to the good feeling that must have prompted those generals to erect in 271 the column and statue in their Queen's honor alongside Odenath's in the Grand

Colonnade. There is, it is true, an unsubstantiated tale that in this same year Zenobia lost her son Vaballath, but whether any connection exists here is for the historians to decide.

Though we know nothing about the arrangements that must have been made for burying Odenath, we may be fairly sure that Zenobia held the beliefs about life after death that were current in the third century. She would, no doubt, have had Odenath's body embalmed, placed in a sarcophagus, and borne through the streets of Palmyra to the City of the Dead.

VI

The City of the Dead

In imagination we now see Odenath's funeral procession passing slowly through the Grand Colonnade. Drawn by twenty pairs of legionaries, ten Roman, ten Arab, the low-wheeled platform bearing the sarcophagus moves steadily on toward Palmyra's City of the Dead. Behind, row on row, marching men bear lifted palm branches. The women and children, who line the colonnade, are comforted when they see half-reclining on the lid of his sarcophagus the effigy of their King; they know that even in the After World he will still be their protector.

In Rome, people were dancing in the streets. Some god, jealous of Odenath's growing power, had struck him from his high pedestal and saved the Empire. So Pollio interprets the assassination at Emesa. But the rejoicing of the people dropped to a lower key, when they remembered that Zenobia was still alive. Their joy flared again, however, when they heard that a favorite general of theirs, who called himself Aurelian, though only peasant blood ran in his veins, had proclaimed in his rough soldier's voice that, if he had his way, he would quickly bring "that woman in Palmyra" to heel. The epithet had caught the fancy of Rome; men began to shout it in the streets, and women flung it from roof-top to roof-top.

But in Palmyra, unaware of what was happening in Rome, Odenath's procession went its way, paused briefly at the triumphal arch, to let the King of Kings take his leave of the god Bel, then turned westward to start the long slow journey out into the desert, where Odenath would sleep with his forefathers in the City of the Dead.

We do not really know if the men in Odenath's funeral procession carried palm branches, but that they did may be assumed since the palm tree has long been a symbol of immortality. An example of its symbolical use in Palmyra occurs on a marble stele—an upright slab often set up to mark a grave—on which was carved the name of Aitibel.

Clothed in a toga-like robe, Aitibel stands in a recess cut into the upper part of his stele. To indicate to the spectator that Aitibel is separated from the living, the artist has carved on either side of the figure a palm tree. Knotted fast to the trunk of each palm and falling in soft folds between them hangs a funeral cloth that conceals the lower part of Aitibel's body. Cloth and palms show that Aitibel is no longer among those who dwell on earth.

A fresco from a tomb in the City of the Dead, known today as that of the Three Brothers and dated in the early part of the third century, represents the hero Achilles among the daughters of the King of Scyros. A mosaic in a house east of the temple of Bel illustrates the same legend.

The legend is connected with the effort of King Agamemnon of Mycenae and his brother, King Menelaus of Sparta, to persuade their fellow-chieftains to join them in the famous expedition to recover Helen from Troy. All, including the youthful Achilles, were eager to go. But the hero's mother, loath to part with her son, sent him off to the island of Scyros.

The King of Scyros, who may have been aware of the plot, persuaded Achilles to exchange his masculine dress for that of a maiden and join his daughter's spinning circle, where no one would think to look for him. The wily Odysseus, however, in the guise of an itinerant trader, gained access to the women's quarters and began displaying his trinkets. Suddenly he held up a sword. The "maiden" stretched out an eager hand, then threw aside his concealing dress.

Both the fresco and the mosaic represent Achilles in the act of tossing aside his clothing. This action of his has been variously interpreted. Some scholars think it symbolizes the *nafsa*, or soul, shedding its earthly garments for those of a better world. But this notion of the survival of the soul was not, as Starcky points out, characteristic of Semitic belief, nor would the survival of the soul alone be an enviable fate.

For those who longed to believe in the soul's survival there were the mystery religions, such as Mithraism and the Eleusinian rites. Both had many adherents throughout the Greco-Roman world. So far, no Mithraum has been discovered in Palmyra. If one should appear, the interpretation of the Achilles fresco might be more easily understood.

The temples and the tombs of Palmyra and of Doura are almost our only sources of information about the architecture, the sculpture, and the painting of Zenobia's day. They are also the chief sources of our information about the religious attitude of Zenobia's people, and perhaps of Zenobia herself. For her beliefs about those whom we call "dead" must have been the beliefs of her day.

Since sacred architecture usually conforms to the beliefs that currently actuate a people, we should expect to find as much difference between the temple architecture of the Semites and that of the Greco-Romans as we find between their beliefs. The temple of the Babylonian god Bel is a good example, because here there is a mixture of styles that conforms to the mixture of beliefs held in the third century.

The ruins of the great temple of Bel, the best-preserved in Syria or in Lebanon, lie on a slight elevation, and this situation is the clearest indication of the Semitic origin of the temple. To commune with his deity, Biblical history tells us, Moses went up on to a "high place," similar, we may imagine, to one of those in Petra.

Whether the Emperor Tiberius understood the Semitic custom or not, he did, at any rate, rebuild the temple on the same elevation. The only change he made was to follow the new Greco-Roman trend of adding columns with Corinthian capitals, and a propyleum, or stepped entrance. Chief among the features he left unchanged is the great parklike enclosure, or *paradisos*, around the temple.

Tiberius may have known that this enclosure would recall to the Semites their lost Eden and its palms. Since the ruins of the sacrificial altar and the sacred basin may still be seen, obviously he did not disturb them. Many other Oriental features also remain unchanged. Reconstructed in this fashion, the temple of Bel in Palmyra would be intelligible to both East and West.

Palmyra's strange City of the Dead is unlike any other burial place in the Fertile Crescent. Most of the tombs that have been excavated lie in a narrow valley that runs between two hills, following what may have been an old camel track in and out of the city. Through this valley Odenath's cortege would have gone to reach the tomb of his ancestors, whether it lay in the valley itself or high up near one of the sand dunes.

The first monuments to Palmyra's dead began to appear during the age of Augustus and Tiberius, when ancient Tadmor had grown into one of the most brilliant cities of the Fertile Crescent. One of the oldest, if not the oldest, of the tomb inscriptions dates from 9 B.C. At that time the city was growing so rapidly that the sulphur springs on which the population had long depended for their water supply had begun to dry up. The city fathers were being obliged to bring in underground water from the surrounding country.

Obviously Tadmor in the Wilderness no longer sufficed for the needs of Palmyra, the caravan city, whose mausoleums, stretching farther and farther underground, and tower-tombs, reaching higher and higher into the skies, bore witness to her growth and to her wealth. During the excavation of the tombs hundreds of funeral statues and bas-reliefs were found. Almost without exception the artist has represented his subjects full front. The two halves of the face are symmetrical; the eyes, if open, are wide-open, the eyelids well-defined; two concentric circles mark the iris and the pupil of each eye. The pleated lines of the clothing are geometrically precise. The artist appears to have taken such infinite pains to produce realistic portraits that any one of his subjects would surely feel apologetic if he failed to recognize himself or his friends in the After World.

Starcky sees a purpose in the artist's mind; he has duplicated his subject, yes, but he has at the same time spiritualized him. In other words, the statue or bas-relief is the individual's *nafsa,* his imperishable Self. Starcky reminds us that on such a statue there is often written in Aramaic characters: *"This is the nafsa of So-and-So."* We may infer, then, that So-and-So expects to recognize himself and his friends, when they awaken and meet one another in the After World. For their so-called tombs in the City of the Dead are literally their sleeping-places, their *koimeteria,* (Greek for cemeteries).

For those who know "cemetery" only in its modern connotation, the picture the word presents is not accurate, at least for ancient Palmyra. If you stand with your back to the temple of Bel and look almost directly westward, expecting to see rows of white headstones, with here and there a monument, you will not find them. Instead, you will see broken stone towers set at infrequent intervals in the midst of a desolate waste of scrub and sand dunes. The contrast with the tall honey-colored pillars of the Grand Colonnade is so great that you may be inclined to agree with the traveler who spoke of the whole panorama as an "almost inhuman landscape."

Some of these towers, the "apartment-houses of the dead," must have been originally seventy feet high, or even higher. Today more than a hundred and fifty are still visible, though some are half buried in sand. Archaeologists think that when Palmyra outgrew its site many families built their houses out here beyond the walls. But since in earlier days the inhabitants of the Fertile Crescent could not believe that the dead were really dead, the habit of keeping the deceased in his own home developed, and it persisted well into Zenobia's time, as some of the dated inscriptions show. To keep the dead in their houses necessitated, however, adding story upon story, until finally the living occupied the lower stories, and the non-living the upper ones.

The desperate refusal of mankind to accept death as the primal condition of all existence has been called the most pathetic fact in the history of the human race. This obstinate disbelief has given rise to many familiar and widespread legends of the origin of death and of varied attempts to outwit the grisly reaper, Time.

Perhaps we might pause a moment here to consider the origin of Time as a "grisly reaper." An ancient confusion between two letters of the Greek alphabet is responsible for transferring the reaping-hook from the hand of Kronos, an early agricultural god worshipped with barbarous rites, to the hand of Chronos, the philosophical abstraction of Time, who would not have been able to hold anything. Greek art added to the confusion by representing Kronos with a curved object, traditionally interpreted as the knife he used on his father, but quite as easily interpreted as a reaping-hook. Time continues, however, at least in literature, to be the "grisly reaper."

The legend connected with the Garden of Eden ascribes death to man's first act of disobedience against his Creator. A legend known to some early tribes of the Philippine Islands attributes death to a god's curse. Certain tribes of New South Wales believed that people were meant to live forever. Here, as in the Biblical story, a woman was the cause of death's entry into the world.

The legend runs that wild bees had hived in a certain hollow tree that no one was allowed to touch. But the women craved the honey. Finally, in spite of repeated warnings, one woman attacked the tree with her "tomahawk." Out flew a huge bat. From then on, the bat roamed the world, and anyone he touched with his wings died.

Though we have no evidence for Palmyra, it is quite likely that there, as among other early peoples, the death-like appearance of a corpse was accounted for by the belief that the soul had temporarily deserted the body. To make sure that the soul had indeed departed, the Greeks and the Romans called three times the name of the dead person. Today the custom has survived, crystallized into the practice of calling three times the name of a deceased Pope.

Since it was customary in Palmyra to make an effigy, or image, of the deceased, it may also have been customary to entreat his soul to return and make the effigy his home. From the belief that a soul could return may have developed the practice of inviting the deceased to attend whenever the family feast was held. What a surprise it would have been if the perhaps long-buried person had appeared to demand his share of the food. The evidence of burial customs, of sacrifices to the dead, and of family meals at the tomb strengthens the comforting belief in the continued existence of the soul after it has reluctantly left its earthly home. Only by nourishing this belief can the inescapable fact of death become acceptable to man.

The ancient Etruscans seem to have believed that when they were carried into their tombs, they would remain there until they were transformed into gods. How long this period of "suspended animation" was supposed to last we do not know, nor, of course, did they. But, when their transformation did come about, they expected to enter into the life everlasting which the blessed gods enjoyed.

During their later and more sophisticated days, the Etruscans must have lost this simple, happy belief of theirs. Then terror of the hereafter plagued them, and they dreaded the arrival of the demon of death, whom they thought of as beating his helpless victims with his club.

There exists sufficient evidence, epigraphical and monumental rather than literary, to indicate that the ancient peoples of the Fertile Crescent must have believed that they, too, would continue to live after their so-called death, but not, as in Christian belief, in bodiless form. Whether they also believed, as did the Etruscans, that they would themselves become gods, we have no means of knowing, for no written records have, as yet, been discovered.

Since burial customs in Palmyra seem to have been similar to those in other parts of the ancient world, Zenobia would have had her husband embalmed, probably in the Egyptian way, wrapped in a winding-sheet—scraps of cloth, often silk, such as one sees in the Damascus Museum, have been found near mummified bodies—and placed in what Starcky calls a *demeure d'éternité*, a "resting place for all time."

We do not know where Odenath was buried; his resting place might have been a tower-tomb, a temple-tomb, or a mausoleum. His effigy would present him to his people as they had known him, in full armor or clad in royal garments, adorned with jewels and stretched at full length or reclining, less comfortably, on one elbow. Forever afterward, Odenath, King of Kings, will be recognizable in the After World.

Though we hear nothing of familiar objects being buried in a grave or tomb that the dead person may have something more by which to identify himself in the After World, it seems safe to assume that the inhabitants of Palmyra and of other localities in the Fertile Crescent did not differ from other ancient peoples. For lack of evidence to the contrary, early man seems always to have conceived of the After World as a copy of what he sees around him in daily life, bigger and better, perhaps, but recognizable; and for that other life he made his preparations. Some one has suggested that in Palmyra, during the early years of our era, this better world was visualized as the kingdom of the Sun-god.

Without wings to reach this better world, man must devise some other way. Perhaps if he built as high into the air as possible and had himself placed aloft, when his time came to leave his present life, he might be close enough to span the intervening space and enter that blessed abode.

We know that tower-tombs were not confined to Palmyra; they have been found elsewhere in the Fertile Crescent. But they are thought to have reached their full development only in Palmyra. The two tower-tombs most often visited are the Jamblichus tomb and the tomb of Elabel. Both are off in the desert, and though one can visit them on foot, it is almost impossible to escape riding out in one of the numerous cars the guides have ready.

The Jamblichus tomb is on the summit of a low sand dune. It was built after Palmyra had come under Roman control. Four stories are still standing. From the top, you can see to the southeast the ancient sulphur springs, so enlarged now that Arab boys plunge into the waters to bathe, and to the west the remains of many other tower-tombs, including the tomb of Elabel. To reach it, you jounce over the dry bed of the Wadi, once crowded with house-tombs that have completely disappeared.

The tomb of Elabel is unique; it has two entrances, one at the rear, the other at the front. The rear entrance leads down to a subterranean burial-place long ago despoiled of its contents. The front entrance opens on a ground floor with forty-eight separate spaces for sarcophagi. Fluted pilasters topped by Corinthian capitals, all once brightly painted, separate the individual spaces from one another. The ceiling is coffered, and ornamented with white roses on a blue background.

Above the front entrance stood the bust of Elabel's son, who was the curator of the tomb. The other members of the family were also represented; each bust stood at the entrance to the recess where his sarcophagus lay, and each was marked with its owner's name. We do not know how high this tomb was, for it has lost its roof and all but its four lower stories. To the left of the front entrance a staircase leads upward—"Mind the breaks," the guide warns as you start to climb; "once a lady fell."

As you climb the open staircase, you pass story after story, each less well decorated than the one before. No sarcophagus is to be seen; the skeletons, too, have been taken away because they disturbed visitors. The third story has a kind of balcony. Seen from below, it resembles a sarcophagus, or perhaps, as some think, a cell in the catacombs of Rome. Though we cannot estimate the exact height of Elabel's tomb, that it was an expensive project for a family to undertake we may be quite sure. In Palmyra the high cost of dying must have been as exorbitant as it is with us today.

A tale one often hears is that a certain enterprising citizen of Palmyra met the high cost of burying one member of his family after another by selling space to strangers, and that his descendants continued the lucrative practice. This profitable tomb is the one guides used to consider Zenobia's. Unfortunately, the inscriptions found there prove that the guides were mistaken.

Temple-tombs, or house-tombs, and mausoleums must have been just as expensive, or almost so, as the more conspicuous tower-tombs. House-tombs, since they could serve a double purpose, were perhaps the least expensive, but that would depend on how elaborate the house was.

Many so-called temple-tombs have been found in Palmyra. Part of the pillared façade of one stands at the far end of the Grand Colonnade. The bases of four columns, surrounded by a court about twenty feet square, show the position of the sanctuary, or *cella*. Underneath the stone floor of this *cella* the excavators found places where sarcophagi had been, and near by a chamber for the customary funeral feasts. The places for the sarcophagi added up to about eighty, if, as it is supposed, the sarcophagi were put one on top of the other. The nearby chamber had been profusely decorated with carved and painted reliefs that represented persons at a feast. Here the families of the deceased gathered at regular intervals for their funeral banquets.

Excavations in Palmyra have shown that at times a low mound of earth will conceal a mausoleum with a series of palatial rooms, where men came long, long ago bringing their sarcophagi or their cinerary urns.

One subterranean mausoleum was carved out of the solid rock. Its central peristyle, or court surrounded by columns, resembles that of a Hellenistic house. Around this inner court were found thirty-five sarcophagi, each in its rock recess. Another mausoleum had a hall almost forty-five feet long. The two rooms that opened off the hall were filled with sarcophagi, each with its sculptured effigy, several low sarcophagi platforms, and innumerable busts on pedestals.

The mausoleum of the Three Brothers had space for at least three hundred and ninety bodies. The brothers who built this mausoleum for themselves, and presumably for their families, finished it almost a century and a half before Zenobia was born. Its shape is that of the letter T upside down. The entrance is at the middle of the crossbar. You enter on a ramp that slopes sharply downward to a hinged door set upon a foundation slab. Inscriptions, written in Aramaic, mention the various people who have from time to time owned space in the mausoleum. Some spaces have belonged to three different owners, in turn.

At either end of the short hallway that forms the crossbar of the letter T there is a room, or exedra, where sarcophagi once rested on their platforms. The exedra to the right had contained three sarcophagi arranged as a triclinium, the U-shape that the Greeks and the Romans preferred for their banquets. Above the sarcophagi were frescoes that represented the brothers enjoying a banquet in the After World.

The exedra to the left held a single sarcophagus; its inscription shows that it was intended for one of the brothers. Unfortunately, when the mausoleum was opened, only fragments were to be seen. At the base of the T another sarcophagus was in sufficiently good condition for its effigies to be recognized: two male figures carved side by side on the lid, at the feet of one, the bas-relief of a woman; the reliefs above were of children.

The frescoes that portray the ghostly banqueters are thought to belong to the early part of the third century. To the same period may belong the Achilles fresco and another, painted on the pilaster facing the entrance, that shows an "evil eye," with birds and scorpions attacking it. Other pilasters are decorated with pictures of women, badly defaced, but recognizable.

Some years ago the tomb of a certain Yarhai—it antedates that of the Three Brothers—was excavated, transported entire to Damascus, and installed in a rectangular basement room specially designed for it. If you turn to your right as you enter, you will see Yarhai, his wife, and his children, Yarhai himself half-reclining on an elevated sarcophagus, his wife at his feet, and his children ranged above. Funeral busts cover the walls on either side of the sarcophagus. There are no frescoes, nor has the museum made any attempt to exhibit a banqueting room.

In both Palmyra and Doura, the excavators found small clay tokens, some inscribed with a name, which they think may have been entrance tickets to the funeral feasts. The name may have been that of the deceased to whose ritual banquet the ticket-holder had been invited. It would be interesting to know whether he was expected to attend the sacrifices that provided the banquet food. If so, he may also have been expected to provide a sacrificial animal or other suitable food.

Though we do not know what these sacrifices were, we may suppose that they provided meat for the living and bowls of blood for the dead. The white-robed priests who conducted the sacrifice doubtless regarded themselves as officiating for the deceased. In the absence of texts, we can only surmise the liturgy, but we may venture to suggest that the more elaborate the liturgy and the feasts, the better sustained would be the memory of the deceased, and perhaps the higher his status in the After World.

An interesting relief appears on a dated sarcophagus found in an underground mausoleum. The date is 229. According to Starcky and other scholars, the height of the relief, its appearance of suppleness, and the graceful stance of the youthful figure portrayed there all point toward the West rather than toward the East. Fully alive and at ease with himself, he looks out upon the world and finds it good.

The mausoleum belonged to a certain Atenatan, but whether our handsome young man was Atenatan himself, we do not know. His rich clothing makes one wonder if he could possibly have been the father of the young prince of Palmyra, Odenath, whose destiny it was to grow up, marry Zenobia, and, still in the prime of exuberant life, fall by the hand of his own kinsman.

In the years after Odenath's death, Zenobia, if she held the beliefs of her time, could take comfort from the fact that her husband lay asleep in his sarcophagus, his effigy on its lid, and supplied with recognition tokens that would enable her to find him when she, too, reached the After World.

BOOK TWO

ZENOBIA, THE QUEEN

"Wise, steadfast, firm, and generous."
TREBELLIUS POLLIO

VII

Zenobia on Her Way

Odenath's sudden death had left Zenobia in a precarious situation.
Her stepson, Herodian, had been killed with his father, and
Maeonius soon afterward. The army, stunned by the triple blow,
had made no move to put Vaballath on the throne. Zenobia knew
she had no time to lose. We have no evidence that she got in touch
with the Emperor Gallienus, but it is reasonable to infer that she
did, for Gallienus had paused long enough in his orgies to recognize
Vaballath as heir to the throne and Zenobia as the boy-king's regent. And Palmyra seemed content.

One morning shortly after these events had taken place, we must
imagine Zenobia, now Queen of Palmyra in her own right, alone in
her private suite in the palace. Though we do not yet know where
the palace stood, it was probably near the tetrapylon and the
caravansery. Like other mansions in Palmyra, the palace was doubtless built of native stone, its windows high and narrow, possibly
of opaque glass, and its doors of polished olive wood, kept
closed and guarded. Officials, messengers, and visitors would pass
through a front court, then an inner court, present their credentials,
and either be refused or escorted into the palace.

On this particular morning Zenobia is pacing restlessly from
room to room. Even if her eyes fall, from time to time, on brightly
frescoed walls, on floors and couches strewn with Persian rugs,

many of them from Sapor's captured tents, or on massive plate studded with precious stones, it is doubtful whether she sees anything. She is thinking of Vaballath, now in his early teens. He should have a tutor, since he no longer has a father to teach him the ways of war and of diplomacy. His Greek is poor, his Latin worse—her fault, because she has, as yet, spoken only Aramaic or Arabic with him. She must try again to teach him to hunt, out in the desert where leopards are still to be found.

Vaballath; a smile might have touched the corners of her mouth as she recalled Odenath's laugh when she told him the name she had chosen for her first-born son.

"In Aramaic, the gift of Allat, our goddess of wisdom," she had explained, knowing it to be unnecessary. "I want him to be all Arab, like me."

"He looks like you even now," Odenath had replied seriously.

When the Greeks in Palmyra heard the name of the small prince, they translated it into their own tongue, Athenadorus, the gift of Athene, their goddess of wisdom. And for them the boy remained Athenadorus, for all that he was a citizen of Rome, as Odenath had been, and as she herself must perforce be, but not for long, she vowed, remembering how docile she had once been. Odenath had curbed her willfulness. She had not resented it; he had been so much older and wiser than she. But she must now think for herself, and for her people.

A discreet knock on the door interrupted her train of thought. Her new Greek secretary, Nicomachus, entered, a parchment roll in his hand. He bowed, waited for permission, then knelt and presented the parchment. Zenobia accepted the roll, but not until she had smilingly dismissed the man did she seat herself at a small inlaid table, and break the seal.

A swift glance told her the news.

Murder again! A group of generals had assassinated the Emperor Gallienus; they had taken advantage of the resentment of the people, who were blaming Gallienus for all their calamities, including the plague, and had banded together to kill him. The Senate had decided not to deify Gallienus; his vicious life had not fitted him for godhead nor for the worship that would have been his due.

Gallienus murdered, and just after he had recognized Vaballath's claim to his father's rights. Who would be the new Emperor? She turned back to the parchment. The conspirators had made their choice, but without giving the legions a chance to make known theirs. Infuriated by the deliberate slight, cohort after cohort had mutinied.

The conspirators had wavered between two men. Each had risen from the ranks. One, Marcus Aurelius Claudius, had a mild disposition; the other, a shock-headed Illyrian general who had acquired the name of Lucius Domitius Aurelianus, was a severe disciplinarian. With an eye to placating the soldiers, the generals chose Claudius. But the soldiers refused to be placated, and the generals had to buy their consent.

In March 268, Claudius became the new Emperor of Rome. Shortly afterward, he appointed Aurelian commander-in-chief of the army. This stroke of political genius met with complete approval, and the soldiers allowed the generals' choice to stand.

One of the first adjustments Claudius made was to set aside his predecessor's decision about the boy-king of Palmyra. Quite possibly it was at about this time that Longinus came to Zenobia's court. A Greek philosopher of the Platonic school in Athens, Longinus was now in his middle fifties, a cultivated man who had had the advantage of travel and study in Athens and in Alexandria. History knows him as the tutor of Zenobia's children, but according to Professor Seyrig's theory the two younger boys were already dead. Probably Longinus tutored Vaballath and assisted Zenobia in her study of Greek and Roman authors. Since Zenobia is said to have composed a history of Egypt, Longinus may have suggested that she occupy herself in this way while she was consolidating her position in Palmyra.

One of the first questions Longinus would have asked was whether Zenobia regarded herself as her son's regent or whether she had ambitions for herself. This was the question that was agitating the Empire. Longinus must often have had to remind her, when he became a member of her advisory council, that she was the first woman to control the fortunes of Palmyra, and that much depended upon how she used her power.

That Longinus did in time become the Queen's most trusted adviser is well known. Perhaps she learned through him that she was being accused of complicity in her husband's murder, for the gossip that was fast spreading throughout the Empire had to come to her through some channel. She could not have remained long in ignorance.

The question of Zenobia's involvement in Odenath's murder has long been a subject of controversy, but so far the problem has never been solved. Most modern laws presume a person innocent until he is proved guilty. Since we have no dependable evidence, either pro or con, that Zenobia instigated her husband's murder, and Herodian's too, we must, in justice to the Queen of Palmyra, consider her innocent. This, I venture to suggest, would have been the opinion of the philosopher, Longinus, for he seems never to have swerved in his loyalty to her.

Whether Longinus or some other member of Zenobia's court acquainted her with the current gossip does not much matter. Sooner or later it would have come to her ears, for gossip must have added as much spice to third-century life as it does to our own today.

In Palmyra, too, gossip must have been rife, though Longinus would have done his best to stifle it, as would Zenobia's chief general, Zabdas, who always remained loyal to his Queen. History tells us that Zabdas, as well as Longinus, served as one of Zenobia's counselors. If there is any truth in the tradition that Antiochus was the Queen's father, we should expect to find him, at this period in her life, also mentioned as a counselor. Instead, we find the name of Vorodes.

The exact position that Vorodes occupied in Palmyra after Odenath's death is hard to determine. When Zenobia had to be absent from the city, he probably acted as her deputy, since that had been his relationship to Odenath. There is some slight evidence, though, that Vorodes may not have been completely loyal to the Queen.

A year or so later, when Zenobia began to plan her ambitious campaign against Rome, she must have been surprised to learn that her treasury had what almost amounted to a deficit. Though the shortest and cheapest route through the desert still ran through Palmyra, and caravans still halted in the oasis city as they had been doing for years, Zenobia's revenues were dwindling. The taxes levied upon the Prostitutes Guild, which had always poured lavishly into the treasury, had become a mere trickle. Business was poor, the Guild's manager informed the Queen. Then her spies reported that some of the city officials were pocketing the water taxes and the salt taxes. Doubtless they thought that since they now had only a woman to deal with, they could falsify their returns without undue risk.

The executioner's axe proved that all these worthies were mistaken. Soon the revenues rose to an unprecedented height, and Zenobia could continue with her preparations.

The death of Gallienus must have convinced Zenobia that she now stood alone; only she had the will and the resources to protect her son's rights. And so she decided to finish what Odenath had begun, extend Palmyra's dominions to north and south, rather than embark upon another disastrous siege of Sapor's capital.

Some historians regard Zenobia's decision not to renew the attack upon Ctesiphon as a repetition of Odenath's mistake; they believe Claudius would have been glad to have Zenobia pull his chestnuts out of the fire. Whether her judgment was right or wrong, she did not lead her army east. She went north and attacked Antioch, which, after Sapor's death, had returned to the Imperial fold. She must have felt that Claudius would be too occupied with the Goths, as indeed he was, to pay attention to her activities in Syria.

Antioch offered little resistance even when Zenobia ordered the mints to stop issuing coins in the name of Claudius, assuring the officials that in future all coins would bear her name and that of her son Vaballath. Rome was stunned! The Queen of Palmyra had defied the Emperor of Rome.

To be flouted by a woman who was scarcely more than a child herself, as Claudius may have thought of Zenobia, would naturally be intolerable to a man of humble birth who had just been elevated to the highest seat in the civilized world. We do not know what reply, if any, Claudius made, when Zenobia said that she was not a weak woman, and she did not intend to be dictated to.

At this time, the leading figure in Antioch was its bishop, Paul, who came, as Lucian did, from the Semitic town of Samosata on the Euphrates. In Antioch, Paul was accused of being a heretic, and Zenobia seems to have roused some resentment both there and in Palmyra by insisting upon Paul's right to believe what he chose. How much of all this Claudius knew is difficult to say; he did not, however, make any move to wrest Antioch from Zenobia, nor did he interfere with Paul. Claudius was probably astute enough to realize that the unrest in Antioch would eventually make the citizens understand how much better off they would be if they were loyal to the Empire. At present he had more important problems: barbarian pressure from the West and Gothic invasion from both East and West.

Claudius and his new commander-in-chief, Aurelian, now decided, rightly, as it proved, that they must without further delay drive back the Goths from the Danubian frontier. The barbarians in the West and Zenobia in Antioch could be attended to later. With Aurelian an able second, Claudius disposed of the Goths so successfully that they withdrew in haste, leaving fifty thousand dead on the field—fifty thousand is a popular number with the biographers.

Claudius was still congratulating himself on having rid the Empire of the Goths when word came from Rome that another woman was causing trouble. At first Claudius may not even have known the woman's name. She was called sometimes Victoria, sometimes Vitruvia. While he was trying to collect information, a popular demonstration in the streets of Rome roused him to action. Armed with whatever they could lay hands on, huge crowds marched to

1. *Columns of Grand Colonnade, Palmyra, inscribed with Zenobia's name. Courtesy of the National Museum, Damascus, Syria. Photograph by Adnan Bounni.*

2. Frescoes from the Tomb of the Three Brothers, Palmyra. Courtesy of the National Museum Damascus, Syria.

3. *Hypogeum of Yarhai, Palmyra. Courtesy of the National Museum, Damascus, Syria.*

4. *Funeral bust of the third century, Palmyra. Courtesy of the National Museum, Damascus Syria.*

the palace and shouted their disapproval of the two women Pretenders to the throne. The Pretender Victoria the rioters seemed to consider a schemer rather than an open risk; Zenobia they regarded as a menace, and the Emperor's apparent lack of interest in her they considered weakness. Not content with seizing Antioch, Queen Zenobia intended to claim for her son the whole province of Egypt, just because Gallienus had been foolish enough to hand it over to Odenath. The Queen herself had disappeared, up to mischief somewhere else, but Zabdas was reported to have left Palmyra with a huge army and to be on his way south. Claudius, the angered people of Rome insisted, must protect the Empire against over-ambitious women.

"Claudius Augustus, save us from Victoria and Zenobia!"

"Claudius Augustus, save us from Palmyra!"

"Claudius Augustus, nothing has Tetricus done!"

People shouted themselves hoarse in the streets. The Imperial guards had to disperse them.

Claudius knew who Tetricus was, and why the people were angered, but he had never expected to have to deal with the man. An ex-senator, Tetricus had succeeded in getting himself appointed governor of Aquitania in Gaul. He had administered his province capably enough until he fell into the hands of the woman Victoria, who wanted a "front" for her political activities. Pollio does not say how Claudius managed to pacify the shouting crowds. He must have succeeded, for we hear nothing more of Tetricus until after the death of Claudius, when Tetricus threw himself upon the Emperor Aurelian's mercy and begged for help.

In the spring of 270 the Western Goths again crossed the Danube, and Claudius again marched against them. By this time Zenobia's cry of freedom from imperialism must have made many converts, for we hear of city after city throwing off the Roman yoke. Soon some of the most reliable provincial troops began defecting to her. When the Roman Senate demanded that their Emperor explain why his campaign against the Goths was going so badly, Claudius wrote that he was ashamed to admit the true reason: Zenobia had won over most of his archers.

Claudius was not able to finish his campaign against the Goths, but he did prevent most of them from escaping through the Straits. This he did at the expense of Egypt, for he withdrew Probus, the governor, appointed him admiral of the Roman fleet, and sent him to the Straits. The departure of Probus from Egypt left Zenobia an open field. She would attack Lower Egypt at once. She must have been in the midst of her preparations, perhaps training more archers, when the startling news came that Claudius had succumbed to the plague that the northern barbarians had brought in with them and that he was being carried home to Sirmium to die.

Soon the expected news arrived: the Emperor Claudius was dead. His reign had lasted just twenty-eight months and had never been free of trouble. It was some consolation to Rome that he, at least, had not been murdered. A romantic story went the rounds that his death had been a voluntary sacrifice—to save Rome.

Zenobia, angry spies reported to the Roman Senate, was elated by the news of the Emperor's death.

"Even the plague is on my side," she had cried.

Rome was in a turmoil. No one knew where Zenobia was or what she was doing. She was often seen in several places at once, sometimes on camel-back or on that white Nubian horse of hers, sometimes driving herself in her war-chariot and wielding a sword like a man. Tales of her exploits roused awe, admiration, and dislike. She was emulating Julia Maesa, the oldsters muttered, and, even if she had no grandson as Julia had to intrigue for, she had a son and she wanted to make him the Emperor of Rome.

Though it was well known that Claudius, on his death bed, had designated Aurelian his successor, his soldiers disregarded his wishes and proclaimed his brother Quintillus their new Emperor. At Rome the Senate also disregarded their dying Emperor's wishes, acknowledged his brother's right to the throne, and ordered coins struck in his name.

Quintillus ruled seventeen days. As an Emperor, he proved to be only a pale reflection of his brother, totally unfit to command soldiers or to rule an empire. In those days it was customary for a newly appointed Emperor to come to Rome and be formally invested by the Senate. Quintillus did not appear.

By this time the war with the Goths had already lasted twenty years, frustrating and exhausting to both sides. Finally Aurelian, who, under the Emperor Quintillus, was still the commander-in-chief of the army, took matters into his own hands, met the Goths, who were now trying to retreat across the Danube to their own country, and inflicted a rousing defeat upon them. His enthusiastic soldiers at once proclaimed him Emperor, perhaps by the time-honored army method of tossing him in a blanket. This occurred in the spring of 270. For a few days there were two Emperors, but when his own soldiers deserted him for Aurelian, Quintillus committed suicide by opening his veins.

Aurelian, already in his late fifties, was now the sole ruler of the Roman Empire. His biographer, Flavius Vopiscus, bases his account (written only sixteen years after the Emperor's death) on documents in the Ulpian Library at Rome. Vopiscus describes him as a "comely man . . . rather tall . . . very strong in his muscles . . . endowed with manly grace . . . a little too fond of wine and food." On the field of battle, his red general's cloak made him an easy target, but he seemed to bear a charmed life. Such was the man who intended to crown his spectacular career by capturing the arrogant Queen of Palmyra.

It is doubtful whether Longinus was personally acquainted with Aurelian, but he must have known the man's reputation for cruelty and for iron determination, and he would have thought it his duty to warn Zenobia to be on her guard at all times. Even without this warning, Zenobia would surely have instructed her spies to report everything they could find out about the new Emperor. Soon she would have learned the most salient facts of Aurelian's life.

His mother had been a priestess of the Sun-god; she had made her son's swaddling clothes from a small purple mantle that had been an Imperial gift to the god. One day, closely wrapped in the purple, the infant had been lifted from his cradle by an eagle and placed on an altar that, fortunately, Vopiscus remarks, "had no fire on it."

Before he became Emperor, Aurelian had been the only commoner to own an elephant; Claudius had sent him as an envoy to Sapor's court in Ctesiphon and Sapor had given him an elephant, a gift normally presented to an Emperor, since elephants by tradition were royal creatures. Prudently, therefore, Aurelian dispatched his bulky gift to the Emperor Claudius.

For Zenobia, the significance of the elephant story would have been that Aurelian had already formed an advantageous relationship with Sapor. She must try to make a rift between the two men, now that Aurelian had become Emperor. Meanwhile, she insisted upon daily reports from Rome.

A report soon came that the Goths were suing for peace and that a treaty had been drawn up. To make sure that the treaty would be observed, Aurelian demanded and received two thousand horsemen and all the sons and daughters of the Gothic chiefs. The young men Aurelian enrolled in his Imperial guards. Later he gave them Roman wives, who were expected to civilize them. The young Gothic women he married to some of his chief officers, among them a general who was said to be able to "drink with the Goths and learn their secrets."

With the Goths under control, Aurelian returned to Rome, for the Senate had not yet ratified his new position. Then, to the surprise of Longinus and to the satisfaction of Zenobia, Aurelian recognized Vaballath, conferred upon him the titles his father had borne, and made him ruler of a small province in Armenia. He even ordered coins struck with the boy's portrait on one side and his own on the other.

History regards these gestures of Aurelian's as merely diplomatic, since so far as we know, he paid no further attention to the boy-king. But to Zenobia, because Aurelian had followed the usual custom of associating another person with himself—he had no son —the striking of these coins meant that he regarded Vaballath as

86

co-ruler with himself. She had some justification, for Gallienus had elevated Odenath to the rank of Augustus, and she considered herself still an Augusta.

Aurelian's recognition of Vaballath did not cause Zenobia to change her intentions toward Lower Egypt; she was waiting a favorable moment to strike. When she heard that Egypt's substitute governor was not proving satisfactory, and that Alexandria was ripe for revolt against Rome, she decided the time had come to send Zabdas to Egypt.

Aurelian was in Rome, his attention fully occupied with domestic matters. Corruption and thieving on the part of the officials of the royal mint had made it necessary to close the entire establishment, temporarily, and reorganize the whole financial administration of Rome. Aurelian did not anticipate trouble.

History has not recorded how many troops accompanied Zabdas to Egypt, only that when he withdrew he took with him seventy thousand. Later, Zenobia ordered him to leave a tactical force of five thousand in charge and to bring the rest back to Syria. She probably needed them for the northern campaign she had in mind.

Nor has history recorded that in the year 271 the caravan road between Palmyra and Bosra, though seldom used after the haltingplace had been shifted to Palmyra, had now become an excellent military road to the south. The shift had made both Bosra and Petra, who had lost her trade to Bosra, jealous of Palmyra's growing wealth and power. She also knew that Petra, now under a Roman governor, had not forgotten its Nabataean origin, and she wanted to discover whether Roman domination had, over the centuries, quenched the desire for freedom that had originally led the Nabataeans to Petra. In that rocky stronghold they had built a civilization so remarkable that they had long withstood Rome. If a spark remained from those distant days, she might fan it into a devouring flame that would bring Petra over to her side in the coming struggle with Rome. To best Aurelian would be harder than it would have been to best Claudius; still there were ways of dealing with men of his stripe.

Without confiding her plans to anyone except Zabdas, Zenobia set out with her troops for Bosra; Zabdas would take them on to Alexandria. She herself with a small detail would cross the strip of desert between Emesa and Petra, size up the Roman governor there, sow a few seeds of discord, and ride back into the desert, the only place where she felt completely at home. Perhaps on her way back to Bosra she would have time to hunt a leopard.

VIII

Rose-Red Petra

Zenobia could hardly have failed to know that the Nabataean Arabs, though they developed the city of Petra, had had an excellent foundation to build on: the ancient civilization of the Edomites who are said to have founded Petra in the eleventh century B.C. And so when the Nabataeans arrived about the middle of the seventh century B.C., they found a flourishing city ripe for plucking.

The famous "rose-red" city in the Siq, as the Arabs call the deep gorge which the mountain streams have cut through the high sandstone cliffs that encircle Petra, was not known by that name to either Edomites or Nabataeans. The earlier name may have been the Sela of the Second Book of the Kings, for in Hebrew Sela means rock, and in Greek Petra has the same meaning. Some Biblical scholars think the name may have been changed during the Greek occupation of Syria when Tadmor became Palmyra.

Whether the identification is correct or not, the fantastic city of Petra, now in ruins, lies in the southeastern part of what was once Edom, but is now the Hashemite Kingdom of Jordan. The entrance to the rock-cut city, whether you go on foot at the risk of a turned ankle, or take one of the sorry horses, is still through the outer Siq.

The Edomites were a far more talented people than has, until recently, been generally recognized. In 1964, a scientific expedition of the Israeli Government found in southern Israel sandstone implements, rotary hand mills, three complete furnaces, the ruins of several others, and copper deposits. Dr. Rothenberg, who headed the expedition, thinks the copper plant might either have been one that King David destroyed during his war with the Edomites, or a later plant of King Solomon's that the Egyptians wrecked when they invaded the country. The expedition dug up one of these ancient furnaces, wrapped it in cloth and adhesive tape, and trucked it to the Haaretz Museum in Tel Aviv, where it is now on view.

Under the Edomites, Sela, or Petra, had become a convenient halting-place for the caravans. During the next few centuries, however, the Assyrians and the Babylonians appeared on the scene. They thought the caravan trade would be less costly if the route through the desert were shortened and the halting-place shifted to the more centrally located Tadmor (the name had not yet been changed to Palmyra). By paying large taxes to whichever country was in power, the Edomites managed to keep their caravan trade for a time and so bolster up their economy.

But when the Nabataean Arabs came along, they either drove out the Edomites or made life so hard for them that they abandoned Petra to the newcomers.

We have no evidence that Zenobia visited Petra in 271, but since it was then that she made her first move southward by sending Zabdas to attack Egypt, which was one of the wealthiest provinces of the Roman Empire, it is reasonable to infer that she may have taken the opportunity to accompany him as far as Bosra. From there, with a small retinue, she could cross over to Petra—west of Bosra and on the fringe of the desert—become acquainted with the political situation and the Roman governor's attitude, plant some spies in strategic places, and return to Palmyra to wait for Zabdas to report that Egypt was safely on her side.

Zenobia's husband had been dead about three years; Vaballath was fourteen or fifteen years old, and she herself, we assume, barely thirty, with an enviable war record of many years. Aurelian had been Emperor of Rome about a year, but before that, as commander-in-chief of the Imperial legions, he had earned such a reputation for cruelty that his men had admiringly dubbed him Old-Sword-in-Hand.

Bosra had long since inherited the caravan trade from Petra, and Palmyra had inherited it from Bosra. Both cities were jealous of Palmyra, especially so since a woman, who called herself Queen, headed the government there and had raised an enthusiastic army to do her bidding. Petra, even if she had lost all but a fraction of the caravan trade, was still strong enough to make her Roman governor fear, at times, for his head.

And so it may not be too far-fetched to imagine that with Alexander's successful expedition in mind, Zenobia had decided to try her luck first in Nabataean Petra. For Petra, though now under Roman control, had resisted for generations the steady encroachments of the expanding Empire. She might be ready to throw off the foreign yoke and become Palmyra's ally against further domination by Rome.

As sole ruler of Palmyra, still in the Roman orbit, but the foremost city of the Fertile Crescent, Zenobia would not have gone to Petra unannounced. Hers would have been a state visit. She would have gone with a retinue and with gifts, not as precious as gifts intended for an eastern potentate, but suitable to the rank of a Roman governor.

Pollio has left us a description of Zenobia, the Queen. "Her face was dark and of a swarthy hue, her eyes were black and powerful beyond the usual wont, her spirit divinely great, and her beauty incredible. So white were her teeth that many thought that she had pearls in place of teeth. Her voice was clear and like that of a man. Her sternness, when necessity demanded, was that of a tyrant, her clemency . . . that of a good emperor."

Elsewhere in his account, Pollio writes that Zenobia wore a helmet "girt with a purple fillet, which had gems hanging from the lower edge, while its center was fastened with the jewel called cochlis, used instead of the brooch worn by women, and her arms were frequently bare."

The cochlis that Zenobia wore was probably a gold jewel in the shape of a snail's shell. Pliny, who was interested in precious stones, explains in his *Natural History* that eastern kings often attached these massive snail-shaped jewels to the frontlets on their horses' heads. Perhaps Zenobia decorated her white Nubian in the same way.

It is interesting to hear that Queen Elizabeth I of England is said to have adorned the foreheads of her coach horses with diamonds and their bridles with pearls. Their manes and tails were dyed orange. Elizabeth herself wore a crimson robe. Zenobia, though, since no ruler in her day would have undertaken such a journey as hers unprotected with armor, would surely have worn her customary chain-armor, no doubt highly burnished.

Dark-eyed, tall and slender, her gold jewel on her forehead, a squad of mounted warriors at her back, Zenobia must have roused the admiration of all who saw her riding through what is thought today one of the most awe-inspiring gorges in the world.

When Rostovtzeff in 1932 entered the Siq to visit the ruins of Petra he took his life in his hands. The stream of water through this narrow gorge could suddenly become a torrent and sweep away whatever lay in its course, whether rock, or beast, or man. But this danger may not have existed in Zenobia's day, for the remains of paving blocks have led some scholars to believe that the Nabataeans diverted the mountain streams into a catch-basin, or reservoir, the remains of which may still be seen. This not only kept the gorge from being flooded during the spring rains, but provided an abundant supply of water for the inhabitants.

The combination of a natural reservoir with the almost impregnable mountain walls that surround Petra soon made the city an ideal clearing-house for the caravan commerce of her day. When the ingenious system that had been devised to keep the Siq dry fell into disrepair, and the water resumed its torrential course, the caravans must have had to take a chance or enter through other gorges. Lawrence of Arabia, who took refuge with his Arabs in Petra, felt that whole armies could have been "lost in the length and breadth of it." Nor does the danger exist today, for the Royal Jordanian Government has renovated the ancient Nabataean system. Now the water, even in flood time, is carried off through pipes set in the gorge walls.

The Roman governor of Petra, with his aides, would have met Zenobia at the entrance to the Siq, on horseback probably, since it is about four thousand feet long and in some places too narrow for an official four-horse chariot. Other entrances to the rock city appear to have been seldom used. And so the Siq was generally crowded with people going to and fro, just as it is still with horses, donkeys, men on foot, and today an occasional supply jeep. Zenobia's coming may have attracted an unusual crowd, eager to catch a glimpse of the much-talked about Queen of Palmyra.

Zenobia would not have been plagued by guides; the governor's aides would have brought along soldiers to see that no one came close enough to harm the distinguished visitor. We may be sure, too, that, as Zenobia rode along between the governor and his chief aide, every eye would have been upon her. Seldom had anyone seen so beautiful a woman!

The governor was probably so entranced with his guest that he may have given away to her more information than he should have. Facts and figures seemed to be all she was interested in. Yes, Roman armies frequently marched through the Siq; no, the rolling stones did not bother them. Easily defended? Yes; of course, when the uncivilized Nabataeans lived in Petra, they must have defended the gorge by rolling down huge rocks from above; she could see for herself, said the governor, how the almost perpendicular walls curved in at the top; easy to send rocks crashing down.

Would the Queen like to stop a moment to examine the massive tombs and temples carved into the gorge walls? Crumbling a little now, with all those wild flowers and weeds growing out of every crevice. And since these monuments were unlike any in Palmyra, Zenobia would have been as impressed as any modern sightseer.

"Nabataean?" she asked.

93

"Yes," the governor replied, a trifle reluctantly, one imagines, since no one could have known better than he that, though the Nabataeans had been good enough architects for Rome to have made use of their skill, they had been a troublesome people, easily stirred up, and always ready to fight.

No doubt Zenobia quickly mollified the governor by admiring the extraordinary streaks of brilliant color that ran in wide horizontal bands along the face of the rock wall. They looked almost as if they had been painted there: blue, crimson, yellow, orange, each melting into the other. The bands and streaks were fascinating to watch, they seemed almost alive, so quickly did their colors shift. Zenobia would have compared them to watered silk, had she known of that material. Silk, of course, she knew; her husband's body had been wrapped in fold upon fold of heavy silk.

"They say the Nabataeans used to live in those places," said the young aide on Zenobia's left.

"Well, why not?" said Zenobia. "They would be warm in cold weather. They could keep their dead with them, too; leave them there, perhaps, when they moved out."

"That is not the Roman way," the governor said quickly. "Now, over there you can see a Greek temple. It has an enormous inner chamber that must be at least sixty feet long and fifty feet wide. There is room enough inside for hundreds of sarcophagi."

"It does not look like a Greek temple," Zenobia replied, "with that urn on its pediment."

"The urn is carved out of the rock, like the temple. The Nabataeans must have had a reason for putting a huge urn up there. You will see another presently."

By this time the party would have almost reached the place where the Siq makes a sharp turn to the right and broadens out into the valley, which was once the industrial center of Petra. The Romans had changed all that. Zenobia would have seen no merchants in striped gowns bustling about, bargaining in the markets for slave girls and spices brought from the Far East, no camel-trains coming and going along the river-road. Now wherever she looked, she would have seen helmeted Roman soldiers, arrogant ladies, and tattered, whining beggars.

"Trajan made a mistake," she said suddenly. "The Nabataeans were loyal allies of Rome until he decided that Bosra would be a better halting-place for the caravans. That ruined Petra."

"But benefited Palmyra, later on," the younger official ventured.

"Yes, of course," Zenobia agreed. "But it was hard on Petra." She reined in her horse. "Is that Pharaoh's Treasure-house?"

"The Arabs call it the Khasna," replied the young official. "Those Nabataeans were marvelous architects. Just look at that, carved right out of the face of the cliff! That urn up there on the pediment is at least eleven feet high. The total height must be well over a hundred feet. The Bedouins sometimes shoot at the urn; they think there is gold inside."

"But it's solid, isn't it?" said Zenobia.

"Yes, of course, but you can't convince the Bedouins. I think we might show the Queen the Deir temple now. It's not far from here."

The famous Deir would have left Zenobia speechless with amazement. Larger than Westminster Abbey, the Deir stands on a plateau one hundred and sixty feet high. Its columned front is half again as wide as that of the Abbey. The doorway is twenty-six feet high. Inside there is an enormous empty chamber about thirty-eight feet square and thirty-three feet high.

Zenobia would surely have wanted to see the rock-cut Palace; Odenath may have told her that it might once have been the home of her ancestors.

"Its upper story is masonry," she exclaimed, when the enormous Palace was pointed out to her.

"Yes, the cliff was not high enough," said the governor. "It is a Roman building, you know."

"The architects were Nabataean, though," Zenobia replied.

Desert-bred and possibly desert-born, Zenobia must have been fascinated by this whole mountainous region. Before her, now that she had left the narrow part of the gorge and had turned to the right, lay the wide, rocky, and uneven plateau, rimmed by high, precipitous cliffs. Through this plateau had dashed, unchecked, the great stream that over the centuries had cut its way down from the "high places," which once had been holy sanctuaries.

Archaeologists have now found seven of these places where sacrifices were performed. The largest of them is five hundred and twenty-eight feet long and ninety feet wide. It lies about seven hundred feet above the plateau where the ancient town once stood. Such places, as Zenobia would have known, were characteristic of Nabataean religion. Men cut their houses out of rock wherever they could, but when they wished to sacrifice, they sought a "high place." Palmyra's great temple of Bel was built, as Zenobia knew, on an elevation.

The highest of Petra's rocky peaks is Mt. Hor. Here, as Zenobia may have heard, Aaron, the brother of Moses, is said to have been entombed. Since it was too hard a climb up from the valley floor for the governor to undertake and since horses could not be used, his younger colleague volunteered to go with Zenobia and her retinue. He took them to the very spot where Yahweh had ordered the sceptical Aaron stripped of his clothing and left to perish. Aaron's tomb, the young Roman told Zenobia, proves the truth of the story. He admitted, though, that the similarity between Aaron's name and its Arabic counterpart, Jabel Horum, might have given rise to the legend.

Before Zenobia left Mt. Hor, her escort would have told her the legend of the Siq. In Arabic tradition, Mt. Hor is the rock Moses struck with his rod and brought forth water for the Israelites when they were escaping from their Egyptian masters.

Early in their flight, usually dated in the fifteenth century B.C., the Red Sea had blocked their escape. But Yahweh had bidden Moses lift up his rod, and the fugitives had walked dry-shod between walls of water.

Plodding on beyond the Red Sea, the Israelites had left the Wilderness of Shur—as that part of the Arabian Desert was then called

—well behind them. By this time their throats were sorely parched, for the infrequent wells had disappeared and by day the sun dried up what moisture the night had brought. Men, women, and children, flocks and herds, all were perishing of thirst. Now a mountain reared its head high in the air before them, and there was no water anywhere in sight. In despair, the Israelites called upon Moses to save them.

A voice that seemed to come from the mountain peak spoke directly to Moses.

"Lift thy rod. Smite the rock."

Moses obeyed. With a tremendous crack the lofty cliff-head split. A great stream of water gushed forth, and the famous Siq was born. One of the Greek historians tells us that because of her springs and rivers Petra could grow the date palm. He also reports that in a certain region balsam grew, and that it became an excellent source of revenue, since it could be found nowhere else in the world. We now know, however, that the "balsam of Gilead," or Mecca balsam, is a tree that grows in Arabia and Abyssinia, and that in Zenobia's day, possibly earlier, the Nabataeans used balsam to make various kinds of drugs.

Though we have imagined Zenobia taking the occasion of her attack upon Egypt to visit Petra, it might be going too far to assert at this point that she succeeded in sowing any seeds of discord. She might have found, later on, a friendly ear in some of the younger people there or have tried in other ways to win over the cities of the Fertile Crescent. Zenobia does seem, though, to have had their support when, after Zabdas had gained control of Lower Egypt, she set out for northern Syria.

We have no evidence that Vaballath accompanied his mother, that beautiful spring morning in 271. Palmyra had lost one heir to the throne; perhaps Zenobia thought it wise to leave her son at home with Longinus. She does not seem to have been the kind of person to worry overmuch, but even she might have wondered, while she led her troops through the city gates, as she and Odenath had done so often in the past, what the future held in store for her fatherless son and for herself. Perhaps she turned for a last look at her beautiful city, softly nested in its grove of palms. The dates were already beginning to ripen; they would still be green in Antioch.

IX

Antioch the Golden

Zenobia had defied Gallienus, she had defied Claudius, and now both were dead. An assassin's hand had disposed of Gallienus; the plague had carried off Claudius; Aurelian remained, a peasant's son turned Emperor, tougher and stronger than any of his predecessors. She would defy him, too, no matter what the cost. Egypt was hers; Petra and most of the cities of the Fertile Crescent were ready to follow her. Emesa and Antioch would fall into line. She leaned forward and touched her horse's neck. He whinnied softly.

The Sun-god had not yet appeared in the sky over the desert, and the air was cool and pleasant. Zenobia with her troops was making good time toward Emesa. She would pause there briefly before going on to Antioch to pick up additional men. Zabdas, mounted as usual on his great black stallion, rode beside the white Nubian. The two horses were as good friends as their owners were. Cohort after cohort of mounted archers followed, their bows slung on their backs. Then came rank upon rank of armed infantry. The loaded camels with their drivers and their guards brought up the rear. The tinkle of their bells assured Zenobia that they were safe.

The news from Rome was good. Corrupt officials and thieving workmen had made it necessary to close the mints, and hundreds had been thrown out of work. Beggars filled the streets. A German tribe, the Alamanni, had taken swift advantage of the disturbances

99

in Rome and had crossed the Alps by the Brenner Pass. Forty thousand horsemen and twice as many infantry were spreading devastation through the whole region between the Danube and the Po rivers. At any moment they might descend upon Rome, Zenobia's spies had told her.

Aurelian had asked the Senate to deal with the angry mint-workers and had hurried off to stem the enemy's advance. The Alamanni retreated to the Danube. Overloaded with booty, which included stolen women, they were about to cross to their own territory when the Roman legions sprang from ambush and attacked them. Aurelian had reached the river first. He had concealed his men, in crescent formation, on the opposite bank, and ordered them to hold their attack until at least half the enemy had crossed. He himself had given the signal for the horns to strike; the rear lines had swung forward, and the trap had closed. Few had escaped the Roman butchers.

If Aurelian's strategy at the Danube had been familiar to Zenobia, she might have been able to guard against it, when later it was used against her, not at the Danube but at the Orontes near Antioch. The Alamanni were good fighters, she had heard, but her own troops were better trained, she told herself as she urged her horse to a quicker pace.

Emesa's citizens seem to have accepted Zenobia and to have provided her with food and whatever else she required, though it meant hunger afterward. They feared that if they refused, they might be held responsible for King Odenath's murder. Besides, Emesa in its palmiest days had looked up to the Julias as being somewhat above the ordinary stature of women. Queen Zenobia was fully equal if not superior to the Julias. She would surely help them throw off the Roman yoke.

Encouraged, Zenobia pressed on to Antioch. She was anxious to see for herself if the city had recovered from Sapor's raids, and to have a word with Paul, gather fresh supplies, and be on her way as soon as possible to the Syrian Gates, the entrance to the pass through the Taurus Mountains. The country beyond would be new to her, and she wanted to consult an oracle she knew of in Cilicia.

Like others of her day, Zenobia probably looked forward to re-entering Antioch, and perhaps paying one more visit to Daphne, the celebrated playground of the East. She knew Antioch's history, probably better than most of her generation, and what she had not learned for herself, Longinus would have supplied. She may have had another reason for visiting Daphne. The suburb lay on a hill above Antioch. From there lookouts could keep watch on all roads leading to the city. Enemies, she knew, had often been checked at Daphne.

No one of Zenobia's generation, though, could have known the epithet that was applied in the fourth century to the pleasant city of Antioch on the Orontes River. Libanius, one of her most famous sons, called his native city Antioch the Golden, and in his day the city fully deserved its name. Fortunately, Libanius has left us an excellent description, almost the only one we have.

Antioch's history is fascinating. Her situation on the triangular island in the Orontes is unique. Some accounts state that Alexander the Great first noted the strategic position of the island and decided to make it the capital of his empire. Other accounts run that after Alexander's untimely death two of his Macedonian generals, Seleucus and Antigonus Cyclops—old One-Eye, his soldiers called him after he had lost an eye in battle—claimed that distinction.

Each general chose the location he favored and started to build. A picturesque story makes Seleucus station elephants where he wanted to build his towers. To mark where the connecting walls were to rise, he sowed wheat. His rival, Antigonus, was well started on his city when he met Seleucus in battle and was killed— he had already named his future city Antigonia. Seleucus stole from the unfinished Antigonia the material he needed to complete his unfinished city on the left bank of the Orontes. He named it Antiochia in honor of his father Antiochus. This is the city we know as Antioch.

During the summer of 360 the local Olympic Games were held

in Antioch. Libanius, a Greek rhetorician, celebrated the event in a long, eloquent speech. "My native city is the fairest adornment of the land that is fairest under heaven," he wrote. The pride Libanius took in the eminence and beauty of his city illuminates the speech that he delivered to the great crowd who packed the stadium where the Games were held. Almost a hundred years had passed since Zenobia had failed to hold the city against Aurelian, but what Libanius tells us applies equally well to the land, the city, and the life of Zenobia's day.

Since the fertile plain the Orontes flows through existed long before its inhabitants, Libanius opens his speech with a description of the land. Level like the sea into which the Orontes tumbles, the land is deep and rich and soft, yielding easily to the plow. The "mountains work for us; they provide wood to stoke the fires that bake our bread; our rivers, lakes, and streams also bring their riches to us. Over so fair a land as ours the Seasons dance harmoniously and do not spoil its charm by any unseemly conduct on their part."

To explain how men first came to live in this golden land of prosperity, Libanius follows the example of early Greek and Roman annalists and turns to myth. The wanderings of Io, the horned maiden of tradition, provide him with a talking point, for Daphne gained its name from two myths, the story of Io and that of Apollo and Daphne. A mosaic found in a house at Daphne illustrates the connection the citizens of Antioch may have felt between the two legends. The mosaic shows three figures, the shepherd Argo, the revengeful goddess Hera, who transformed Io into a heifer, and Io herself, in human form but with two small, almost imperceptible horns.

By recalling the myth of Io, Libanius draws attention to Antioch's distant past when gods and heroes honored the city by their presence. He does not mention the myth, possibly because his audience was well acquainted with the exact tree, for ancient guides would often point it out and explain that it had once been a frightened maiden, who, pursued by Apollo, cried aloud for help. Responding gallantly to her entreaties, the gods transformed her into a tree, and probably laughed uproariously when they saw the foiled lover tenderly clasp a tree in his eager arms.

For us, the mosaic found in Daphne has an additional interest; it shows the kind of Oriental dress that was worn in Zenobia's day. Argo's brief tunic, in red, blue, and yellow, has short sleeves and is worn with a belt. His mantle is blue-green and fastened, as usual, on the right shoulder. His trousers are striped, his shoes grayish-white, and he wears a light blue Phrygian cap. Hera wears a greenish-yellow chiton (woman's tunic), a light yellow mantle that almost covers her person, an orange-colored necklace, and sandals. Her head is bare. Io's blue chiton is also fastened on her right shoulder. Her cloak is violet. She, too, is bare-headed and wears sandals.

Libanius reminds his listeners that in the olden days Antioch's fame had spread as far as the island of Cyprus, beloved of the gods. But the gods wished to leave their island and emigrate to Antioch. The oracle at Delphi, when consulted by Antioch, gave permission. Draftsmen went to Cyprus and asked to be allowed to make reproductions of their gods. These they substituted for the originals and so brought the Cyprian gods to Antioch. Forgeries, it seems, are as old as the gods themselves.

"And what brings more glory," Libanius asked, "than to have the gods decide that it pleases them to sojourn in this land."

Libanius told his hearers, that long-ago day when Antioch celebrated the Olympic Games, that a strong swimmer could leave the island at sunrise, reach the sea, and return with fish by the time the sun stood midway in the sky. Others say the journey required a full day. Today the Orontes is not even navigable, but in ancient times the river traffic is said to have played such an important part in turning Antioch into a flourishing center of trade that by Zenobia's time the population had mounted to almost a quarter of a million. This number did not, of course, include women, slaves, and children, probably only the adult free males.

Five miles south of Antioch, and on a somewhat higher level overlooking the Orontes, Daphne with its shade trees, its gardens filled with flowers, and its cool mountain waters flowing over high aqueducts into the city, early became a pleasant summer resort. In addition to Daphne, there were other suburbs, where excavators have found remains of luxurious villas, baths, and churches. Though Libanius knows of several famines that occurred in his day, during the century before while the city was still loyal to Zenobia, crop failures are not heard of. Garden vegetables were plentiful, beans and peas, and the cucumbers for which Antioch was famous.

During the last days of the Roman Empire Daphne's temples and pleasant groves became the haunts of those who lived on the fringes of society. To "go to Daphne," passed into a proverb, its meaning easily understood. In the temple that Seleucus built to the Pythian Apollo, society's outcasts could seek and find asylum. Libanius has painted a glowing picture of the city of his birth, and of the beauty and the luxury kings and emperors came far distances to enjoy, but behind the jeweled façade there existed, as always, the darker picture of the slum where filth, disease, and corruption bred.

The external story of Antioch and its suburb covers nine centuries of conquests and reversals, punctuated by earthquakes and rebuildings, while its internal story is enlivened by constant revolts against constituted authority, sums of money appropriated for erecting statues of gold, then recovered in times of stress by melting them down and turning them into the coinage that had been so wasted and then so needed.

One of the most extravagant of Antioch's rulers was Antiochus IV, better known as Antiochus the Mad. He was a brilliant, erratic ruler proverbial for his love of display. In 167 B.C. he celebrated games at Daphne that astounded even the sated Greco-Roman world.

Antiochus was determined to outdo the magnificent display that a Roman general, the year before, had inaugurated to celebrate his victory over the Macedonians. To make sure that all who had witnessed the Roman show should have an opportunity to see his own, Antiochus sent lavish invitations throughout Greece. Polybius, a contemporary Greek historian who lived in Rome, must have been among those who went to Antioch, for his description of the almost incredible procession that opened the Festival impresses one as being that of an eye-witness. This description Zenobia herself may easily have read alone or with Longinus.

Five thousand men in Roman armor led the processional march into the Olympic stadium. Behind the armored Romans came the same number of Mysians, and behind them three thousand Cilician light infantry, each soldier wearing a gold crown. Three thousand Thracians and five thousand Gauls came next. Ten thousand Macedonians carried golden shields, five thousand bronze, and five thousand silver. Two hundred and fifty gladiators followed, then thousands of horsemen in gold and silver trappings. Fat cattle and cows and goats formed part of the procession.

Horse-drawn and elephant-drawn chariots, thirty-six of the great beasts lumbering along in single file, eight hundred young men wearing gold crowns and carrying ivory tusks that had been presented to Antiochus, images of gods and heroes all dressed in gold-embroidered garments, slaves carrying gold and silver booty, hundreds of women sprinkling perfume from gold bowls, others riding in litters with gold or silver supports, all followed one another in endless lines through Daphne's great stadium.

Libanius speaks of an enormous hippodrome at Antioch, one of the finest in the Roman Empire, in which gladiatorial combats were held, of summer baths and winter baths, of public fountains, of elaborate houses three stories high with covered arcades to protect the citizens against rain and sun. In Antioch, Libanius says, there is no need for even the poor to go hungry, for the rivers that flow through the city are well supplied with fish. No doubt the poor had no silver platters for serving their fish, such as we see in a mosaic found in a house at Daphne that shows a large and splendid fish with two round loaves of bread near by.

After Antiochus IV, the Seleucid kingdom steadily declined. Antioch changed hands again and again, as claimants to the city appeared and disappeared. Finally, about the middle of the first century B.C., Antioch along with Syria passed into the hands of Rome. From this time on each succeeding Emperor, from Octavian to Hadrian, adorned the city with so many temples, theaters, and colonnades that it came more and more to resemble a Roman metropolis.

The economic recovery of Antioch began with the Roman occupation. Roman merchants established themselves, coinage was revived, public utilities were restored, an aqueduct was built to supply water to the people who lived on the mountain slopes, and property taken from the Jews was returned. The Parthians invaded Syria and captured Antioch, but within two years were forced out by Mark Antony, who brought Cleopatra to Syria and married her, it is believed, in Antioch. Seven years later, in 31 B.C., Antony committed suicide in Alexandria.

During the reign of the Emperor Augustus, Antioch like Palmyra began to play a role in international affairs. Strabo writes of seeing ambassadors from India on the streets of Antioch. The mint, no longer local, gained Imperial status. The local games became Olympic Games, and Rome flocked to them. Peace and prosperity went hand-in-hand, so people must have thought.

Early in the first century of the Christian Era, a series of disasters struck Antioch. A severe famine, caused by crop failure in Egypt, Palestine, and Syria, affected Antioch for several years, dependent as it was on supplies from the countryside. In the midst of the famine, an earthquake overthrew houses and temples and destroyed part of Daphne. To protect the city against future quakes, a prophylactic column of porphyry, obtained from the west coast of the Red Sea, was set up in the middle of the city. The column did not placate the anger of the underworld any more than did the enormous bust, called the Charonian, that was carved on the mountainside overlooking the city to drive away a fearful pestilence.

Toward the end of the second century, the Olympic Games that the Emperor Marcus Aurelius had abolished to punish the city for a political misdemeanor were restored. In Antioch, the principal official of the Games was regarded as a representative of Zeus, in whose honor the Games had first been performed. This official, writes Glanville Downey in his book, *Ancient Antioch*, "carried out an ascetic ritual of sleeping in the open air . . . on rush mats . . . spread on the ground. He wore a white robe ornamented with gold, a crown adorned with rubies and pearls and other precious stones, and white sandals, and carried an ebony rod." The secretary of the Games also wore a white robe. His gold crown was made "in the shape of laurel leaves."

Antioch did not enjoy her restored Games long. The Emperor Septimius Severus, with whose family Odenath had been connected, moved the Games from Antioch to Laodicea—to destroy potential sources of disorder, he said. The explanation satisfied no one; Antioch considered herself grossly humiliated to have had one Emperor restore the Games and another, only ten years later, remove them entirely, especially to its ancient rival, Laodicea, whose gardeners boasted they could grow better lilies than Antioch's gardeners could.

Severus also deprived Antioch of its proud position as the capital of Syria and bestowed that honor upon Laodicea. Most historians consider that he was justified in making this change, for political factions in Antioch were rapidly becoming sources of possible revolution against the Empire, especially dangerous at a time when the Parthians were again making trouble. Within two years, using Antioch as his headquarters, Severus was able to drive out the Parthians from Syria. Early in the third century, he paid a state visit to Antioch to show, apparently, that the city was no longer in disgrace, but he did not restore the Games. That became one of the first acts of his son and successor, Caracalla.

Caracalla was well-disposed toward Syria, probably because his mother, Julia Domna, one of the three powerful Julias, had been born in Emesa. Caracalla did much to compensate Antioch for her earlier humiliation. He restored the Games and was seen constantly at them. He is said to have indulged himself so passionately in his various pleasures that he undermined his health, and, the gossips said, his beard fell out. During most of his short reign—five years —his brilliant mother had to manage all affairs of state.

Like his father, Caracalla was obliged to battle the ambitious Parthians. He invaded their country in the summer of 216. In Antioch his mother had full charge, attending to all official communications and doubtless forwarding only what she considered essential. While campaigning against Parthia, Caracalla was assassinated. A certain Macrinus, the pretorian prefect, next in authority to the Emperor, gave the order for his murder. Four days later, the soldiers proclaimed Macrinus Emperor.

Dio Cassius, a Roman historian who was a native of Nicaea, the city near the Straits Zenobia hoped to capture, reports that when the news of her son's death reached Julia Domna in Antioch, she tried to commit suicide. With the help of the soldiers she had at her command, she then plotted to seize the Empire. When Macrinus heard of Julia's activity, he ordered her to leave Antioch. She defied him and either starved herself to death or let a long-standing disease run its course.

The changing situation in the Roman provinces, the rise of the Sassanid Persians under Sapor, the fate of Valerian and of Gallienus, the constant Parthian attacks upon the caravans, the loss of Antioch, and now the threat of a Palmyrene empire under the fearless Zenobia—all these, despite the loyal support of his legions, must have weighed upon Aurelian's mind as he struggled with rioters in Rome, another uprising of the Alamanni, and an imminent attack by the Vandals.

His scouts had, however, assured him that, though Zenobia and Zabdas had reached Antioch and seemed to be in control, the city would not resist the Roman eagles. The people might even welcome him, hoping he would put down the endless squabbles between Jews and Christians. No one seemed able to comprehend that Rome demanded only one thing, full and complete recognition of the Emperor's divinity. And from this neither Paul nor Zenobia was exempt.

X

Zenobia's Protégé Paul

Gossip about Antioch's heretic bishop, Paul, had been rife throughout Syria ever since the Emperor Gallienus had approved his election to the bishopric. To sign the official letter sent to Paul had
been one of the first Imperial acts Gallienus performed after his
father's death in 260 had put him on the throne. Since political
considerations probably motivated Gallienus, the gossip that soon
broke out in Antioch would not have troubled him, even if it had
come to his ears.

As the head of the Christian community in Antioch, Paul had an
episcopal palace to live in and a full staff of servants, and enjoyed
the usual perquisites of high office. So far as we know, he was un-
married. What qualifications he had for his office not even Eusebius
in his *Ecclesiastical History* tells us. We know that a bishop was
supposed to exercise general supervision over his flock, to symbolize
the unity of the Church, to be blameless himself, and above all, to
guard against schism as against sin itself. We hear of no laying on
of hands, that had passed with the apostolic age, and of no ordina-
tion, for that was yet to come.

Within three years after his election Paul had become the leading figure in Antioch. He represented the power of the Roman Empire; he also represented Palmyra, for Gallienus had rewarded Odenath's loyalty to Rome by granting him the title of Imperator, which

made him the virtual ruler of all Syria. Though one of the early accusations brought against Paul was that he "consorted with women," we have no knowledge that Zenobia's name ever entered into the growing whispers. Nor have we any record that Aurelian ever concerned himself in Paul's affairs until he heard that Zenobia was protecting him against all attempts of the church Synod to remove him from office. Ecclesiastical power in Zenobia's day was not supreme over the temporal, since Christianity was still an illicit sect. Zenobia, therefore, as the ruling power in Syria, had every right, from her point of view, to side with Paul. The Synod had been holding meetings in Antioch because, ever since the fall of Jerusalem and the destruction of Solomon's Temple in 70, Antioch had been the metropolis of Christianity. And so it was natural that when Paul's "errors" were brought to the notice of the Church officials, a Synod should have been held in Antioch to discuss them.

The error that may have appealed most to Zenobia was Paul's constant appeal to the Christian community of Antioch to uphold the teachings of the historical Christ and reject all metaphysical interpretations. This may have found in Zenobia's mind an intellectual response. She may also have approved of the appointment of a religious teacher from Samosata who had Semitic leanings, as some think she herself had.

This first Synod, called by the Bishop of Tarsus, inquired into Paul's religious teaching and into his conduct, both private and public. Paul succeeded in allaying their suspicions and promised the assembled bishops to reform.

For a few years all went well with Paul. Then Odenath and his heir were assassinated, Zenobia came into power, Claudius died of the plague, and Aurelian became the Emperor of Rome. And Aurelian, Paul's private sources of information informed him, was bent on depriving Zenobia of all that she and Odenath had won. If that happened, Paul would lose his favored position as a royal protégé.

Paul's critics were quick to take advantage of the new situation. in 268 the Bishop of Tarsus called another Synod, also at Antioch. This time some eighty bishops attended. At the earlier meeting

Paul had been able to disguise what the bishop called his heterodoxy, since few of them were sufficiently well-versed in Church doctrine to understand what Paul meant by stressing the "unity of God and the manhood of Christ." But all were well-schooled in the rumors of his scandalous private and public life. A letter, written and circulated throughout the Empire, had greatly troubled them.

Now at that time there was at Antioch a school of rhetoric whose head was a certain Malchion, a skillful dialectician who had sufficient background to penetrate Paul's attempts to disguise his religious beliefs and to bare them to the Synod. The Synod was horrified. A heretic in their midst!

They took up the contents of the letter.

"He misuses the church funds . . . he struts in the market places . . . he reads letters and dictates others in public . . . attended always by a bodyguard . . . preaches in a theatrical manner . . . smites his hand on his thigh and stamps the tribunal with his feet . . . changes the sacred hymns to sound as though they were addressed to himself . . . has them sung by a chorus of women!"

Women's voices raised in church!

The bishops could not vote fast enough. They excommunicated Paul, bade him vacate the episcopal palace, and nominated his successor. Paul, still relying on support from Zenobia, refused to cooperate.

Clearly, the monotheistic beliefs of such a recalcitrant bishop, however much the Jewish population may have approved of them, could not have helped Zenobia win the support of the Christians in Antioch who opposed Paul. In 269 a third Synod was held. The bishops confirmed Paul's excommunication, and reiterated the demand that he hand over the bishopric to his successor, the son of the deceased bishop Demetrianus, whom Sapor had carried off to Ctesiphon and who had died in captivity.

Paul again refused to give up his office. Obviously he still expected protection from Zenobia, though we know of no move she made to enter the controversy. The complaints of the people in Antioch continued. Paul had made himself wealthy through extortion; he acted as though he were a king, even an emperor; people had to salute him in the streets.

It should not be surprising to find a man of Paul's stature preaching heretical ideas in Antioch. The Christians and others living there in a city that was one of the great commercial centers of the world would necessarily come into contact with beliefs unlike their own.

In such fertile ground heresies of various kinds would sprout and grow vigorously. Gnosticism, for example, came to Antioch as early as the first century, and flourished there as fruitfully as did the later offshoot of Paul's heretical teaching, Arianism. Gnosticism, an eastern theosophy, which became a more serious rival of the Church than the later Arian heresy did, promised its converts complete knowledge of the workings of the universe and eternal salvation in a happier world. This was to be attained through knowledge (*gnosis*), not through faith in a man who claimed to be the long-awaited Savior of the world.

These heresies were troubling Antioch when Zenobia and Zabdas entered with their troops. For a time the influx of hundreds of military men, bent on marching to the Straits and establishing a port, overshadowed the theological squabbles. But they soon revived, stronger than ever. Delegations waited on the Queen.

Let Paul believe what he chose, the Christians clamored, but let him take his Jewish ideas elsewhere. The old bishop's son was the rightful bishop; let him have the episcopal palace to live in. Meanwhile, though officially excommunicated by the Church officials, Paul steadfastly refused to yield either his office or his residence. Whether he continued to "strut in the market places," or to let women sing in church, we do not know.

For a time Antioch had two bishops, one orthodox, the other heterodox. Where the rightful bishop found a place to lay his head has not been recorded. Zenobia, anxious to continue northward, no doubt had more important affairs to attend to than the squabbles of two angry ecclesiastics. Nothing further about her part in the matter has come down in Church history. The problem became Aurelian's.

Zenobia on her way from Antioch to Tarsus, through which she would have to pass to reach the so-called Syrian Gates, may have wondered what she should do if another Synod were called in Antioch. Without her there to protect Paul, the Synod might forcibly eject him from his episcopal palace. But more pressing problems probably drove him from her mind. There might be snow in the pass. The pine grove through which her troops were now marching was pleasantly cool, though the horses' feet occasionally slipped on the needles. They would encounter rough stony ground soon enough, her guides kept warning her.

At last, without too great loss of life—the camels could not manage at all and had to be slaughtered—the troops reached Tarsus and settled down to rest. They must have had little to eat except the tough stringy flesh of the camels they had butchered, and nothing except water to wash it down with. Fortunately the taverns were well-stocked, the brothels too, and few of the men suffered.

In Tarsus, Zenobia learned that men constantly risked their lives tramping through the Cilician pass, which lay ahead of her, in search of the copper and silver of the mountains. Originally, the pass had been only a narrow gorge wide enough to carry the waters of a small tributary of the Cydnus River, which flowed through Tarsus. It was in the cool, swift waters of the Cydnus that Alexander had plunged, after a long day spent hurrying through a hot, malarial valley. Fed by melting snows from the mountains, the river was icy cold, and Alexander paid for his recklessness with two weeks in bed, racked by cramps and burning fever. We do not know whether any of Zenobia's men were equally reckless.

Somewhere in Cilicia, perhaps near Tarsus, there was in Zenobia's day a well-known oracle that many people came to consult. Zosimus tells us that twice during her struggle with Aurelian Zenobia consulted oracles, and that one of them was the shrine of Apollo Sarpedon in Cilicia. The other was that of Venus Aphaca in Lebanon. The two occasions were a year apart. Unfortunately, Zosimus does not say which one of these oracular shrines Zenobia consulted first.

It seems reasonable to assume, though, that since she had to pass through Cilicia to carry out her program of northern expansion, she would have taken the opportunity to find out from the oracle there what the future held. She may have thought that Sarpedon would look with favor upon her venture. During the war between the Trojans and the Greeks, the hero Sarpedon had tried to help Troy hold the Straits against the marauding Greeks. When he fell in battle, his men had rescued his body and sent it home to Lycia. There his burial place had become a shrine. But nearby Cilicia had also preserved his memory, and there his shrine, since it housed a hero, had become greatly favored by the god Apollo. With the passage of time, the shrine developed oracular powers.

Apollo Sarpedon failed to justify Zenobia's trust. We do not know the question Zenobia put to the oracle, but the response was clear: "The Palmyrenes are imposters and Aurelian is the falcon that makes doves tremble."

The priests and priestesses who controlled oracular responses were only human, and oftentimes their heads depended upon the pleasure of those who sought their advice. The most celebrated example is, of course, the response a certain Persian monarch received from Delphi. The monarch was told he would destroy a great kingdom. He did, but the kingdom was his own.

Zosimus explains that a year elapsed between the two occasions when Zenobia sought the oracles. If Zenobia consulted Apollo Sarpedon on her way through Cilicia, she must have consulted Venus Aphaca after she returned to Palmyra. Starcky, to whom I am indebted for these references, says there was once, somewhere in Lebanon, a temple of Venus Aphaca (aphaca is a kind of bean that grows abundantly in Turkey and the Near East). Near the temple there was a sacred spring that fed a small lake. The waters of this lake were not quiet; they rose and sank. Pilgrims who came to the shrine of Venus Aphaca brought with them splendid gifts: gold and silver, jewels and precious stuffs. These they cast upon the waters of the lake. If the gifts sank, they were acceptable and, we assume, the response was favorable. If they floated, they were rejected. Since Zosimus tells us that both oracles foretold the Queen's defeat, we must infer that whatever gifts she sent were rejected.

Zosimus says that Aurelian, apparently as anxious about the future as Zenobia was, consulted the Druids in Gaul. His anxiety, however, did not concern the outcome of his war against Palmyra, but the fate of his descendants—would they follow him upon the Imperial throne? The Druids were the core of the rebellion of the Gallo-Roman Empire against Roman domination. This, of course, Aurelian must have known, and yet he consulted them about the future. The answer, strangely enough, was in the affirmative. Yes, his descendants would succeed. Judged in the light of succeeding events, this reply of the Druids is understandable.

We do not know whether Zenobia's spy-system was so well organized that she was aware of Aurelian's favorable reply, nor do we know whether he, in his turn, learned that she had received two adverse responses. But the two antagonists were still running neck and neck and Zenobia seemed about to spurt ahead.

The Syrian Gates, or lower pass, which Zenobia and her men had negotiated without too great difficulty, had prepared them somewhat for the Cilician Gates, or upper pass, that provided the only possible approach to Tyana, the capital of Cappadocia. Unfortunately, though from early days the pass has been in constant use, no ancient writer has left us as satisfactory an account as that of D. G. Hogarth, a former director of the British School in Athens.

In 1896, Hogarth traveled this same steep wagon road that Zenobia and Zabdas, and afterward Aurelian, led their men over. Hogarth describes the Taurus Mountains as a "very desert of the damned, ridge upon ridge of rock, like the picked bones of the earth." The ascent to the summit, over six thousand feet high, was hard enough for a man on foot, but for Hogarth's companion, who was desperately ill, and had to be carried in a wagon, the climb must have been torture.

But the descent, Hogarth writes, was far worse. "The wagon

takes flying leaps from boulder to boulder, crashes across gullies, and rocks like a ship at sea." Two dervishes in a wagon passed Hogarth and his train, and narrowly missed plunging over the cliff when one wheel slipped.

Zenobia probably sent scouts ahead to apprise the governor of friendly Tyana that she was coming through the pass, for she appears to have met with no opposition, except that of nature itself. Here in Tyana once lived the miracle-worker, Apollonius, who had erected a monument to drive the plague out of Antioch. Ever since then friendly relations had existed between the two cities. The fame of Apollonius was widespread. His followers declared that his powers equalled those of his contemporary, the Man of Bethlehem, who had stirred up so much trouble he had had to be crucified.

The citizens of Tyana believed that when their Apollonius died, his body had been translated to the skies. In times of crisis he appeared to them. He was not a faker, as the Christians said; he was the most illustrious citizen Tyana had ever had; he was a philosopher, a purifier of religion, and known throughout the whole of the civilized world. Wherever he went, people flocked about him, begging him to drive out demons, heal the sick, raise up their dead.

To honor their famous miracle-man, his fellow-citizens had built him a temple in Tyana. Here some paid their respects to him as to a god. And this worship, if the city ever became a part of the Roman Empire, they would have to continue in secrecy, as the Christians had to, for Rome's state religion took precedence over all other beliefs.

Signs and portents had attended the birth of Apollonius. His mother had been bidden to go at a certain time to a specified meadow and there her child would be born. She obeyed, and in the meadow amid springing flowers and to the sound of music—the musicians were swans—the child was born. It was here in the meadow that his temple had been erected, and the town grew out to enfold it.

When Apollonius was sixteen, he became a follower of the Greek philosopher Pythagoras. Soon he dedicated himself to the monastic life, renounced meat and wine, and condemned the sacrifice of animals, a stricture hard to obey in a time when the village priest was also the butcher, and only sacrificial meat could be eaten. Later, Apollonius became a healer of the sick and a religious reformer. He spent five years in complete silence, traveling everywhere without speaking a word. He professed to understand the language of birds and animals, as well as all spoken and written languages without having studied them.

There is no record that Apollonius practised his healing skill upon those who, if they drank the water of a nearby spring after they had sworn falsely, were sure to contract dropsy and other incurable diseases. Its reputation for bringing to light perjurers was almost as great as that of Apollonius for reforming the beliefs of those who did not agree with him.

In his romantic biography of Apollonius, Philostratus, who lived in the second century, includes an act of what we might call spiritual healing. Rudely addressed by a young man whose conduct marked him as possessed, Apollonius ordered the demon to remove himself, and the demon obeyed.

That tradition has made Apollonius able to converse with birds and animals should not surprise those who know that the same facility was ascribed to St. Francis of Assisi. And today in this twentieth century groups are gathering together to talk with one another in "strange tongues" which all, though without previous knowledge, insist they can understand.

In this birthplace of Apollonius, a city that wanted only one thing, freedom to live and think as it wished, Zenobia was undoubtedly a welcome visitor. She had protected Paul's rights; she would protect theirs. But whether the capital city of Cappadocia dared go to the extent of sending a contingent of armed men along with Zenobia we do not know. Perhaps Zenobia needed only a friendly reception and supplies for her troops.

From Tyana, Zenobia now had to strike northwest through Galatia and Bithynia, a distance of some four hundred miles as the crow flies. She had completed perhaps half of her march, and so far had met with no opposition. When this news reached Aurelian, he must have found it difficult to concentrate on what had to be done nearer Rome.

Though Zenobia's triumphal progress enraged Aurelian, he could not pursue her because the Alamanni had risen again and were marching on Rome. Aurelian met them near Piacenza, just north of Rome, but the battle resulted in such heavy losses to the Romans that many feared the Empire would fall. At the same time riots began again in Rome. No one seemed to know who instigated them. People were so panic-stricken by the reports of Zenobia's progress toward the Straits and by this second appearance of the Alamanni that the wildest rumors were being passed from mouth to mouth. No one would have wanted to face the truth, that the men who had been thrown out of work when Aurelian closed the mint were the leaders. But this, as it turned out, was not the whole truth. Some dissident Senators, who thought the loss of so many men at Piacenza indicated weakness on Aurelian's part and who did not want to sponsor a loser, had abetted the rebellious mint-workers.

While the rioting at Rome was at its worst, Aurelian's spies reported that Victoria's protégé, Tetricus, against whom the people had warned Claudius, was embroiled in a civil war in the West, and that in the East more cities were welcoming Zenobia as their champion. But Aurelian could not leave Rome until he had put down the riot. Finally he urged the Senate to consult the Sibylline Books in the temple on the Capitoline Hill. When the reply came that the plague had left behind an evil that must be eradicated by purifying the city, many Senators objected to the expense that would be involved. The price of sacrificial animals had gone up, they said. Aurelian offered prisoners, but there is no evidence that upon this occasion human blood was shed.

At last, after much bickering, the Senate yielded and voted the necessary funds. To purify Rome, it was the ancient custom to consecrate a pig, a ram, and a bull, lead them along the outer limits of the city, and then sacrifice them on the public altar.

The oracle had clearly been right; obedience to it brought a lull on both the western and the eastern fronts. The lull gave Aurelian the opportunity to strike at the Alamanni, who, encouraged by their success at Piacenza, had reached the Umbrian plain near Perugia. It took two hard-fought battles to dislodge them; in the end a few escaped across the Alps. Aurelian did not pursue them. He returned to Rome to deal with the Senators who had abetted the mint-workers. Some citizens accused these Senators of being the same men who had objected to consulting the Sibylline Books. Whether this was true or not, Aurelian had some put to death; others he ordered to hand over all their property to the State. Many historians have thought that Aurelian meted out such severe punishments because he still needed money for his campaigns against Victoria and Zenobia.

It was not consistent, however, with Aurelian's long-range policy to punish the Senators and overlook the mint-workers. They, too, must acknowledge his right to act in the interests of the Empire. And so Aurelian himself led a carefully selected force against their entrenched position on the Caelian Hill and finally dislodged them. He must have been aghast when his casualties amounted to seven thousand men he could ill spare.

With peace so hardly won in Rome, and Italy freed, for the moment, from invaders, Aurelian decided to reinforce Rome's divinely protected barriers by more substantial fortifications. With the consent of the Senate, Aurelian set the building corporations, or guilds, to work. They were to extend the earlier wall to enclose the whole city and make it so strong that barbarians would be discouraged from pouring through the passes of the Alps to attack Rome.

Rome's great wall, which Aurelian would never see completed, but Zenobia would, was to be twenty feet high and twelve feet thick, with rectangular towers at intervals, and to have eighteen gates; it would be comparable, as Aurelian planned it, to Hadrian's Wall in the British province of the Empire. Since soldier-workers could not be spared, Aurelian allowed the builders to draw upon commoners and slaves for unskilled labor.

When the work on the wall had reached a point where Aurelian felt he could safely leave the city in the hands of the Senate, he launched his campaign against Victoria and Tetricus in the Gallo-Roman Empire. One can easily imagine that Aurelian, who appears to have been a hot-blooded man, would have preferred to deal first with Zenobia, and some chroniclers think he did. Victoria, as a woman, could not have interested him. She was too old. Zenobia, from all he had heard about her, was young and beautiful, and Aurelian, despite his age, must have been eager to get his hands on her. Not that he thought of himself as old. He was not much over fifty, still young enough for any woman.

All the way from Italy to Gaul, driving with his charioteer over the military roads, tossing at night on his rough army bed, Aurelian thought about Zenobia. Roman gossip called her a descendant of Cleopatra, Mark Antony's old flame. No truth in it, of course. Suppose there were, ancestry—here Aurelian must have paused, remembering his own lack of ancestry. His father had been a *colonus*, a peasant farmer who tilled the land of a wealthy Roman Senator from Sirmium; since the Senator's name had been Aurelius, he himself, though his father's legitimate son, had when a lad been called Aurelianus.

His spies had told him that the Palmyra woman called herself Septimia Zenobia, but that her real name was an outlandish Arab or Semitic word no true Roman could twist his tongue around. She was not a Semite, they told him, but she protected Jews. Once in Palmyra a rabbi had been haled before her, and she had let him go in peace.

Aurelian had heard the ancient prophecy that Zenobia was actually the long-expected desert child "sprung of the fiery Sun and the flexing Moon." Another prophecy said she was "man born woman and woman born man." Not that Aurelian believed these old women's tales; still, his peasant blood told him he could not altogether ignore them.

The important question to be resolved was whether Zenobia had murdered her husband or had been a party to his murder. To kill a disobedient slave or a captive taken in war was one thing; to murder in cold blood an official of the Empire, for so Aurelian had to consider Odenath, was a criminal act and punishable by death. Odenath's treacherous kinsman had already suffered the full penalty; Aurelian knew that. Still if Zenobia had been an accessory. . . . The Semitic code was an eye for an eye, a tooth for a tooth; even though not a Semite, Bath-Zabbai should be able to understand that.

Naturally, if those old prophecies meant that she was the daughter of a great desert chief, a Ras, she probably could not be brought to justice, even if she were guilty. She called herself a Queen; but she was also a widow, with no man around. That Longinus of hers did not count. Neither did the heretic bishop in Antioch. Still, together they might make a good pair for burning.

Soon Aurelian, the peasant's son, may have begun to dream dreams. Long ago, in his early youth, an affluent landowner who thought him promising, had given his daughter Severina to him, with sufficient dowry to banish forever all thought of poverty. She had been a worthy person and had borne him a daughter, but their love-making had not been altogether satisfactory. Still, it had not been like that of Odenath and Zenobia, if the tales that circulated in Rome about the married life of this strange "half Arab, half Semitic" couple were true. Indeed Aurelian would have found it impossible to believe that any woman could have restrained her passions to the extent that gossip attributed to Zenobia. Some day Zenobia would fall into his hands, of that Aurelian was sure. Then she would discover she could not impose her will upon him, as she was said to have done upon her compliant husband. Doubtless Odenath had, at such times, taken his pleasure elsewhere in the palace at Palmyra.

Apparently Zenobia and those archers of hers who had so terrorized the Romans had found it easy to capture Antioch. But Aurelian did not intend to leave Antioch in a woman's hands, not so long as he himself still had his. Nor did he intend to allow the mint there to continue striking out those coins she had ordered.

To invade a troublesome province like Egypt and go away leaving a garrison of only five thousand men was a performance Aurelian could only consider the utmost folly. Perhaps her general thought so too, but Zabdas, from all reports, was fanatically devoted to Zenobia. It was a pity that Claudius, in his campaign against the Goths, had had to send Egypt's governor to the Straits. His strategy had helped, though, for Probus had destroyed the whole Gothic fleet.

Those of the Goths who had escaped drowning were nicely settled now in Thrace and in Macedonia. The plague had helped, too; it had killed off multitudes, including Claudius, and had given Aurelian his chance, at last. Aurelian remembered thinking at the time how fortunate it was for the morale of his soldiers that so many young Gothic females had escaped the sickness; each soldier could have two or three for his own use.

Perhaps that woman in Palmyra had heard rumors of what happened to females the Romans caught, and would stop short before running the risk of capture. Aurelian certainly would not have wanted that; he meant to catch Zenobia himself, if not at Nicaea, which Claudius had had the good sense to strengthen before he died, then surely at Antioch, but catch her he would.

We do not know where Aurelian was when he received his first disturbing communication from Tetricus, but it made him stop thinking about Zenobia and dash off to Gaul to undo the mischief Victoria had caused.

XI

Pursuit

Zenobia, who, though rather tall, seems to have been fragile-looking, often dismounted from her horse and marched four or five miles with her troops. Pollio's statement does not tell us whether this habit of the Queen's endeared her to her men. Perhaps some admired her courage and endurance, while others may have thought she exposed herself to danger unnecessarily. There is no record that she ever allowed Zabdas to accompany her. She trusted her men. But surely to see their fragile-looking Queen—this is the impression we receive today from those gold coins that show her portrait—pacing them mile upon mile could not have failed to raise the spirits of many a soldier.

During the long, tedious journey through river valleys and wide plains from Tyana on its hilltop to Ancyra on its higher hill, Zenobia must have dismounted frequently. Ancyra, the capital of ancient Galatia, now Ankara, the capital of modern Turkey, stands about five hundred feet above the plain. Today third-century Ancyra and twentieth-century Ankara have only two features in common, a natural hill and a man-made monument.

History-minded as she was, Zenobia would have been less interested in the hill than in the monument. Today the monument is in ruins, but in the first century of our era it was a beautiful marble temple that the Emperor Augustus built when the city became the capital of a Roman province. Inscribed on its walls was a full account of the Emperor's life and deeds. Written in Greek and in Latin, the inscription would have presented no difficulty to Zenobia. If the temple was still intact when she arrived in Ancyra, she doubtless managed to crowd in a visit to it while she was arranging to continue her march to the Straits.

We do not know how Ancyra received the Queen of Palmyra and her thousands of troops. Nor do we know where or when she received the puzzling news that Aurelian who, as she knew, had left Rome on the first leg of his march to the Straits, had suddenly changed his course and had gone west instead of east. Her spies would soon have discovered for her that he was on his way to Cologne, the capital of the Gallo-Roman Empire, to help the Pretender Tetricus put down a rebellion. The whole procedure would have mystified her.

We who have access to documents unknown to Zenobia are less mystified. Pollio, for example, excuses himself for his indiscretion in listing Victoria and Zenobia among the Pretenders by saying that "the ways of Gallienus brought it about that women, too, should be deemed worthy of mention." This is, certainly, at the very least, a backhanded compliment that provides Pollio with a cover for what appears to be a secret admiration for the lady Victoria's political ability. It also classes Victoria with the three Julias of the previous century who made and unmade Emperors.

We do not know whether Zenobia was personally acquainted with this remarkable woman of her own day, but Pollio intimates that when she first confronted Aurelian she told him she believed Victoria to be a woman like herself. "I, too," she is supposed to have said, "desired to become a partner in the royal power, should the supply of lands permit."

Rome had never recognized the Gallo-Roman Empire, of which Tetricus was now the nominal head. This so-called Empire comprised the provinces of Spain, Gaul, and Britain, and they had early become, in that order, respected members of the Roman state. From mines that were seemingly inexhaustible, Spain had sent into the treasury gold, silver, copper, iron, and lead. Spain, therefore, ever since the days of the Emperor Augustus, had enjoyed full employment, peace, and security. Gaul and Britain had not been so easily won over. Only after bloody and savage battles had they succumbed.

Still, matters had gone along without too much rebellion until Gallienus became the Emperor of Rome. The demands he made upon the provinces, merely to fulfill his own vicious desires, finally drove them to open revolt. The storm had broken over Claudius' head, but the plague had carried him off before he could cope with the situation he had inherited from Gallienus. As with many other problems, this one had become Aurelian's.

Riding steadily westward in his chariot, Aurelian tried to recall what he had heard about Victoria's relationship with Tetricus, the ex-Senator. Victoria's husband, he knew, had governed the provinces with an iron hand. Victorinus, his son and successor, had been an excellent ruler of men. Unfortunately, he had also been an excellent seducer of women, especially those of high rank. In 267 a coalition of jealous husbands at Cologne murdered him and so put an abrupt end to his illicit pleasures. Though Victorinus' son seems to have been too young to share in his father's pastimes, the outraged husbands killed him anyway. Victoria survived both these mishaps.

Though neither her husband nor her son had been recognized as anything more than Pretenders, Victoria had assumed the Imperial title, Augusta, and an additional title of even higher distinction, Mother of the Camps, which, hitherto, had belonged only to Empresses. She also, according to Pollio, had minted in her own name coins of copper, of silver, and of gold.

For some three years after her son's death, Victoria was the sole ruler of the Gallo-Roman Empire. During this time, the nominal power was in the hands of her two "fronts," a certain Marius, an iron-worker, and Tetricus, an ex-Senator of Rome. Gibbon reports that Victoria ruled both these stooges with a "manly vigour." Marius (his full name was M. Aurelius Marcus Augustus) is believed, according to at least one source, to have preceded rather than followed Victoria's son. Except for statistical purposes, his place in the Imperial list matters little, since he ruled only three days.

Pollio adds to the three-day tradition Cicero's famous jest about a Roman consul who once held office—as a substitute—for six hours during the middle of the day:

"We have had a consul so stern," Cicero jested, "and severe that during his term of office no one has breakfasted, no one has dined, and no one has slept."

Tetricus, when Victoria called him, reluctantly gave up his governorship to become the ruler of the Gallo-Roman Empire, which at that time comprised Britain and Gaul. According to Pollio, Victoria urged Tetricus to take a further step and set himself up as a rival to the legitimate Emperor Claudius, "solely that she might always be daring the deeds of men." This Tetricus refused to do.

Unfitted to rule, Tetricus spent four of five unhappy years trying to learn to manage an army whom he feared and who later despised him. At the time, though, that he assumed the purple, his soldiers may only have disliked him because they knew he had gained his insecure seat upon the throne through a woman's influence.

Victoria's death, which has never been satisfactorily accounted for, seems to have occurred either while Tetricus was in office or immediately after his decision to abandon all pretence of being a ruler. Some writers say that Tetricus killed his benefactor, others that she "succumbed to the destiny of fate." We do know, however, that she did not suffer the humiliation of being displayed to the people of Rome as Tetricus was, when Aurelian shortly afterward made his triumphal entry through the gates that led to the Sacred Way.

The misplaced Tetricus, either before or after Victoria's death, decided that the only way out of his predicament as a rival Emperor with no desire or aptitude for Imperial power was to throw himself upon Aurelian's mercy. He took the risk of pouring out all his troubles in a letter to Aurelian and proposed to him a method of rescue.

Aurelian was an experienced military man. He must have understood, Gibbon thinks, his own predicament as well as that of Tetricus. If their secret correspondence fell into the hands of the powerful Roman army, both would lose their lives. In those days, Kings and Emperors did not step down from the eminence they had attained. Had Tetricus done so, he would have been "guilty of treason against himself."

Tetricus saw one way out. He pretended that civil war was brewing and that he needed help to put it down. If Aurelian came, he would pretend to oppose him. Aurelian arrived with his legions. Tetricus posted his men in the most disadvantageous places he could manage, and so assured their defeat.

Early in the engagement, Tetricus and a few chosen friends deserted. The army, outnumbered and abandoned, fought on desperately until, almost cut to pieces, they surrendered. History has not recorded how Aurelian received the survivors. Nor do we know whether these "barbarians" were aware that their so-called Emperor had grossly betrayed them.

Word of the betrayal at Cologne may have come to Zenobia while she was still in Ancyra. She may also have learned, to her surprise, that Aurelian, though he considered Tetricus a traitor, had heaped honors upon him. She, too, from Aurelian's point of view, was a Pretender, but she would not stoop to betrayal to gain her ends. That Aurelian would always put the good of Rome before all else probably did not, at this time, enter into her thinking.

The distance from Ancyra to the Straits, depending on the roads Zenobia took, was between two and three hundred miles. She seems to have started on this second part of her march at just about the time when Aurelian returned to Rome from Cologne, probably bringing Tetricus along, to save him from being murdered by his betrayed army.

Aurelian returned to Rome, where, for the time being, the Senate and the people were satisfied. Except for minor disturbances, the western part of the Empire seemed secure. The Senate, naturally, knew that the other woman, the one from Palmyra, still defied

Aurelian, but they trusted him to attend to that detail in good time. He could quickly dispose of her.

Vopiscus, though he admires Aurelian, admits that he often used wrong methods in putting down revolts, that when he closed the mint in Rome, he marred his excellent reputation as an Emperor of whom great things were expected by putting to death without full proof of treason some of the Senators who had abetted the mint-workers and by confiscating the property of those he had not condemned. His action left whole families beggared. Vopiscus adds that Aurelian was a "good physician indeed, but the methods he used were bad."

Historians agree that Aurelian had meant his closing of the mint at Rome to be an initial step toward reorganizing the financial administration of the city. But since the first consequence of this had been to throw thousands out of work, his intended reform merely helped to increase the city's disorder.

All this, however, seems to have been forgotten by the time Aurelian returned to Rome and announced to the Senate that his defeat of Tetricus had restored the West to the Empire. He might have hoped, at this great moment in his life, to imitate Claudius and other Imperial predecessors by extending the *pomerium*, the ancient boundary line of the city, but since as yet he had not added any foreign territory to the Empire, the law forbade him.

Word came that the Alamanni wished to send ambassadors to treat with the Emperor of Rome. Aurelian, who seems to have been a born showman, decided to make a lasting impression upon the Germanic mind. He ordered the Alamanni to send their ambassadors upon a given day, when he would receive them outside the closed gates of Rome.

The ambassadors arrived as commanded. Helmeted and in full armor, his red general's cloak draped over his left shoulder, Aurelian sat in state upon a throne that had been specially made and gilded for the occasion. On either side of him were the principal leaders of the Imperial cavalry, eyes straight ahead, statuesque on their well-trained horses. High into the air behind the throne, men raised

on silvered pikes the consecrated images of Claudius and his predecessors. And above the long lines of massed legions shimmered the
golden eagles of Rome, with the name of each legion written large
on its standard.

Not a sound broke the stillness. The ambassadors fell on their
faces in the dust. The Emperor bade them rise and set forth their
mission. Through their interpreters, they offered a peaceful alliance,
provided the Emperor reimbursed them for their losses. These in-
sulting proposals Aurelian scornfully rejected. He bade the ambassadors take word to their people that they must choose either total
submission, or punishment.

"We have spoken," the Emperor said coldly.

News of a Vandal invasion into Pannonia, the Roman province
where Claudius and Aurelian had been born, made it impossible
for Aurelian to wait until the ambassadors returned; he had to trust
his lieutenants to carry out his orders. They were to kill the entire
Alamanni force outright or else cut them off from all means of
subsistence and let them starve. In Pannonia he was astounded to
hear that neither order had been carried out: the Alamanni had
eluded their guards and had spread themselves from the Alps to the
Apennines. From there they were preparing to descend upon Rome.

Rome was close to panic. Aurelian had earlier ordered the governors of the northern provinces to strip the country of all food
supplies and to store everything in the cities. This order had been
obeyed; and its precautionary measure had its effect, for when Aurelian finally confronted the Vandals, he easily conquered them.
With the consent of the soldiers, the defeated Vandals were guar-
anteed safe conduct home, and food as long as they were on Roman soil. Aurelian stipulated that both their kings should surrender
their sons as hostages and furnish a "contingent of two thousand
horsemen to the Roman auxiliary services."

Aurelian now began preparing for serious war against Zenobia.
In the midst of his preparations, he heard that Zenobia, when she
left Antioch, had assured the heretic Paul of her full protection
and had declared that even if he held strange ideas at variance with

those of the Christian community there, he need not resign his bishopric. This interference of Zenobia's, Aurelian's spies told him, meant more trouble in Antioch.

Aurelian was disturbed. He knew that for generations men, women, and children had been flocking to Antioch, bringing with them their strange faith, turning that pleasure-loving city of the Romans into their spawning-grounds. He began to wonder whether Zenobia herself had become a member of the new sect.

At this time Zenobia's empire consisted of two parts: the provinces Odenath had governed in the name of Rome, and the countries she had won over since her husband's death. These countries included Lower Egypt, Western Asia as far north as Ancyra, and the recently won cities that lay between Ancyra in Galatia and Nicaea in Bithynia. Nicaea itself she expected to capture without difficulty. She does not seem to have known that Aurelian had planned his campaign against her as soon as he received authentic reports about her movements. He sent his trusted general Probus—not the unfortunate official by the same name who had committed suicide by opening his veins—to Alexandria, where there was a strong pro-Roman party, with orders to do whatever was needed to restore Lower Egypt to the Empire.

Probus made swift work of the small token force Zenobia had left there, and so by the autumn of 271 Egypt again belonged to Rome. How soon Zenobia learned of her loss, we do not know. She may have learned, somewhere during her march across Bithynia, that Nicaea would not be captured as easily as she had expected. Nicaea's importance lay in her strategic location; whoever controlled the city could seize Chalcedon and Nicomedia. Both were flourishing ports on the Straits. News of the order to strengthen Nicaea seems never to have reached the Queen of Palmyra. Aurelian was well aware of the Emperor Claudius' forethought; it may, of course, have been Aurelian's forethought. When Claudius sent him to Sapor's court, his route would have taken him through Nicaea, and he may have noticed then that the city was especially vulnerable on the eastern side.

Aurelian's next move was to assemble his army on the Danube River. From there he led them through Thrace, paused temporarily to drive back some rebel Goths to their own territory across the river, then headed for Byzantium on the Straits. To reach Chalcedon on the other side, he would have to transport his army across that narrow stretch of water with its unpredictable current.

Under previous Roman Emperors, Byzantium, known for centuries as Constantinople (Constantine's city), but of recent years as Istanbul, had greatly suffered. Originally a Greek city, it had not lent itself easily to conquest by either Alexander the Great or by a succession of Roman Emperors, who had from time to time partially destroyed the city. Angered by some trivial omission on their part, the Emperor Gallienus had put most of the inhabitants to the sword. When Aurelian arrived, the unhappy city was still struggling to recover.

Vopiscus does not tell us how the Byzantines, who could not have been overjoyed to see another Roman army at their gates, received the Emperor Aurelian, of whose reputation for cruelty they must have been well aware. Nor does Vopiscus tell us how Aurelian transported his army across the Straits. Since Aurelian had no quarrel with Byzantium and merely wanted to get his army to Chalcedon, the chances are that the city was spared further brutality. Besides, Aurelian knew he would need all his men in the coming tug-of-war with Zenobia. He also knew that unless he crossed the Straits when the swift current ran in the right direction, he might have trouble, and he could not afford to lose men by mistake.

His engineers managed the crossing well. Soon the entire army was marching toward Chalcedon, originally a Greek colony nicknamed the *Blind*. Its founders had been too short-sighted to realize that the site across the channel, where Byzantium was later built, was superior to theirs.

In Chalcedon Aurelian learned that Zenobia had been unable to capture Nicaea and had turned back. No one in Chalcedon could tell Aurelian why she had left so abruptly. The governor of Chalcedon seems to have admitted that if Zenobia and her troops had appeared at his gates, the citizens might have forced him to surrender the city.

Neither man, so far as we know, had ever seen the Queen of Palmyra. Aurelian must have seen her portrait on those coins she had circulated in the East. If he had, he probably underrated her as a commander of men. His scouts would have told him, though, that her army was loyal and well-staffed.

Aurelian marched on to Nicaea. The city had been built in the form of a square; from a monument in the center its four gates, each in the middle of a wall, could be kept constantly in sight. When Aurelian arrived, the governor probably took him at once to the monument and from there pointed out how the walls had been raised, in some places doubled, and the gates fitted with heavier bars.

"Where did the lady Zenobia appear?" would surely have been one of Aurelian's first questions.

"Yonder, at the east gate."

Zenobia, in full armor and astride her white Nubian horse, her great jewel glittering on her forehead, would have been a sight to call forth cries of admiration from Nicaea's people, had she come upon any other errand than to demand their surrender. Beside her were Zabdas and her other generals, and behind them thousands of eager warriors, ready to charge at the word of command.

That word was never given.

Zenobia and her generals must have realized at once that, though they had been successful so far, the odds were now against them. The high walls bristled with armed men, with catapults, and with machines for hurling fire-balls. At intervals stood great earthen jars of burning oil. Zenobia's scaling ladders were too short, and she had no siege-engines. Though Aurelian could not claim the honor of having forestalled Zenobia, still in this struggle between the man from Rome and the woman from Palmyra, the first round had gone to the man.

Chagrined and apparently without striking a blow, Zenobia turned away from the city she had thought to take so easily and ordered a retreat. She would have to relinquish, temporarily, she must have hoped, her dream of a port on the Straits. Discouraged, but not daunted, she led her troops back to friendly Galatia.

With his prey in flight, Aurelian had no time to lose. He pushed on.

Though we do not know enough to enable us to follow, step by step, Aurelian's pursuit of Zenobia from Nicaea through the mountainous country that lay between Bithynia and Galatia, we may be sure that he encountered opposition from the cities that had accepted the Queen of Palmyra in preference to the Emperor of Rome.

Galatia, southeast of Bithynia, had received its name from the Gallic peoples who had once overrun that part of the East. As a Roman province, Galatia had for centuries been steadfastly loyal to the pagan Empire. The establishment of Christian churches and the resultant conversion of Gentiles to the new faith not only caused a rift within the Church but caused many to rebel against Rome. The rift within the Church concerned ritual and circumcision, some members insisting that both should be obligatory for all converts. This Rome regarded as a family quarrel and so took no part.

Defection from the Empire was another matter. In the second century Hellenic ways and modes of thought had fanned the winds of freedom in Galatia and in Cappadocia, and this prepared the way for Zenobia's cry of political freedom. Many cities in both provinces obviously preferred Zenobia as an overlord rather than a dissolute Roman Emperor. But when in the unstable third century Aurelian appeared on Zenobia's heels, neither Cappadocia nor Galatia, with the exception of Ancyra, appears to have had the courage to remain loyal to Zenobia. Both reaffirmed their allegiance to Rome.

Some historians have felt that if Galatia and Cappadocia had remained loyal, Zenobia's chances of setting up a rival Empire in the East might have been good. There were precedents: Semiramis reigned forty-two years over Assyria and left a well-regulated kingdom to her son; the Cleopatras of Egypt are well known; Victoria

133

and the Julias were powerful women. But none of them had to contend with an Aurelian backed by all the resources of the vast Roman Empire. Pollio says that during the few years that Zenobia ruled after her husband's death she proved herself an excellent administrator. At times he seems to rate her above Odenath. Had Zenobia succeeded, the entire history of the Near East might have been different.

Since the first round in the struggle between Emperor Aurelian and Queen Zenobia had, because of Roman foresight in fortifying Nicaea, gone to Aurelian, he had a ready-prepared springboard from which to leap upon the provinces that had gone over to Zenobia. The first to feel the fury of his attack was Ancyra.

Traces of Zenobia's passing had met Aurelian all through the mountainous country between Chalcedon and Ancyra. Wherever he looked, he saw discarded clothing and sandals, broken spears, whitened bones, even a corpse or so from which angry vultures rose. Now and then his scouts captured stragglers, tortured them for news, and threw them aside. But though Aurelian pressed his men hard, with no mercy to spare for the sick or wounded, he could not overtake Zenobia and her retreating army. They knew the terrain; he did not.

Ancyra, looking down from her rocky hilltop, though terrified to see a Roman Emperor toiling upward at the head of his men, closed her gates and prepared to resist. She never had a chance. Finally Aurelian accepted the hostages that were proffered, demanded food, and hurried southward through the desert toward Tyana in Cappadocia and the narrow, rocky pass through the Taurus Mountains.

At Tyana a surprise awaited the Emperor Aurelian.

XII

Kill All the Dogs

The gates of Tyana were closed. On the high walls, silhouetted against the western sun, appeared long lines of armed and helmeted soldiers. They might have been carved out of stone, so motionless and silent they stood, with not even a downward glance as the foremost of the Roman legions breasted the steep hill on which, long before Zenobia and Aurelian had been born, men had built their city and walled it against their enemies.

Aurelian, with his staff officers beside him, stared up in disbelief at the closed gates and the armed soldiers. He had come to free men from the intolerable yoke of a woman, and this was the way they received him, their city girded for war, and no governor in sight. Days ago, Aurelian had sent couriers ahead to warn the governor that he expected suitable provisioning. It was the custom, and Rome paid well.

One of the couriers he had sent to Tyana approached him, saluted, and gave him the governor's message: he had been forced to hand over to Zenobia and her troops all the food he could spare; there was nothing left in the city; the Romans would have to live off the countryside.

Aurelian's temper flared.

"In this city I will not leave even a dog alive," he shouted.

Vopiscus has preserved, without comment, this angry exclama-

135

tion. Whether true or not, it is in character with what we know of Aurelian.

Perhaps Vopiscus found Aurelian's shout recorded in the same documents from which he learned that Apollonius, the famous mystic of Tyana, appeared in ghostly form to Aurelian and warned him not to destroy the city. Aside from the account in Vopiscus, our only source for this interesting tale is a Greek writer, Philostratus, a contemporary of Septimius Severus, who wrote a book on the life and miracles of Apollonius.

Apollonius, we learn from the book, was a traveled man, a man of education, and a follower of the philosopher Pythagoras. But when Apollonius finally returned to the East, he was less revered as a philosopher than as a magician. This two-fold reputation of the mystic from Tyana led Philostratus to dedicate his book to Julia Domna, in appreciation of her wide acquaintance with literature, art, and philosophy; to which she added a lively interest in miraculous events; in fact, in everything that savored of mysticism.

Apparently because Philostratus dedicated his book to Julia, she was accused of fostering an upsurge of mysticism throughout the East which was already in a turmoil over the miracles attributed to the Man from Galilee.

Whether Zenobia was a mystic or not is beside the question; she must have been well acquainted with the fear that even the bare mention of the mystic's name aroused. She must also have known the disaster that Ancyra had suffered for her sake and have been determined to save Tyana from a similar fate.

If the peasant-born Aurelian could be made to believe that the long-dead Apollonius still watched over the city of his birth, ready to punish a transgressor, he would surely spare Tyana. And so, since the ancients have not attempted to explain the apparition of Apollonius, but have merely accepted it at face value, we may be allowed to ascribe it to the quick-witted Queen of Palmyra. She would have left the visible defense of Tyana to the governor and his militia, while she herself set about inducing the wraith of Apollonius to appear to Aurelian and warn him of his peril if he harmed

Tyana. We do not know what kind of black magic or human persuasion Zenobia employed, but Vopiscus assures us that an apparition, which Aurelian recognized as that of Apollonius, came to the Imperial tent.

Zenobia, of course, would not have waited to see the outcome of her scheme. With Zabdas and her troops, she passed quickly through the Cilician Gates, probably cheered on by the guards posted upon the cliffs, and retraced her way to Antioch, where she had decided to take her stand. There she would have the advantage of being able to choose her battle ground.

Enraged by the escape of his prey, by the sight of armed men on the walls of Tyana, and by the governor's refusal to provide him with food for his men, Aurelian must have been, momentarily, at a loss. Zenobia, the governor said firmly, had ordered him not to let the Romans enter the city nor negotiate the pass through the Taurus Mountains.

Aurelian knew he could not force a passage without first securing provisions; and he could not get provisions without besieging Tyana. The countryside had nothing left, for first Zenobia's army and then his own had ranged over a wide area. He would have an excuse for storming the city, if the citizens were concealing Zenobia from him. But all reports from the pass agreed that she had gone through. He would have to decide quickly, for he had promised his legions a fair share of the booty. They were already restless, hungry too, for food and dissipation in the city.

Aurelian had no choice. He had fought through hostile country, had crossed rivers and mountains and deserts. Now the city of the dead Apollonius was blocking his way. Yet only through this narrow pass could he reach the Syrian Gates at the other end and march against Antioch. Though Aurelian knew why he hesitated to put into practice his angry shout that he would leave not even a dog alive, his men did not. And so Aurelian kept hoping desperately for a sign, an omen, anything to prove that he had a right to destroy Tyana.

Hesitation, Aurelian knew, was fatal, especially since he could offer no explanation that even his centurions would accept. And they were growing as impatient as the men; they, too, wanted to carry out their commander's threat.

So it was that with loud cheers even the centurions finally heard Aurelian give the order to attack. At last all would have the chance to fill their hungry bellies and attend to other needs as well. Sober historians state that, though the troops vigorously pressed the attack, they were unable to make much headway until, through the treachery of a disloyal citizen of Tyana, they were enabled to occupy a height above the city, which then capitulated.

Vopiscus tells us that the disloyal citizen was a wealthy man who hoped to save his own life if the city were forced to surrender. He advised the Emperor to dress himself in full regalia and climb up to the top of a nearby hillock. Aurelian did as the man suggested, and "holding aloft his purple cloak he showed himself to the townsfolk within and the soldiers without, and so the city was captured, just as though Aurelian's entire army had been within the walls."

Vopiscus does not vouch for the truth of this account; he lets us infer that the mere sight of the Emperor Aurelian caused the frightened citizens to clamor for surrender. Perhaps they felt that a ghostly Apollonius would not be able to cope with an Emperor in the flesh. If they had any such thoughts, they were certainly mistaken, for that night, after Aurelian had retired to his tent, his ghostly visitor arrived.

The recognition was mutual.

Vopiscus is careful to assure his audience that he found this remarkable incident mentioned in his sources in the Ulpian Library. Aurelian, he feels, could not have failed to recognize Apollonius, for he must often have seen statues and portraits of the mystic in his temples both at Rome and elsewhere.

Apollonius must have known which Emperor of Rome he was addressing, for he spoke to him in Latin, Aurelian's native tongue, calling him by name, not only once, but three times, as was the custom when calling upon the dead. The ritual terrified Aurelian:

"Aurelian, if you wish to conquer, there is no reason why you should plan the death of my fellow-citizens."

"Aurelian, if you wish to rule, abstain from the blood of the innocent."

"Aurelian, act with mercy if you wish to live long."

"And so, stricken with terror," Vopiscus adds, "he promised him a portrait and statues and a temple, and returned to his better self."

The next day, when Aurelian merely announced that he had decided to spare the city, his soldiers were so indignant at being deprived of their expected booty that they caught the traitor and killed him. Their appetites still unsated, they reminded Aurelian that he had said he would not leave a single dog alive.

"I did indeed declare," Aurelian replied, "that I would not leave a dog alive in this city; well, then, kill all the dogs."

Now follows, in the biographer's account, an ambiguous statement: "Notable, indeed, were the prince's words, but more notable still was the deed of the soldiers; for the entire army, just as though it were gaining riches thereby, took up the prince's jest, by which both booty was denied them and the city preserved intact." Though the Latin text is clearer than the translation, we are still not entirely certain how the soldiers interpreted Aurelian's permission.

In a letter Vopiscus says Aurelian wrote afterward to a friend, he is quoted as saying he was glad to learn that his soldiers had killed the traitor. "He who spared not his native city would not have been able to keep faith with me," he added.

Unfortunately we cannot ask Aurelian why he did not put the Pretender Tetricus to death. Tetricus betrayed his army to their deaths; and not only did Aurelian not punish him; he rewarded him. Yet, according to his lights, Aurelian was a just man. Perhaps we should not blame him if his lights flickered somewhat during the long, tiresome march with the elusive Zenobia always just beyond his grasp. For, obviously, while Aurelian was being held up at Tyana, Zenobia and her army went through the mountain pass on their way to Cilicia.

Vopiscus commends Aurelian for his leniency toward Tyana. The traitor, he remarks, received his just reward, but Aurelian allowed his family to escape the customary punishment. "I did not confiscate the man's property," Aurelian wrote in the letter to his friend, "but restored it to his heirs." The Emperor did not want any one to be able to say of him, Vopiscus explains, that he permitted a "rich man to be slain for the sake of his money."

After impressing upon the citizens of Tyana that loyalty to the Empire meant adherence to the state religion, Aurelian set out for the pass through the Taurus Mountains. Disgruntled because their kill in Tyana had been limited to the city dogs and one traitor, Aurelian's army followed him sulkily through the rocky pass toward its southern exit, the Syrian Gates. Here Aurelian may have expected to find that Zenobia and Zabdas had posted a rearguard, but he appears to have encountered no opposition. His men, professional soldiers all of them, were now spoiling for a fight, not against dogs, but against armed men who would resist them. They may have been somewhat mollified when those who knew Antioch assured their fellows that the Syrian city was wealthier than the Cappadocian Tyana.

Zenobia's men were equally disappointed, for they too had expected to add booty from Tyana to what they had already acquired. By the time they reached Tarsus their morale must have been indeed low. If any inkling had reached them of Zenobia's discouraging reply from the Cilician oracle, their morale would have sunk to a lower level. Aware of the feeling of their men, Zenobia and Zabdas announced that they would stand and fight at Antioch.

And so, though the pine needles were as slippery underfoot as before when they marched so hopefully north, few of the men even noticed them, buoyed up as they were by the recollection of the fertile plain and the Orontes River. There, on the left bank, would be Antioch. Those of the soldiers who called the city home would have been proud to hear from their less fortunate fellows that they, too, had heard of Daphne and its delights; their Queen would give them time off for Daphne.

Aurelian, we imagine, arriving in Tarsus with a victorious army

at his back, may have received a rather dubious welcome. But when
the city fathers learned that he only wanted news of Zenobia, they
were doubtless glad to be let off so easily. Shopkeepers opened their
doors. Soon business, at prices double the normal amount, found
its way to the soldiers' pockets and swiftly emptied them. As for
Aurelian, the chances are that his spies found out for him that the
Cilician oracle had characterized him as a falcon and Zenobia as a
dove.

Aurelian may also have learned that at Tarsus a Roman centurion, known as Saul, had turned aside from the state religion to
join the new sect; he had had a vision, people said, and afterward
he had changed his name to Paul. Though two centuries had passed
since Paul died for his faith in Rome, Tarsus had not forgotten its
son any more than Tyana had Apollonius; and Aurelian must have
heard many accounts of him, both favorable and unfavorable.
Vopiscus includes none of them in his biography of Aurelian. Perhaps the books he consulted in the Ulpian Library contained nothing Vopiscus wanted to use about a centurion who had changed
his name from Saul to Paul.

Paul believed in monotheism, and in this Aurelian would have
supported him, though he would have disagreed with him concern-
ing the nature of the deity to be revered.

Among the third-century pagans (a misnomer indeed), monotheistic tendencies were active, and the re-introduction of the worship of the Sun that Aurelian officially established afterward in
Rome gave expression to these tendencies. It is worth remembering
that it was the great temple of the Sun-god in Palmyra that Aurelian
ordered restored in all its original grandeur. And at Rome he appointed Senators to serve as high priests in the temple he built there
to the Sun. He also instituted games in honor of the Sun; but he
never went as far as Julia's son Elagabalus of Emesa, who identified himself with the god he served. For Aurelian the re-establish-
ment of Sun-worship meant strengthening the state religion, since
to him they were one.

During the few days that Aurelian allowed to his troops to recuperate in Tarsus from their passage through the mountain pass, he might have heard more about the theological argument that was causing trouble in Antioch. Bishop Paul had upset the Christians by denying that the founder of their own religion could claim divinity. Next thing, the fellow would deny the Emperor's claim, and that would indeed be serious. Perhaps at this point, Aurelian chuckled; his scouts had also reported that a few years ago the chaste and beautiful Zenobia had become Paul's champion in Antioch. To Aurelian that meant only one thing, an affair. And Daphne was just the place for them to meet. The mere thought of that must have made Aurelian's temperature rise to a higher point than was safe. His spies assured him that in Antioch the greater part of the Christian community would support him, since Zenobia had alienated most of them by her friendship with Paul.

XIII

She Was No Dove

Zenobia's situation in Antioch (she and Zabdas reached there considerably before Aurelian) was a complicated one. The Jews were hostile to her because they thought her indifferent to Paul, and since his religious stand closely approximated their own, they resented her attitude. The Greeks were hostile because she would not yield to their entreaties to surrender the city before it was too late. Her own soldiers, though, stoutly maintained that they could hold Antioch against Aurelian. Some citizens doubted these assurances; they said they preferred to trust the "talismans" Apollonius had given them.

Apollonius, it seems, was famous for talismans: various objects that were engraved with mystic symbols supposed to avert evil. Once while in Antioch, he had presented some of them to the city. To protect people against the north wind, he advised setting one up on the eastern gate. Because scorpions often plagued people, he made a bronze scorpion, and this they set up in the middle of the city. Glanville Downey, to whom I am indebted for this information, adds that Apollonius also "prescribed an annual ceremony that would act as a charm against gnats."

We do not know how much trust, if any, the Christian population of Antioch put in these magic symbols.

The wound their recalcitrant Bishop Paul had inflicted upon the

Christian community had not healed; instead, it had become a festering sore. Paul would not budge from his theological position. Neither would he give up his episcopal palace to the Synod's appointee. And no one except Zenobia had the right to dislodge him. Delegations from both sides again waited upon her; she talked of the danger to the city, and oddly enough asked questions about Daphne. No one knew what to think.

It was midsummer when Zenobia's spies told her that Aurelian's advance scouts had appeared on the road that skirted the eastern shore of the Lake of Antioch. It was obvious to Zenobia and Zabdas that Aurelian meant to strike from that direction. The talisman on the eastern gate was intended to protect the city against the north wind, as they both knew, not against enemy attack; still, since many people believed implicitly in their talismans, Zenobia may have thought it wise to let the news leak out that Aurelian would approach from the east.

"We have retreated far enough," Zenobia probably said to Zabdas, "now we shall fight."

Perhaps, at this critical moment, the response of the Cilician oracle may have recurred to Zenobia. She had been acting like a "dove," a sitting dove, really. Now the falcon was about to swoop. His wings must be clipped before he crossed the Orontes.

Though we have no evidence of this decision, it must have been made, for somewhere along Aurelian's road he encountered Zenobia's cavalry. Despite the heat, her horses and men wore chain armor, and the heat in Syria must have been as intolerable in the third century as it is in the twentieth. The sun rises early and sets late. The wind whips sand into your face and fills your mouth, unless you muffle yourself, as the Bedouins do, with a neckcloth drawn close to your nostrils.

When Aurelian saw that enormous mass of metal moving toward his lightly armed cavalry, he must have thought the Sun-god had sent the excessive heat his men had been complaining about that he, Aurelian, a devotee of the god, might win the day's fight. His

Romans would be far less hampered by the heat than would Zenobia's sweating cavalry. The Sun-god was on his side.

Aurelian's habit seems to have been to send his cavalry in first, to "soften up" the enemy, then throw in his infantry. This time he reversed his strategy. He knew that neither his cavalry nor his infantry, least of all his infantry, could stand against mailed horsemen, and so he sent his infantry across the river first. The cavalry followed, with orders not to engage the Palmyrenes but to pretend fright and withdraw along the road away from Antioch.

The maneuver succeeded. Zabdas and his heavily burdened cavalry pursued the "fleeing" Romans in the general direction of the small village of Immae, some thirty miles from Antioch. When Aurelian saw that the Palmyrene cavalry was tiring, he ordered his own cavalry to wheel and charge. Worn out by the heat and the weight of their armor, Zabdas and his men fell an easy prey to the Romans. The survivors—we have no record of the numbers—kept in order by Zabdas, escaped to Antioch. Riderless horses that galloped home may have been Zenobia's first news of the disaster.

Some authorities think that this battle near Immae, in which Zenobia's army was thrown back, could have been only a preliminary skirmish, and that the second one (at Emesa, modern Homs) was the decisive one. To Downey, the first battle, as preserved in the account of Zosimus which he follows, was the deciding factor.

The withdrawal to Immae, according to Downey, though the actual ground covered may have been only a few miles, must have been long enough under a blazing sun to take the heart out of even fresh troops, let alone men weighted down by heavy armor. Another reason for the defeat at Immae, which seems to have received little consideration except from Downey, might have been that Aurelian was with his troops, and, so far as we know, Zenobia was not. She seems to have expected, originally, that the decisive engagement would take place at Antioch itself.

Aware of the delicate situation in Antioch, Zabdas did not acquaint the city with the defeat of the Palmyrene army at Immae. Instead, he let a rumor circulate that he had met the Romans and had routed them. As proof, he paraded through the streets a man who resembled Aurelian. The trick succeeded, and Zenobia and Zabdas were enabled to withdraw, during the night, the survivors of Immae and the rest of the army without arousing suspicion.

Their withdrawal, or rather retreat, Zosimus states, lay southward past Daphne to Emesa, where they obviously expected to find loyal support. At Daphne they left a rearguard on the heights, doubtless with the hope that even a small force might be able to delay for a time Aurelian's pursuit.

In the morning Antioch awoke to find itself without protection. The only gate the army could have taken was the so-called Golden Gate—actually the gate leading toward Daphne was not gilded until many years afterward. One wonders whether the gate-keeper was bribed, or otherwise forced to keep silent, for surely the retreat of an army even at night could not have passed entirely unobserved.

Expecting any moment to hear the blare of Roman trumpets and the sound of heavy Roman boots, many people fled from their city to seek refuge anywhere rather than remain penned up behind their walls. There seems to have been no thought of civil resistance. As matters turned out, no resistance would have helped.

Aurelian, naturally, learned of Zenobia's flight. He gave up his intended attack upon the city and, unopposed, marched in with his legions. Whether he was surprised by the enthusiastic reception he met, history has apparently not thought it worth while to record. His first act was to issue a proclamation in which he promised a general amnesty. It seems that Apollonius had again appeared to Aurelian and advised him to spare the city. At least that is the reason Aurelian's biographer gives for his lenient treatment of Antioch.

When the people who had fled heard of Aurelian's proclamation, they returned to their city. Downey regards it as a "tribute to the strength of Aurelian's military discipline that he was able to keep his troops from plundering the city."

Zosimus states that Aurelian, before starting to pursue Zenobia, issued "such orders" as were necessary to stabilize the internal affairs of the city; he does not specify what such orders were for a people as torn by factions and as subject to pogroms as Antioch was. His greatest problem may have been Zenobia's protégé, Paul. Possibly he would have preferred to sidestep the problem. But, since Zenobia had been supporting Paul, Aurelian had to do something. It has been pointed out, though, that Aurelian did dodge the main issue, that of deciding between the two rival bishops. Actually, Aurelian merely decided that the house belonged to the ecclesiastical representative who had been elected by the Synod as Paul's successor. Paul now drops out of both ecclesiastical and secular history. Doubtless he applied his talents elsewhere.

That Aurelian left behind him a strong garrison to keep Antioch in order must be assumed. He himself with the rest of his army set out by way of Daphne to pursue Zenobia. To his surprise, when he reached Daphne, where in his youth he may have spent some pleasant hours, he found the heights already occupied, but the main part of Zenobia's army nowhere in sight. To scale the heights in the face of a well-entrenched enemy able to take full advantage of the rocky terrain, Aurelian knew would be no easy task. But it had to be done.

He selected men skilled in mountain fighting, formed them into a closely packed mass, each with his heavy shield over his head, shield overlapping shield, and sent them up. Protected against anything Zenobia's rearguard could throw down upon them, the soldiers gained the top of the hill and attacked.

Outnumbered and outmaneuvered, the rearguard fled; some were sent crashing down from the peaks, to be finished off by the waiting Romans below. The rout was complete. We hear nothing about the disposal of the dead on either side, nothing about the care of the wounded, only that Aurelian and his troops marched south following the only road Zenobia could have taken to Emesa.

The road led through Apamea, Larissa, Arethusa, and Laodicea. The first three cities threw open their gates and welcomed the Emperor of Rome. There is no record that Aurelian stayed any length of time in these places, perhaps only long enough to rest his horses and men, before taking the road for Laodicea and Emesa. His spies had reported that on the plain outside of Emesa, Zenobia and Zabdas, with a force of some seventy thousand men, would make their stand.

Aurelian, if unsuccessful at Emesa, would have to strike across the desert to Palmyra. He was accustomed to desert fighting, but the crossing would be easier and probably faster for Zenobia than for him, since she would be in friendly country with food and water plentiful, while he would have to fight for what he could get. He would have to reckon with wind and dust and hostile Bedouins.

Laodicea received Aurelian, if not with enthusiasm, at least with a trust that was not misplaced. Though the city had not retained the honor earlier bestowed upon her of being made the metropolis of Syria in Antioch's stead, Laodicea was still one of the three Syrian cities that were not required to pay tribute. This was an exemption that, under the Roman system of provincial government, was permitted to residents who were not full Roman citizens but who possessed "Latin rights." As such they were like guests at a banquet who were seated "below the salt."

Emesa, also exempt from tribute, was the home of a family who had held for centuries the hereditary priesthood of Elagabalus, the Sun-god. Because of this, the family claimed to be a royal dynasty. The famed Julia Domna, Caracalla's mother, had been honored with the title of *mater deorum* (mother of the gods). During her lifetime she had even been worshipped as the Heavenly Juno.

Aurelian, as a worshipper of the Sun-god, must have known that the god was believed to be incarnate in a black conical stone. He must also have known that the chief priest of Elagabalus was the grandson of Julia Domna's sister. The boy had become the chief priest of the Sun-god when he was about fourteen. Robed in floating garments of purple and gold and decked out with jewels, he performed the religious ceremonies of the cult. A moral pervert from his early teens on, the boy-priest was soon foisted off by his grandmother upon the Roman Senate as the natural son of Caracalla, and therefore heir to the Empire.

As Emperor, the boy imagined himself to be the god whom he had served, and insisted on being called Elagabalus. During the few years of his reign, he practically made a career of sexual license and debauchery; and Rome's wealthy society eagerly followed where their young Emperor led. He removed the black fetish from Emesa to Rome, where he built two magnificent temples, one on the Palatine, the other in the city's suburbs. At midsummer all Rome would join in celebrating the Sun-god's festival. Echoes of its grandeur permeated all Syria, including Emesa, whose citizens must have grieved over the senseless rape of their god.

By Aurelian's time, however, the black conical stone had been returned to its home in Emesa and the excesses at Rome's summer festival almost forgotten. Judging from the description of one of these festivals that has come down to us, it must have been long talked about. The procession started from the Sun-god's temple on the Palatine Hill. A chariot, drawn by six white horses—no visible charioteer—and richly adorned with jewels, carried the god to his temple outside the city. The young Emperor, robed in his priestly garments, ran backwards in front of the horses, his eyes fixed adoringly upon the fetish. Behind the chariot streamed the people. When the religious ceremonies were over, the Emperor distributed the largess the people were waiting for: "gold and silver, beasts and raiment that had been collected for the deity."

Now, fifty years after Elagabalus had been made Emperor by his grandmother, had married (within three years) and divorced five wives, including a Vestal virgin, Aurelian was marching into Emesa, intent on ridding the Empire of a woman, who, though reputed to be impossibly chaste, was, in his estimation, as troublesome a mischief-maker as Elagabalus' grandmother. And what he would do with Zenobia when he caught her, Aurelian at this time may not have decided.

Before Aurelian reached Emesa, his spies reported that the city had remained loyal to the Empire. Zenobia and her army had been admitted, but when the city fathers made it plain that they would not assist her in any way, Zenobia and Zabdas did not stay. In fact, they seem to have departed so hastily that Zenobia abandoned some booty she had meant to take along.

Zenobia had not gone far, Aurelian's spies added; she was waiting for him in a broad plain nearby, with a force of cavalry and infantry said to number in the thousands. Sympathizers from the general vicinity had greatly swelled her ranks. Their leaders may have worn helmets similar to an unusual one found at Emesa and now in the Damascus Museum, labelled "The Helmet of Emesa." Its date is the first century of our era. With its face mask made of silver and with silver ornaments, this is no ordinary headgear, but a helmet for a distinguished person, perhaps a ranking general. Experts think it was manufactured in Antioch, where there were numerous gold and silver shops.

The course of the great battle that was fought on the plain outside the walls of Emesa is somewhat confusing. Zenobia's army of seventy thousand greatly outnumbered Aurelian's. But, according to Zosimus, Aurelian had Dalmatian and Moorish cavalry, and divisions from many Roman provinces, including unusually tall Palestinian troops armed with huge three-foot clubs.

Aurelian's biographer has, as usual, a fantastic story to tell. The Roman cavalry were being driven back when above the field of battle appeared a "divina forma." The cavalry rallied, the infantry rallied, the huge Palestinian clubs came smashing down, and Zenobia's men broke in terror. They hurled themselves upon the closed gates of Emesa, but the gates held fast.

Aurelian, we hear from his biographer, entered Emesa as a conqueror. He went first to the temple of Elagabalus to offer thanks and pay his just dues to the god. And again there appeared to him the same divine being he had seen on the battle field. He seems to have known what form his gratitude should take, for he ordered a temple built to Elagabalus, presented the god with many valuable gifts, and, when all his work in the East was done, he built in Rome a great temple in honor of the Sun-god.

But his work in the East would not have been finished so long as Zenobia and Palmyra remained to mock him. He knew that for him the end was not yet in sight; the desert that lay between Emesa and Palmyra had still to be crossed.

Emesa lies on the western edge of the desert, Palmyra some eighty or ninety miles due east. Now Zenobia would have the advantage; even in retreat she and Zabdas would know how and where to pause, how to spare their troops, keep them fresh and fit for the task that lay ahead, and above all, how to use the friendship of the nomad tribes who were always on the look-out for plunder.

The length of time Aurelian would have needed to cross the desert to Palmyra has been estimated at about a week, under normal conditions. But a desert is unpredictable, especially when oases have been pre-empted, and men's mouths become parched for lack of water. One must also be constantly on guard against nature's dislike of interlopers and her efforts to be rid of them. Her troops are sun and wind and sand, but she can also marshal hunger and thirst. All this Zenobia had known from childhood and little of it could Aurelian have absorbed during his previous campaigns, carried on as they had been under such different conditions.

He had clambered with his men over mountains, waded streams, and besieged cities, but desert warfare may have been somewhat new in his experience. He would have been appalled if he could have foreseen how easily the Bedouins could turn wind and sand against marching men. He was not left long in ignorance.

Alexander Baron in his novel, *Queen of the East*, published in 1956, has painted a graphic word-picture of what seven days in the desert did for the most seasoned Roman army the third century had ever known. Six-deep, chanting their favorite marching ditties, they swung along behind their silver eagles, helmets dangling from their belts, glad to feel the wind on their heads. "A week later," Baron writes, "they plodded in silence, strained dark faces glimpsed within a moving wall of dust."

The wind had become a furnace gust. It stung their eyes; it rasped their flesh; it choked their throats with dust; it filled their hearts with undying hatred for the woman they had come to fight. She swam before their hot eyes; she raced with the Bedouins on their swift camels that appeared and disappeared in clouds of dust; she snatched the food from their mouths; she slaughtered their beasts; she and her Bedouins kept the whole camp in an uproar night after night; how they hated her! "She haunted the army like a spirit . . . from the underworld . . . nervous sentries claimed they had seen her in the night."

Aurelian did not hate her as his men did. The days passed like a dream; he was conscious of only one thing, a consuming desire to get his hands on her, crush her to bits—even that, he knew with a sick feeling in the pit of his stomach, would not help the hundreds of corpses he had to leave behind for the vultures to feast on.

Their week of torture ended the day before they reached the outskirts of Palmyra. The wind had gone, the Bedouins had gone, and Zenobia no longer haunted their dreams. The following day, the men strained their eyes ahead, each eager to be the first to catch a glimpse of the tall palm trees and the springs of cool, refreshing water they protected.

The palm trees were gone, cut to their roots. But the springs still bubbled up. Throats parched with thirst, the men fell on their knees beside the water. A foul smell assailed their nostrils.

BOOK THREE

ZENOBIA AND AURELIAN

"And so Aurelian . . . held Zenobia in chains."
FLAVIUS VOPISCUS OF SYRACUSE

. *Bas-relief of the third century, supposed to be Zenobia, but probably the goddess Astarte.*
Courtesy of the National Museum, Damascus, Syria.

6. El Khasna, often called Pharaoh's Treasury, Petra, Jordan.

Young boy. Bas-relief on third-century sarcophagus, Palmyra. Courtesy of the French Arche-ogical Institute, Beirut, Lebanon. Photograph by Jean Starcky.

XIV

A Message from Aurelian

The struggle between Zenobia and Aurelian for control of the East had already been costly on both sides. Though we have no figures to turn to, men and beasts must have died in their thousands, even before the fearful desert march in which Aurelian's losses must have far exceeded Zenobia's. Emesa and Daphne and Antioch had taken their toll; his army was no longer the splendid fighting machine it had been; the men were disgruntled and, what was more serious, they were frightened. Aurelian was accustomed to taking the temperature of his men; he always knew when it reached the boiling point. He had meant to encamp near the springs. Now he knew that would be impossible.

To lay siege to Palmyra at once was also impossible; yet that would be the only way to bring down the temperature of his men, who were spoiling for booty and for women. To besiege Palmyra would be more costly, Aurelian warned the Roman Senate in his first communication to them after crossing the desert. Zenobia would have the advantage of being able to fight from behind her walls. If he set up his camp too far away from the city, he would be an easy target for the swift nomads; if he went closer to the walls, he would be an easy target for Zenobia's sharpshooters, whose proudest boast was that no one of them ever missed his man.

We do not know where Aurelian finally pitched his camp, perhaps between the springs and the walls. He may not have known at this time that Palmyra had plenty of water, stored in underground reservoirs, and that inside the city there was at least one spring. Water would not be a problem for the citizens.

A Roman camp was a carefully regulated affair, constructed according to definite specifications that seem to have allowed of no variations. Legionaries remained in service for a twenty-year period, seeing their families, if they had any, only at infrequent periods. A man's camp was his home; when he moved from one to another, he found himself in familiar surroundings; he knew who he was and what he had to do. It was comforting, Aurelian knew, especially after a captured city had provided plenty of women. And so the first necessity when the army arrived in a new place was to set up the camp. This time, Aurelian probably drove his men to work at top speed, and promised them extra rations and free wine as soon as they finished.

The camp was a great square bisected with streets that ran north and south and east and west, each legion in its own quarters, hospital tents with doctors ready to hand, disciplined and orderly throughout.

A Roman legionary was paid almost nothing, yet out of that little he knew that deductions would be made, not the least of which would be the cost of his own burial, if he lost his life while in service. To supplement the pittance that remained, he had to depend on loot from the conquered cities. But the loot was not all his; it had to be shared. The Imperial treasury had the first claim, then came the officers, last of all the legionary. No wonder that Aurelian's men had clamored for the destruction of Tyana.

No one could have known his men's demands better than Aurelian; he had destroyed city after city without compunction, sold the inhabitants on the spot, often to the soldiers themselves, who would later re-sell them at double or triple the original price. And Aurelian knew that his men would expect him to follow the same procedure at Palmyra, the wealthiest of all the cities in the Fertile Crescent, the proud city of Zenobia.

Aurelian was faced with a dilemma: he wanted Zenobia, but he wanted her alive. And he must have felt in his bones that she would never surrender, even if he battered her walls to pieces. He had heard that she claimed descent from Cleopatra, and all Rome knew how Cleopatra had died. Aurelian did not want anything like that to happen with Zenobia.

The dilemma Aurelian found himself in did not, of course, prevent him from carrying on a vigorous siege of the walls. His engineers built larger and stronger battering-rams; his director of operations had burning faggots tied to spear-hafts and catapulted over the walls. Zenobia's soldiers often caught them and hurled them back, but now and then soldier, spear, and blazing faggot toppled backward inside the walls. Nothing had any effect upon Palmyra's defenders. Zenobia's men jeered at him from the walls; her sharp-shooters picked off his soldiers as though they were flies; and it was rumored that she herself, though no one ever saw her, was as good a shot as any archer.

During the early weeks of the siege, Aurelian's greatest problems, aside from persistent rumors of an attack by Sapor's Persians, were his commissariat and the Asian climate. He had other problems, too. He had to keep a constant look-out for the desert tribes who, as he soon learned, were accustomed to renew their water-supply from Palmyra's outside springs. He had also to keep open his line of communication with the now friendly city of Emesa, upon which he depended for supplies to eke out what the Syrian country people grudgingly brought him. Prices were rising fast, too. And Aurelian was too experienced a commander not to know that as soon as his men felt the pinch of privation, they would rebel and take the usual way out, assassination. Then all the plunder would be theirs, including Zenobia and her children; he seems to have believed that she had more than one.

Troublesome reports about Zenobia kept drifting to his ears; that the Nabataean merchants who had made Palmyra's fortune kept their caravansery stored with food and goods of every kind. They were as fiercely independent as their ancestors had been and as their Queen still was. They would never surrender, even if their Queen did. Their Zenobia was not only attractive; she was clever and ingenious, and the merchants looked up to her; she even understood why tariff laws were necessary. Soon he heard other reports.

Zenobia was capable of great physical endurance. Though she enjoyed marching on foot with her soldiers, she usually rode a horse or a camel; she detested litters, and used a carriage only on state occasions. In a drinking bout with her generals, she could hold her own. Pollio adds, with a touch of humor, that she drank with Persians and Armenians only to "get the better of them." She was not fond of ostentation, but at her banquets she used "vessels of gold and jewels, and she even used those that had been Cleopatra's."

No such costly vessels have been found in the excavations at Palmyra, but they were not unknown in the luxurious East. An entire dinner service, each piece studded with jewels, that formerly belonged to the Sultan of Turkey has been on view for some years in one of Istanbul's museums. Zenobia's dishes may have resembled the Sultan's.

Third-century mosaics found in Daphne show the kind of food Zenobia and her guests may have eaten: fish on a silver platter, artichokes, pigs' feet, boiled eggs in cups, a joint of ham with round bread cakes to eat with sliced ham, a roast fowl or so, and, of course, plenty of wine.

While trying to discover all he could about Zenobia, Aurelian may also have learned of an old Nabataean custom that prevailed at drinking bouts, when a chief entertained those whom he wished to honor. The chief always served his guests with his own hands. Did a feminine chief follow the same custom, Aurelian wondered?

Each guest was warned at the beginning that he was strictly limited to eleven goblets, and one final drink served in a golden beaker. Afterward, if he could stay on his feet, each one must sprinkle on the altar in the inner courtyard a handful of frankincense. Vopiscus says that Aurelian was a hard-drinking man, but he must have wondered whether he could keep up with Zenobia if she followed the ancestral custom at her banquets.

To sprinkle frankincense on an altar would have met with Aurelian's approval; he probably meant to go at once to the great temple of the Sun he had heard so much about; it would be his first act of worship in Palmyra—after he had caught Zenobia, naturally.

If he could only breach those thick walls and get his hands on that rich city. He need not fear assassination if he could fill his soldiers with food: food and wine first, then women and gold, or perhaps gold and women.

The walls of Palmyra bristled with armed men; sharpshooters, javelin-throwers, war-machines, and what Aurelian's spies told him were terrible engines that could throw huge boulders to great distances. Angered by critics at Rome who wanted to know why their Emperor did not get on faster with one who was after all only a woman, Aurelian wrote a curt letter to the Senate.

"There is as great a force of the enemy as if I had to make war against a man, while she, because of her fear and her sense of guilt, is a much *baser foe*." He enumerates Zenobia's weapons: stores of arrows, spears, stones, machines that can even "hurl fire." He closes his letter, however, by saying the gods will truly bring aid to the Roman commonwealth, for they have "never failed our endeavors."

Aurelian's mention of Zenobia's "fear and sense of guilt" is ambiguous. He may be referring to her rebellion against Rome and her determination to create a free and independent kingdom for her young son, Vaballath. Or perhaps he intends to hold her guilty of her husband's murder, and fearful of punishment if she falls into the Imperial hands. It is also difficult to decide whether the letter really reflects Aurelian's state of mind, or whether the sentiments are those of Vopiscus.

Day after day the siege dragged on. And day after day Zenobia's sharpshooters, with deadly aim, picked off the men who drove the heavy battering-rams against the walls. Finally the soldiers rebelled, and slaves were substituted. They too were picked off. Fire-machines burned the survivors. The machines had long snouts that belched fire down on the struggling slaves. Their screams began to haunt Aurelian's sleep.

But gradually the situation began to change. Defectors from Palmyra began seeping into the Roman camp. Aurelian had them brought before him, examined them, tortured them, tried in every possible way to discover whether they were spies. As far as he could determine, all who drifted into camp were really defectors; they brought tales of disaffection in Palmyra: food was giving out, the water in the reservoir was failing, and morale was low.

From these tale-bearers Aurelian now began to hear palace gossip. The philosopher Longinus was constantly with the Queen. The fellow was a teacher; he had come to teach her children, but he was improving her Greek, too; she preferred it to honest Latin. Longinus attended all her council meetings and spoke his mind on every subject. The thing did not make sense. But then nothing about Zenobia made sense to Aurelian, and this irritated him.

One day he heard something that passed the limits of belief. What he had heard before was incredible enough. Now since Zenobia's biographer has told us what appears to have been common knowledge, unless he was drawing largely upon his own imagination, there seems to be no reason why Aurelian should not have learned what Pollio found out from his sources.

According to Pollio, then, Zenobia was an extraordinarily continent woman. "Such was her continence, it is said, that she would not know her own husband save for the purpose of conception. For when once she had lain with him, she would refrain until the time of menstruation to see if she were pregnant; if not, she would again grant him an opportunity of begetting children."

Pollio also tells us that the eunuchs who served in Zenobia's palace were of "advanced age," and that her attendant maidens were few in number. We do not know whether these maidens were free-born or slave girls bought for palace use. The chances are that they were slaves. That eunuchs should have formed a part of the royal household should not surprise any one familiar with the East. We read of one instance where a Roman father, whose daughter had married a man of high rank, had a great number of young men castrated for her service, that she might have servants befitting her new rank.

Aurelian, we imagine, would have asked how many children Zenobia had. Someone may have given him the same information that we get from Pollio, that she had three sons, and that the two younger ones, Herennianus and Timolaus, she dressed in the purple robes of a Roman emperor when she brought them to public gatherings. Pollio adds that Zenobia attended these gatherings "in the fashion of a man." The manner "of their death," he continues, is uncertain; "for many maintain that they were killed by Aurelian, and many that they died a natural death, since Zenobia's descendants still remain among the nobles of Rome."

No daughters appear in either Pollio or Vopiscus. The names of three (Faustula, Julia, and Livia) appear in a nineteenth-century historical romance by the Reverend William Ware, written in the form of letters from Lucius Piso (a senator) in Palmyra to a friend at Rome, which hints that Piso will eventually marry Zenobia.

Pollio's use of the word *liberis*, commonly translated children, may, it is true, have been intended to cover both sexes. The historian Zonaras, whom Tillemont calls a "bad authority" says that Aurelian married one of Zenobia's daughters and gave the others to noble Romans. A late Christian source mentions one daughter as living in Rome with Zenobia.

Aurelian would surely not have cared to think of Zenobia as the mother of a daughter; there would have been no place for a daughter of hers in the plan that he must have been slowly shaping in his mind. This plan, though, might depend upon whether Zenobia was guilty of her husband's assassination. No one whom Aurelian questioned seemed to believe that the Queen had had any connection with Odenath's death. Even the soldiers who hated her most absolved her of guilt. Those who had seen her on the walls of Palmyra said she did not look like a murderer.

Captured nomads said defiantly that Aurelian would not dare punish Zenobia, no matter if she had killed her husband; they insisted that even if Zenobia did not know her parentage, all the desert tribes did. Her father had been a great Ras, a desert chief with many wives and many sons. From time to time he needed daughters to use in sealing contracts with neighboring chiefs. The girl-child, Bath-Zabbai, had arrived when she was not needed. The Ras tried to get rid of her, but she was hidden away and grew up with the numerous boys in the household. That, said the nomads, accounted for her unusual gifts: hunting wild animals, shooting to kill, enduring all hardships, and yes, bearing children only when she felt ready.

Aurelian tried hard to catch sight of Zenobia on the walls. Occasionally he seemed to hear a voice the soldiers said was Zenobia's, and he had a feeling that she was often up there on her wall looking down at him and laughing. But, so far as we know, Aurelian never actually saw Zenobia in the thick of the fighting.

Vopiscus tells us that at some time during the siege of Palmyra an arrow wounded Aurelian; he does not say how or when it happened. Though Vopiscus only mentions the wound once, and Pollio not at all, we do not know whether it was serious enough to influence Aurelian's decision to try to end his attempt to take Palmyra by storm.

Tradition relates that one day Aurelian was standing near a section of Palmyra's wall when he heard a rough voice shout down to him. An armed guard was jeering at him because his battering rams could not breach the walls.

Beside Aurelian stood one of his sharpshooters.

"Sire," the man said softly, "would you like to see yonder ruffian dead at your feet?"

Without waiting for an answer, the sharpshooter fitted an arrow to his string and drew his bow. An instant later, the guard lay twitching at Aurelian's feet.

How long Aurelian remained camped there below the walls fruitlessly trying to breach them faster than Zenobia's engineers could repair them, neither Vopiscus nor Pollio states. Vopiscus says that finally, "exhausted and worn out by reason of ill-success," Aurelian ordered the siege held up for two days. Then he wrote a letter in Greek, soldier-Greek, perhaps, for we know that he was not an educated man, and said it should be sent the following day to the Queen. In his mood of discouragement, he may have thought the peace party in the city would be influential enough to persuade Zenobia to surrender on the terms he offered. Or he may have been obsessed by fear of losing Zenobia.

"Of this letter," Vopiscus writes, "I have inserted a copy."

"From Aurelian, Emperor of the Roman world and recoverer of the East, to Zenobia and all others who are bound to her by alliance in war. You should have done of your own free will what I now command in my letter. For I bid you surrender, promising that your lives shall be spared, and with the condition that you, Zenobia, together with your children shall dwell wherever I, acting in accordance with the wish of the most noble Senate, shall appoint a place. Your jewels, your gold, your silver, your silks, your horses, your camels, you shall . . . hand over to the Roman treasury. As for the people of Palmyra, their rights shall be preserved."

So wrote Aurelian, the peasant boy of Sirmium, to Zenobia, who, in spite of two reverses, seems to have been confident of holding Palmyra.

XV

The Fatal Letter

For the first time in weeks, Palmyra awoke to an unnatural still-ness. No one knew Aurelian had given orders that for two days the siege was to be lifted. Zenobia and Zabdas must have been as sur-prised as everyone else. One can easily imagine how speedily the city streets filled with wildly excited people. No longer were their ears shattered by the heavy boom of Aurelian's battering-rams; no longer need they dodge the blazing faggots, then rush to quench the starting fires.

Rumors flew from mouth to mouth: Aurelian's wound was seri-ous; he had a high fever; he was on his death-bed. The rumors grew as they spread. No one knew what to believe, Zenobia and her generals least of all. Even their spies were baffled.

The following day brought an announcement from Aurelian; he wished to send ambassadors to the Queen, if she would promise to safeguard their entrance and their exit. Since the biographers have neglected to tell us how Aurelian sent his letter to Zenobia, it seems reasonable to assume that traditional arrangements would have been necessarily observed.

In earlier days a definite procedure was followed before petition-ers were allowed into the presence of an Eastern monarch. The petitioners presented themselves at the entrance to the outer court, were examined and, if passed, proceeded to the entrance to the inner court, where they were again examined.

The Queen of Palmyra, faced with Aurelian's proposal, we assume would, then, have fallen back upon this earlier custom, whether it was still effective or not. To protect the monarch still further, his throne, though it faced the second entrance, stood with its high back against the rear wall of the palace, that no assassin might creep behind and knife his master.

To protect himself still further, the monarch had soldiers posted on the flat roof of his palace. Zenobia, if her counselors insisted on this additional precaution, would have had a detachment of her archers posted above her head. Her archers seem to have already created such fright among the Romans that the very sight of them ranged along the waist-high parapet would have been a protection in itself.

Thus, we may take the liberty of imagining, the stage may have been set for the appearance of Aurelian's ambassadors, bearing the letter he had written asking her to surrender to him before it should be too late.

Zenobia would not have received Aurelian's ambassadors alone. Her counselors would have been with her: Longinus, Zabdas, Vorodes, and of course her Greek secretary Nicomachus, upon whose unlucky head much of Aurelian's rage was later to fall. There would have been others present, too, lesser officials and caravan owners, who must have been as powerful in Palmyra as the merchant class of medieval days in Florence; to this the numerous statues the merchants of Palmyra set up in the Grand Colonnade testify.

Though "children" appears in Magie's translation of Aurelian's letter to Zenobia, the original text uses neither *liberis* (children) nor *filiis* (sons), merely the possessive pronoun *tuis* (your). And so Vopiscus is no more help to us than Pollio is. Pollio, however, seems convinced that the two younger boys outlived their father and that it was in their names that Zenobia held the "imperial power."

Vopiscus, as usual, disagrees with Pollio: "it was in the name of her son Vaballathus and not in that of Timolaus or Herennianus that Zenobia held the imperial power which she really held."

If the rumor of Vaballath's death in 271 is false, then when Aurelian was besieging Palmyra, the boy-king would have been in his sixteenth year, old enough to have taken his legitimate place as his father's successor. Whether he did or not remains unknown.

Judging from the coins that were issued immediately after his father's death and that bear his portrait, Vaballath was a fragile child. His resemblance to his mother is striking. Mother and son have the same delicate features, the same air of fragility which, in Zenobia's case, is contradicted by the strenuous life we know she led. Though no biographer or historian, so far as I know, has drawn attention to the fragility so evident in the child's portrait, we may have here a clue to the otherwise strange omission of his name in all accounts of his parents' activities. Whether he was a sickly child or not, he must have been alive in 271 when Zenobia had those coins issued at Alexandria and at Antioch. They bear the titles of *Imperator* and *Augustus*. To bestow such titles upon her son was, naturally, construed at Rome as an act of rebellion, and made war between Aurelian and Zenobia inevitable.

Our imaginary scene in the inner court of Zenobia's palace might, then, have included three young princes, but of this we cannot be sure. No daughters, if there were any, would have been present. Pollio tells us that Zenobia had "very few attendant maidens." Whoever they were, upon this occasion they, too, would have been absent.

Flanked by her counselors on her right and her secretary on her left, ready with his notebook, Zenobia received Aurelian's ambassadors. There would have been two of them, with a detail of soldiers to guard them. A current joke in Rome today explains why the picturesque *carabinieri* always patrol in pairs: "One can read and one can write."

Whether Aurelian's ambassadors were both able to read and write does not matter, they had eyes in their heads and were certain to have been instructed to use them to good advantage. What their reaction was to the splendidly attired Queen of Palmyra, protected by lines of archers on the roof, we do not know, though it would be easy to guess. But we can be quite sure that they would have been given no opportunity to approach the Queen and deliver in person the roll of parchment one of them carried. Nicomachus would have come forward, received the roll, and held it for his mistress.

We next see Zenobia alone in her private chamber. She is seated at her small inlaid table, the parchment roll in her hand. Hesitant to open it, she delays, as we all do before what may prove unpleasant; finally she breaks the seal. The first sentence would have brought her bolt upright in her chair.

"From Aurelian, Emperor of the Roman world and recoverer of the East, to Zenobia and all others . . ." Blunt and discourteous! She was an Augusta. He could not possibly have thought that to omit her titles would put her into a compliant mood. But then he was only a peasant and ill-bred, even though he had become Emperor of Rome. And certainly not until he conquered Palmyra, could he call himself "recoverer of the East." Perhaps his spies had not told him that her people called her Queen of the East, or had called her, she may have thought ruefully, before she had had to abandon Antioch, flee across the desert, and enter her own gates, almost as a refugee. But against him the very desert had turned!

She would have stayed in Antioch to fight him, if that wretched Paul with his theological hair-splitting had not so divided the city that Zabdas feared she might be treacherously attacked. Zabdas had been right, as usual; she could not have risked it; she had to think of Vaballath. In a sudden burst of rage, Zenobia snatched up a figurine from her table, and hurled it against the wall. It fell in pieces on the floor. She shrugged her shoulders and laughed. She would not break so easily. She would still see her son enthroned before her own time came to join his father in the After World.

Meanwhile, here was Aurelian, this peasant's son who was Em-

peror of Rome, waiting outside her walls for an answer to a letter
that commanded her, the Queen of Palmyra, to surrender her city.
In future, he went on to say, she was to live wherever he should
decide.

"You, Zenobia . . . shall dwell wherever I, acting in accordance
with the most noble Senate, shall appoint a place."

Overbearing and conceited, how could he expect her to trust him,
an Emperor who had had coins struck with his portrait on one
side and Vaballath's on the other, encouraging her to believe in his
good faith? Now he was promising to guarantee the "rights" of Palmyra's people. Well, she would not be duped again.

She would not surrender; she would fight him with her bare
hands. She was young; he was old. Her spies assured her that he
must be over fifty, anyway. (Actually Aurelian was nearer sixty);
he could not last much longer. She would win back all he had taken
from her during the last four years. Apollo's oracle had called him
a falcon; he had swooped down upon her fast enough, but he had
not caught her napping. She would get in touch with her Bedouins
again.

Enraged though Zenobia must have been by Aurelian's demands,
she surely would have remembered how often Longinus had told
her not to risk her cause by antagonizing Aurelian; he was not like
his predecessors. His soldiers boasted that he had once killed forty-
eight men in a single day. He had murdered his own daughter, some
gossips said; others said no, not his daughter, she was still alive;
he had had his niece put to death.

Vopiscus, though he admired Aurelian for his military genius,
cites many instances of his cruelty. He allowed his soldiers to loot
and burn houses, slaughter men, women, and children in the streets,
and leave evil-smelling charred bodies behind to spread disease. He
was equally severe with disobedient soldiers. Vopiscus has recorded
one especially frightful example.

Roman commanders often had found it necessary to billet soldiers in private houses. Once a soldier wronged the wife of his host.
Aurelian ordered the soldier's feet tied to the tops of two trees,

forcibly held down, and the trees released. The body was torn apart. Whether Aurelian was imitating Alexander the Great, who is said to have punished a soldier in the same way, we cannot know.

Zenobia's hunting days and her years of warfare must have inured her to cruelty, but nothing in her history suggests that she would ever have loved brutality for its own sake or would ever have ordered such a horrible punishment for any soldier of hers.

This morning, as Zenobia sat alone in her chamber reading and re-reading Aurelian's letter and thinking about her own reply, she may have remembered that Longinus, shortly after he came to her court, had warned her that the new Emperor had one single thought, to unify the vast Roman Empire. Palmyra would be his chief target; to avenge Odenath's assassination would be only an excuse.

A man like Aurelian, Zenobia must have realized, might well believe that she had conspired with Maeonius to kill her husband. But, even if he thought so, he had no right to call her to account.

Zenobia was not the kind of person to remain inactive long. A decision once taken would have been speedily transformed into action. And so we may be sure she would now have summoned Nicomachus and ordered him to send for Zabdas, Vorodes, and Longinus to come at once to her throne-room.

Pollio states that it was "rather in the manner of the Persian kings that she received worship." This should mean that those who came into Zenobia's presence would prostrate themselves, as cardinals and other high churchmen, upon certain occasions, still do before the Pope. But Pollio lived in the fourth century, when the Emperor Diocletian had introduced eastern fashions into conquered Palmyra. In Zenobia's day, men kept their heads covered, and stood erect in the presence of majesty. The Persian Sapor had ordered Odenath to appear "flat on his face," but Odenath had not obeyed.

Seated on her throne, Zenobia receives her advisers. On her right stands Nicomachus, notebook in hand, on her left an armed guard, in front, the three men, each standing at the correct distance of three paces before the throne. The two military men would have been helmeted and armed, but Longinus would have worn his long-sleeved philosopher's gown.

We have no description of Zenobia's throne, nor do we know what she is likely to have worn upon such an occasion as this. But since the marble plaque that Bounni found and identified as representing the goddess Astarte was first thought to represent Zenobia seated upon her throne, the sculptor may have modelled Astarte's throne upon Zenobia's. The goddess is seated in a high-backed arm-chair, flanked by what appear to be fluted columns; on her left stands an attendant.

Astarte and her attendant wear tall circular crowns. Both are richly dressed in ankle-length gowns, held in at the waist by tightly rolled cords that reach almost to the lower edge of each gown. Astarte wears heavy necklaces, earrings, and embroidered sandals, only one of which is visible. To any one who compares Astarte's rather heavy features with the delicately beautiful face that appears on Zenobia's coins, Bounni's identification of the plaque as portraying Astarte and not Zenobia will seem fully justified.

But we have left the real Zenobia waiting too long. However she was dressed, we know that she would have worn her helmet and that her great jewel would have rested on her forehead.

We have no actual evidence that a consultation such as we are imagining ever occurred, but there are enough hints in the biographers and the historians to make it fairly certain that Zenobia sought advice before she answered Aurelian.

Vopiscus asserts that Nicomachus wrote the letter in Aramaic just as Zenobia dictated it and afterwards translated it into Greek because Aurelian's demand had been written in that tongue. According to Vopiscus, Zenobia's letter contained "more pride and insolence than befitted her station"; he adds that her object was to "inspire fear in Aurelian."

The authorship of Zenobia's letter has long been a matter of dispute. Some scholars have suggested that Longinus may have inspired it, or may actually have written it. Others feel that Longinus may have tried to dissuade Zenobia from even answering such a letter as Aurelian's was, or if she felt she had to reply, to soften her wording. Whatever the truth, surely discussion would have preceded the writing.

Aurelian's demands were clear; he asked for everything, jewels, gold, silver, horses, camels, Zenobia's person, and the persons of her "children." In return, he promised that the citizens of Palmyra should keep their "rights."

"Conquered people have no rights," some one would have observed, as Nicomachus read the letter aloud.

"The right to starve," another might have replied.

"The food situation is already serious in Rome. No food can come from there," Longinus must have reminded them, for he was in constant touch with other countries, Egypt, Greece, and Italy especially. Bread, he could have told them, was strictly rationed. Once a month each person received his allotment, and paid nothing for it, either in money or in services. The ration was not sufficient, though, and people had to supplement it as best they could. As a result, thieving had greatly increased.

To alleviate the situation, Aurelian had announced that he would soon increase the ration, by using the revenues he had now acquired from his re-conquest of Egypt. This, Zenobia knew from her own treasurer to be true; he had told her that the money she needed so badly to keep her army fed and provided with weapons was no longer coming in from Egypt. Aurelian had also promised his people that when he returned from Rome with Palmyra's treasures stowed away in his baggage-train, he would give each citizen two pounds of gold. To keep such an absurd promise, Zenobia knew he would have to melt down every gold and silver statue in Palmyra and in Antioch and in every other city he had conquered.

He had promised not to loot Antioch and Emesa, if the citizens would surrender quietly, but he would be obliged to break those promises if he fulfilled his promises to Rome. All Palmyra's golden days of past prosperity, all that Zenobia had hoped to do in the future, Aurelian now intended to destroy. A hard-hearted and arrogant man, Zenobia must have concluded, a man who would stop at nothing to achieve his desires. And from what she had heard, apparently he had fixed his desires upon her, Zenobia, the Queen of Palmyra. He must be mad.

It is a pity that we have nothing in writing from Longinus to which to turn, at this particular moment while Zenobia's answering letter is under discussion, to learn what Longinus himself thought of Zenobia, of her mental ability, of her character, and of her integrity, so important to us in trying to decide whether she could have been guilty of the charges that have been made against her. Longinus must have tried to teach her the true meaning of the Greek word *Arete,* so ineptly translated by the Latin *Virtus,* but whether she grasped its full truth we cannot, without more evidence, be expected to know.

The discussion in Zenobia's throne-room must have gone on and on. Should the letter be answered or ignored? If it was to be answered, what wording should be used? Contradictory phrases swirled about Zenobia's head. Nicomachus struggled frantically to catch them and transfer them to parchment. Zenobia watched and listened. When the argument reached a stalemate, Zenobia, we may imagine, reached into the girdle-pocket that always hung beside her dagger, and brought out a small gold coin; it was one of those that showed Aurelian's head on one side and Vaballath's on the other. A good likeness of the Emperor, people had called it when the coin was first issued. Zenobia looked closely at Aurelian's pictured face. Hard-hearted and arrogant, selfish, too, probably.

Vopiscus would have agreed, but only partially, with Zenobia's verdict. The following letter which Vopiscus includes in his biography of Aurelian shows another side of the Emperor. The letter is one that Aurelian wrote to an officer of his:

"Restrain the hands of your soldiers. None shall steal . . . each shall be content with his allowance. Let them get their living from the booty taken from the enemy and not from the tears of the provincials. . . . Let them keep their pay in their belts and not spend it in public-houses. Let them wear their collars, arm-rings, and finger-rings. . . . Let them be attended by the physicians without charge, let them give no fees to soothsayers, let them conduct themselves in their lodgings with propriety, and let anyone who begins a brawl be thrashed."

None of this would Zenobia have known that day in her throne-room when she turned over the coin to look at Vaballath's portrait. She should have begun training Vaballath long ago. Odenath had always taken Herodian along on campaigns.

With a swift movement, Zenobia flung the coin to the floor. It spun round and landed at the feet of Zabdas. Startled, he bent down and looked at it. Vaballath's head was uppermost. Zabdas picked up the coin, careful to keep the boy-king's head upright. Nicomachus waited, stylus in hand. Zenobia and Zabdas were staring with unwinking eyes at each other. An almost imperceptible sign passed from one to the other.

On Zenobia's forehead her great jewel danced briefly, then was still. Neither Zenobia nor Zabdas would ever surrender to Aurelian. The letter would go its way.

"Write, Nicomachus," Zenobia ordered.

ZENOBIA'S LETTER

"From Zenobia, Queen of the East, to Aurelian Augustus. None save yourself has ever demanded by letter what you now demand. Whatever must be accomplished in matters of war must be done by valour alone. You demand my surrender as though you were not aware that Cleopatra preferred to die a Queen rather than remain alive, however high her rank. We shall not lack reinforcements from Persia, which we are even now expecting. On our side are the Saracens, on our side, too, the Armenians. The brigands of Syria have defeated your army, Aurelian. What more need be said? If those forces, then, which we are expecting from every side, shall arrive, you will, of a surety, lay aside that arrogance with which you now command my surrender, as though victorious on every side."

Longinus, many think, could not have inspired that fatal letter. He was too gentle and scholarly a man, trained to look carefully at all sides of a problem, to take the middle road whenever possible, and not to be hasty.

Vopiscus comments on Aurelian's reaction when he read Zenobia's letter: he "felt no shame, but rather was angered." We have no record that Aurelian sent a second letter. His reply to Zenobia's "insolence" was to take immediate steps to cut off all aid from other rebellious peoples for the beleaguered city. Some of them, by a liberal use of money, he brought over to his side, others he forced back into the desert.

Soon Zenobia stood alone.

XVI

Zenobia Seeks Help

Aurelian wasted little time over Zenobia's letter. Angrily, yet reluctantly, he ordered the siege renewed. Once more the boom of battering-rams assailed Palmyra's ears; once more blazing faggots started fires in the city.

Palmyra, so far as we know, had never been besieged before, even when the Sassanid Persians were overrunning the Fertile Crescent. For as the Roman Empire declined, the Persian had risen and spread westward, until it engulfed all except a few stubborn cities, which had managed to retain their freedom. The most stubborn had been Palmyra. And so, when Aurelian found that his blazing faggots could not terrify the citizens into surrender, he must have changed his method of attack.

To build enormous wooden towers, put them on rollers, fill them with soldiers, and move them up to a city wall was a favorite device often employed in the East. To guard against these towers, the defenders would construct a moat, across which the besiegers would have to throw a bridge to enable them to land on a wall and engage in hand-to-hand conflict.

Though we have no evidence that Aurelian used towers, or if he did, where he got his material, it is probable that he did resort to towers, because the cost of the prolonged siege in both men and money was making the Roman Senate uneasy.

During her years of warfare Zenobia must have learned how moving towers operated, even if she and Odenath had not used them—and apparently they did not—when they were trying to reduce the walls of Ctesiphon. Since then she had realized that even if they had breached the city walls, they would still have had to batter down Sapor's palace.

Today we may know more about the great palace at Ctesiphon than Zenobia did, for its huge vault was still standing in 1919 when the British captured Baghdad. We do not know whether moats encircled the walls of Ctesiphon, but we do know that during the Trojan War the Greeks protected their seashore camp by building a wall and a moat on the landward side.

Zenobia, since she obviously knew the part Sarpedon had played in the Trojan War, must also have known how the Greeks turned their moat into a death trap for the attacking Trojans. Since we have assumed that Aurelian may well have employed moving towers against Palmyra, we may also assume that Zenobia, as soon as her spies had told her, early in the pursuit, Aurelian might use siege-towers, sent orders to Vorodes to prepare a moat outside the city walls.

Before the Desert Gate, which Zabdas thought would be the first point of attack, the moat was wider than before the other gates. The bottom of this moat Zabdas had reinforced with gravel and small stones; then into it he had driven spears, hafts down, points uppermost. This had been the Greek device.

In the Battle of the Ships, the Trojans threw temporary bridges across the Greek moat. By the third century of our era the prototype of the medieval bridge—drawn up and down by chains, had probably developed to provide an easier mode of entrance and exit from walled cities. Such bridges were common in the days when men had to protect themselves against possible assault. If then Zenobia had provided Palmyra with a moat, she must have had a bridge with chains to manipulate it. And surely she would have had some of the links in the chains loosened just enough to make them too weak to support the weight of a tower. When the moat had been filled with water to keep the spear points from glinting in the sunshine, the bridge was carefully hauled up. Zabdas stationed archers on the walls at either side of the gate, with the fire-spouting machines at a little distance away. All would then have been ready to receive the great tower lumbering across the plain toward the Desert Gate.

Suddenly the tower stopped. Darkness fell, the swift dark of the East. Zabdas had flares set at intervals on the walls, and the long night vigil began. Nothing happened. At daylight the next morning the tower again began its slow journey. Soon it was close enough for the defenders on the walls to see that the wide platform on its top was crowded with spearmen, slingers, archers, and other fighting-men.

When the tower came within shooting distance, Zenobia's archers began to pick off the enemy. But the places of those who fell headlong from the platform were instantly filled by others, as the tower kept moving slowly, inexorably forward to the water-filled moat.

From his place of concealment on the wall, Zabdas was to wait until the tower was opposite a designated place on the drawbridge before giving the signal to the men to lower it. The moment came when from the tower platform a heavy ladder began to slide out. Slowly the ponderous tower trundled forward; as soon as its front rollers were on the bridge the ladder slid farther out and hooked itself to the wall. With exultant shouts the Romans swarmed out on their ladder. Zabdas waited until the first wave had almost reached the wall. Then he gave the signal. The tower staggered; the ladder lost its hold, plunged downward, and hurled its load of men upon the hidden spears. The tower staggered again, lost its balance, and crashed down on the screaming men.

Arrows and fireballs quickly finished off the few survivors who had tried to save themselves by clinging to the wreckage.

But Aurelian built other towers and filled them with men from his seemingly inexhaustible troops. Day after day they attempted to scale the walls, and day after day the towers crashed into the

177

moat. In Palmyra, though the faint-hearted cried aloud for peace, peace at any price, their cries went unheard in the rush to defend the city. Men raised long ladders, women and children climbed up, to hand over to the half-naked, sweating men hot oil or scalding water to dash into enemy faces. Zenobia seemed everywhere at once, darting through a rain of arrows, helping to send scaling-ladders backward into space, and smiling grimly as she saw men fall from their ladders and crash into their mates below.

Aurelian kept urging the city to surrender. He promised again that he would spare the citizens if they would deliver their Queen to him, and with her the officers of her army. But many a wealthy merchant had no faith in Roman promises; he gathered up his family and whatever goods he could take, and fled from the city by secret ways and under cover of darkness.

All business was at a standstill. For months no caravans had been able to enter the gates. The Romans always halted them and forced the drivers to unload their beasts and hand over everything. The camels they either kept and used for transport or killed them for food. In Palmyra wealthy families complained about the shortage of spices and the exotic foods they had grown so accustomed to in the prosperous past that they now felt they could no longer live without them. Some succeeded in obtaining permits to visit relatives outside, saying they could bring back food. Of course they never returned. The countryside, alarmed by the constant inroads the Roman commissariat made upon their dwindling food supplies, flooded into the city to seek safety behind her walls.

To see the country people pour into Palmyra would have gratified Aurelian. More hungry mouths for Zenobia to feed, and less food to put into them would turn the balance in his favor. Palmyra would then surrender, and he could take that stubborn Queen and the rest of his richly earned booty and go home. Meanwhile he replenished his food supplies from the outlying farms that over the years had grown prosperous on land reclaimed from the desert. Here sheep and goats were to be had for the taking.

Zenobia, naturally, would have been aware of the risk she ran in accepting the terrified country people, but she could not have closed her gates against them. Day by day they poured into the besieged city, and day by day hunger clawed at men's vitals. Zenobia had hoped that scarcity of food in the countryside would compel Aurelian to give up the siege. But the men on the walls reported that food kept coming regularly in great desert convoys from the cities and towns that Aurelian had conquered and that were now required to supply his needs. However strong their sympathy for their besieged friends, these people had no choice but to bring Aurelian whatever he demanded.

Fresh rumors now began to circulate through Palmyra. People whispered to one another that the Queen was still a foreigner; she is not one of us, they said. The Romans have no quarrel with us. They want to restore the caravan trade as much as we do; they are rich; they will give us money, and we can rebuild our houses.

So the talk must have run, as in every besieged city, when a man's stomach argues with his head, and when a mother sees her children fighting with each other in the street over a crust of bread. Soon civil war would break out, more terrifying to Palmyra's polyglot people than surrender to the Romans.

Zenobia had now ruled her city for some five years. Though she had had to be absent for considerable periods and had had to leave many things to Vorodes, her administration had been steady and firm, and Vorodes seems to have ably seconded her. Her biographer states that she was so economical that she was sometimes accused of avarice. As a result, she had had enough money in her treasury, after the defeat at Emesa, to pay for another army; but without resorting to compulsion she had found it impossible to gather one together, and so she had had to retreat, knowing, as she must have, that her people had lost the desire for conquests so far from home.

One by one, the cities she had added to her growing empire had gone over to Aurelian. Forced to retire within her walls, she had realized that though her people would fight to the end for their homes and their families, as she was doing for Vaballath, some at least were beginning to think they had been better off as a free city under Rome. They did not know, she must have thought sadly, what freedom meant. And yet they were, most of them, of Arab descent.

While matters were still in this uncertain stage, word came that Sapor was dead. His son Hormizdas was now the king of new Persia. Remembering that shortly after Odenath's death Sapor had suggested his son as a suitable husband for her, Zenobia now began to think seriously of seeking help from Hormizdas. He had some years of experience behind him, he had already served as a governor during his father's administration, and so far as Zenobia had been able to discover, he had not yet taken a wife—a concubine or two, perhaps, but that need not stand in her way. She could manage a Persian husband; anything would be better than being given over to Aurelian.

Shortly after the news of Sapor's death, Zenobia's spies reported that Aurelian had persuaded the nomad tribes to exchange their long friendship with Zenobia for Roman gold. Whether this meant that whatever help Palmyra had been receiving would go to the Romans no one could be quite sure. On the heels of the first report came another. The troops that Sapor, before his death, had dispatched to relieve Palmyra had been turned back by Aurelian, again with Roman gold.

Zenobia again summoned her counselors.

Pollio tells us that Zenobia was a prudent person. Perhaps before meeting her counselors, she may have slipped out of the palace to examine her tariff list and calculate how she stood financially before she finally decided to seek help from Hormizdas. Near the southern gate of the caravansery had stood, ever since she had come to Palmyra as a child-bride, a tall marble slab. In Aramaic letters, it set forth Palmyra's whole tariff list.

In 1881, this marble slab, or stele, discovered in excavations that were being carried on south of the caravansery, was taken to Russia and put in the Hermitage Museum. Its inscription says that the Senate of Palmyra had decreed on April 18, 137 to engrave on stone certain changes in the tariff laws. The stele, according to

Starcky, is about five feet wide and contains more than four hundred lines of text, divided into four panels. The first panel, written in Greek and in Aramaic, refers to the new laws covering taxes on exports and imports, on landed property, and a special tax levied on those who used spring water for their gardens. It is likely that Zenobia's interest in this tariff list was concentrated on figuring how much of the year's income she could afford to offer Hormizdas, if that became necessary. The salt tax was, she knew, a government monopoly, and it composed a large part of Palmyra's income.

Still figuring, she may have noticed some carved figures on a nearby cult monument. A male figure, in Parthian dress, was flanked by strange-looking animals. The animals, seated on their haunches and each with a paw uplifted, were gazing up at their master as if begging to use the short, stubby wings with which each was equipped. For, without permission, they could not fly, since each was chained to the master's staff, tightly held in his hand.

We do not know which of Zenobia's officials served as her tax-collector. Under Odenath, Vorodes had had to perform the duties expected of an official during the absence of his superior. Generally, such men were appointed by the Emperor: they had control, to some extent, of the army; they collected the taxes; they felt the pulse of the community, and reported their findings to the Emperor. The status of Vorodes seems to have been slightly different. For example, there is no evidence that he ever acted as a tax-collector for either Odenath or Zenobia. Probably Zenobia appointed her own official. If she needed advice, though, she may have turned to Vorodes.

To make a decision is one thing, to convince others of its wisdom is quite different, especially if one does not explain the thought process that has led to the decision. And not to explain any more fully than she had to seems to have been characteristic of Zenobia. She must have formed the habit, after her husband's death, of acting as far as possible on her own, not because she considered her judgment superior to that of her advisers, but because she usually had sources of information that were not available to either Zabdas,

Vorodes, or Longinus. And she had decided, as a last desperate effort to save her city, to take what gold and jewels she had and go in person to Hormizdas in Ctesiphon.

Dusk was falling when Zenobia took her final step. She sent word to Vaballath's attendants to dress their young master in full armor and escort him to the door of her throne-room; she would meet him there. She looked approvingly at him when he appeared. Though his silver helmet, topped with bright feathers, his silver breastplate, long baggy trousers, striped blue and red and tucked into army boots, may have made him seem older than his years, he may still have retained the look of fragility we have seen on the gold coins Zenobia had had struck shortly after his father's death.

If Zenobia's counselors were surprised to see the boy-king enter the throne-room with his mother and stand beside her high-backed throne, no one of them would have shown curiosity or alarm, though all knew he was attending the council for the first time.

Her counselors were all present, standing as usual in a straight line three paces away from the throne: Longinus in his simple Greek robe, Vorodes and Zabdas helmeted and armed, and Nicomachus with his notebook. All, except possibly Vaballath, knew that, in spite of Aurelian's recent successes, to which he might soon add the conquest of Palmyra, the Roman Empire was closer to a breakdown than it had ever been. The facts were there for anyone to interpret. The frontiers Rome had established were too extended; local recruiting had barbarized the legions; and the earlier feeling of cohesion under one all-powerful ruler was being lost.

But Palmyra, too, was on the verge of a breakdown—for lack of food, and this Aurelian may have known as well as Zenobia and her counselors did. Some food had got through the Roman blockade, but not enough. And all present in Zenobia's throne-room that summer evening knew that when the animal population of a city has finally disappeared into human stomachs, the end is near.

Calmly, Zenobia informed her counselors of her plan: she would go in person to Ctesiphon and propose to young Hormizdas that this was the moment to ally himself with Palmyra against Aurelian.

Strong, concerted action might yet save the East from succumbing to the power of Rome. She would point out to him that Rome needed the East more than the East needed Rome, that without the caravan trade Rome would lose the West and fall a prey to the uncivilized barbarians from the North.

Zenobia's counselors must have listened to her in unbroken amazement. Every man there knew that their Queen spoke the truth. But to let her start off alone that very night—as she proposed— was unthinkable. She should remember the humiliation the former King, Sapor, had inflicted upon the Emperor Valerian, and that, though the Roman world had cried out against the atrocity, only Odenath had tried to call Sapor to account, and had been grossly insulted for his effort.

Her treasury was not yet empty, Zenobia, with a glance at Vorodes, may have reminded her council; she could offer a good sum to Hormizdas, and her own person, if necessary—better that than surrender to Aurelian, as he had demanded in his letter.

It is unforgivable of Zenobia's biographer not to have given us any inkling of the conversation between the Queen of Palmyra and her counselors on the eve of her valiant effort to save her city by seeking help from the distant city across the Euphrates. Pollio does not even mention her effort; Vopiscus dismisses it in a few words; Zosimus is more interested in explaining why she took "female dromedaries" than he is in her gallantry.

We must now return to Zenobia's throne-room, where we shall surely find the counselors wrangling with one another, half hearing their Queen as she states first that if anything should happen to her, they must remember that Vaballath is their monarch, then that she will ride her swiftest dromedary. No, her horse will not be a better mount; her dromedary can cover as much ground in one day as the swiftest horse in five or six, and it is only sixty miles to Doura on the Euphrates; she can easily cover that distance by daybreak.

Some member of the council, and we cannot take the responsibility of putting the words into his mouth, may have suggested that the Queen's mission might be successful, that Hormizdas might consider an alliance with Palmyra an excellent opportunity for revenge. Twice in a span of fifty years, Roman armies had attacked and destroyed Ctesiphon. The first time they had razed the city to the ground; the second time they had sacked it, killed great numbers of people, and carried off one hundred thousand prisoners.

Some of her advisers may have reminded the Queen that Sapor had flown into a passion when Odenath had presented him with costly and rare gifts. She must not make that mistake with Hormizdas. He, like his father, might hurl into the sea whatever she presented to him.

Some one else may have reminded her that she and Odenath had captured Sapor's wives and concubines and all their jewels, too; that Odenath had given them to Herodian, and that now they were hers.

Her counselors would have also reminded her that even after she reached Doura, the nearest crossing point for the Euphrates, Ctesiphon lay a great distance to the south; five days' journey in all, and meanwhile Aurelian might succeed in breaching Palmyra's walls. Naturally, every one knew that if the Queen insisted on going, no one could forbid the venture. Yet on one point, all must have stood firm: she must on no account go alone.

Finally Zenobia gained her council's full consent, though not approval, to leave Palmyra as secretly as possible and with a small number of armed men speed across the desert to the Euphrates. There the men would find a boat and take her across the river into Persian territory.

Though all accounts agree that Zenobia made this desperate attempt to seek help from Persia, there is no agreement about Vaballath. According to one tradition, he went with his mother and, presumably, was captured with her. It would seem far more likely that the boy-king remained in Palmyra.

XVII

Trial at Emesa

Zenobia, Vopiscus explains, chose female dromedaries because, being fleeter-footed than males, they could be expected to outrun Roman pursuers mounted on horses. How a party, even a small party mounted on camels, could escape the Roman sentries and speed away through the desert we do not know. Some one has suggested that they crawled out through a disused water channel. But they could scarcely have smuggled their dromedaries through with them. It seems more probable that friendly Bedouins provided them with camels outside the walls; clothed in Arab dress and mounted on camels, they could have been just another desert group.

How soon Aurelian learned that his hard-sought prey had escaped him, we do not know. It has also been suggested that one of Palmyra's many prostitutes, known to Aurelian's officers, came boldly to the Roman camp and announced that the Queen had fled from the city. Perhaps the informer gave Zenobia a good lead. All that we know is that the mounted soldiers Aurelian dispatched, with orders to capture the fugitives, did not overtake them until they reached the Euphrates. As to the exact spot where the soldiers caught Zenobia, there is no agreement. Tradition relates that she was jumping into a boat to cross the river. Pollio and Vopiscus merely say that she was captured. Zosimus says she succeeded in getting to the other bank before Aurelian's men caught her.

Alexander Baron makes a good story out of Zenobia's capture. Aurelian, in Baron's version, went with his pursuing party. This is credible. Even a trusted officer might have taken the risk of tricking Aurelian; he could have reported that the Bedouins had concealed her, or that her boat had upset, drowning her and her companions, and that the current was too strong for him to retrieve her body. The rest of Baron's story seems a trifle far-fetched, even allowing for Aurelian's frustration and understandable anger, and perhaps some fear of assassination if Zenobia escaped the punishment his soldiers longed to visit upon her.

When Aurelian caught Zenobia, Baron imagines, he tied her hands, attached a rope to her, mounted his horse, and set off, forcing her to run behind him. When she fell, as of course she must, he dragged her. His later treatment of Zenobia—at Antioch—did not lacerate her body, but it must have inflicted a wound upon her spirit from which—one would think today—no proud woman could ever recover.

Baron does not let Aurelian drag his captive all the way back to Palmyra. After a time, he halted his horse, had his prisoner hoisted up in front of him, and rode on with the still defiant Queen perched uncomfortably close to his horse's neck. And so they rode through the desert, the Emperor of the whole world, as Aurelian styled himself, and Zenobia, the Queen of Palmyra, in complete silence.

Biographers, historians, and Baron seem unconcerned about the fate of the other members of Zenobia's party. If there were others, perhaps Aurelian relieved his feelings by having them all killed, there on the river bank.

Since we do not really know how Zenobia was captured and brought back to Palmyra, we shall accept rather than Baron's account the general belief that the first meeting between Aurelian and Zenobia occurred in the Emperor's tent outside Palmyra. What happened there we do not know. Nor do we know how long Zenobia remained with Aurelian before he took her back to Emesa. We do know, though, that as soon as the citizens heard that their hitherto invincible Queen was in Aurelian's hands, the whole defense collapsed.

The peace party had triumphed. Vorodes and Zabdas surrendered the city and themselves on condition that Aurelian spare the lives of the citizens and not allow his soldiers to plunder their houses or their shops. Other leaders including Longinus and Nicomachus, must also have surrendered. At Emesa all had to stand trial with the Queen.

When the terms of Palmyra's capitulation had been met, Aurelian himself entered the conquered and humiliated city. He is said to have gone first to the temple of Bel, where he gave thanks to the god for granting him his hard-won victory. He then appointed, according to Vopiscus, a certain Sandarion to act as military governor. Zosimus, however, whose account is fuller and perhaps less trustworthy than that of Vopiscus, says that the new governor's name was Apsaeus. Aurelian also left a garrison of six hundred archers billeted in Palmyra to help the governor restore order.

The new governor seems to have pointed out that he could not possibly control the city if Aurelian held his trial of the Queen and her supporters in Palmyra, whether inside or outside the walls. The Queen had risked her life for her city; it was not her fault that she had failed. Emesa, he may have suggested, was the nearest place for a trial.

Before he could take his prisoners with him to Emesa, Aurelian had to engage in mopping-up operations. How long a stay this meant in the vicinity of Palmyra our sources do not make clear. However long it was, we assume that Zenobia remained a captive at Aurelian's headquarters; he could not have imprisoned her anywhere else without risking her life at the hands of his men.

But since Aurelian seems not to have tried to wrest from the Persians those parts of Mesopotamia and of Armenia that they controlled, the mopping-up operations may not have taken long. Aurelian may have merely made sure that Persia would not interfere with Palmyra's present status as a subject city, and then have started

187

on his way back to Emesa, on the first leg of his long overland journey to Italy and Rome.

Perhaps we should let Vopiscus have the last word before we reach Emesa: "And so Aurelian, victorious and in possession of the entire East, more proud and insolent now that he held Zenobia in chains, dealt with the Persians, Armenians, and Saracens as the needs of the occasion demanded."

It is a pity that our ancient writers have left us in ignorance of the many details we should like to have before we leave Palmyra: for example, Aurelian's impression of the beautiful city he had wanted to conquer but not destroy. He must have known that Palmyra had been Hadrian's favorite city, and that he and other Emperors had contributed to her beauty. Now we should like to know how much destruction Aurelian saw, what plans he made with the new governor for rebuilding the broken houses, and, most important of all, what steps he took to make the people understand that all he asked of them was obedience to Roman law and religion.

Aurelian entered the temple of Bel, that we know, but did he enter other temples, at or near the caravansery, and pay his respects? Did he visit the City of the Dead, outside the city limits, and feel a premonition that he would not live long enough to enjoy the fruits of his victory over the East, that after his death men would praise him for completing the task he had set himself, the unification of the Roman Empire, but that few would speak of him with affection?

All this and much more we should like to hear.

To piece together into a clear account the various events that followed the overthrow of Palmyra is not easy. Aurelian appears under a new title, *Parthicus Maximus*, which is taken to indicate that he spent some time in operations that made him the undisputed master of the Fertile Crescent, but whether he engaged in these operations before or after he held his court trial at Emesa nothing indicates.

Nor do we hear anything of Vaballath, whether Aurelian captured him and took him along or killed him, as Pollio thinks. All we are told is that Aurelian left Palmyra some time during the summer of 272. This seems reasonable since he would not have wanted to cross the Taurus Mountains after the snows had begun.

And so, across the desert Zenobia went, not astride her favorite Nubian, not on camel-back, perhaps on the straw-covered bed of a jolting wagon, fettered, no doubt, as though she were the meanest of African slave girls. Weary and heartsick after her futile attempt to seek help from Persia, she must have tried to sustain herself with the hope that her Bedouins would rescue her before she reached Emesa. That was unlikely, for Aurelian probably rode beside her prison-wagon. He may have relaxed somewhat as they neared Emesa, though he would still have feared his men.

Pollio must have learned something of the attitude of Aurelian's men, for he tells us that when Aurelian reached Emesa, "there arose a terrible uproar among all the soldiers, who demanded Zenobia for punishment."

And, when we recall that Zenobia doubtless knew the various kinds of punishments for which Aurelian was famous, we must admit that even her stout heart may have quailed, not only for herself, but especially for Vaballath, whom she had taught to call himself King of Palmyra. If he were still alive, Aurelian might try to force him to testify against his mother, perhaps lead him on by cunning questions to denounce her as his father's murderer. Zenobia, upon entering Emesa, now Aurelian's city, could have been sure of nothing except that in some way she must escape.

Again the details we long for are missing in our sources. We should like to know how Emesa's people received the Emperor to whom they had so recently submitted, whether they sympathized with the plight of a Queen whom they had formerly admired, and how they took the news that Longinus, their most famous fellow-citizen, was Aurelian's prisoner. And we should like to know how long Aurelian waited, after his arrival in Emesa, before he brought up his prisoners for trial. He may have waited to discover, through his spies, how the people of Emesa felt about their erstwhile Queen, and about Longinus, too.

The little we know about what has been called a trial inclines one to think that the word, with its modern connotations of judge and jury, is a misnomer. From our point of view, there was no actual trial. We should remember, though, that in the Roman Empire of the third century the Emperor combined in himself the functions of judge and jury, and that from his verdict there was generally no appeal. The power of the army was enormous, it is true, but it was an illegal power.

The trial seems to have been held in Aurelian's official quarters in Emesa, but whether he had encamped, as before, outside the city, we do not know. Aurelian probably wore his red general's cloak, thrown back over his shoulders and exposing his steel breast-plate with the flamboyant eagles of Rome incised upon it. Helmeted and booted, a sword at his belt, gold bands encircling his upper arms, Aurelian would have been a fine figure of a man, and Zenobia, despite her circumstances, might have thought so in a small corner of her mind. Perhaps, woman-like, she regretted that she could not stand before him in her usual queenly attire, instead of bruised and bedraggled, with unkempt hair and bare, shackled feet. Yet, if Pollio is right when he calls attention to her great dark eyes, to her teeth like pearls, and to her unusual beauty, Aurelian, who was a passionate man, must have had difficulty in restraining himself. But restrain himself he had to, for Zenobia's counselors and other friends were there in the tent with her, and unless they, too, were fettered, they might have sprung upon him.

Pollio reports a brief conversation which he alleges took place between Aurelian and his royal prisoner:

"Why is it, Zenobia," Aurelian asked, "that you dared to show insolence to the Emperor of Rome?"

"You, I know are an emperor indeed, for you win victories," Zenobia is said to have replied, "but Gallienus and . . . the others I never regarded as emperors." (The "others" were especially Claudius and his brother Quintillus who, chagrined because his soldiers deserted him for Aurelian, committed suicide.) Zenobia's answer to Aurelian's question creates the impression that she meant to flatter him; her next words, however, dispel the impression. She refers to Victoria and adds that, like Victoria, she "desired to become a partner in the royal power, should the supply of lands permit."

Pollio has failed to tell us what Aurelian replied to such an astonishing statement from a woman who should have humbled herself before the Emperor of Rome. Instead, she puts herself upon a level with him; she would share his "royal power."

These words that Pollio has put into Zenobia's mouth may well be a clue to what, according to at least one modern historian, she may have had in mind: to restore the Nabataean Kingdom to its former glory and make it a free and independent ally of Rome rather than a subject state which would eventually be crushed by the rising strength of the East. Palmyra had long had a place as a buffer state, but Rome had not had the wit to recognize that place in the entire scheme of government.

Vopiscus adds a little more to our scant information about the trial. Aurelian's soldiers were infuriated when they learned that Zenobia was not to be put to death. Probably they thought little of the Emperor's reply when they insisted on knowing the reason for what they must have interpreted as a lack of firmness.

Aurelian replied that he thought it "improper to put a woman to death." He might have added that neither had he ordered Victoria put to death—she may have died of a broken heart, when Tetricus failed her so utterly. As for Zenobia, Aurelian had other plans for her, and a rude death at the hands of uncouth soldiers was not what he had in mind.

He had also to defend himself before the Senate. To the Senate he wrote that the Emperor Claudius would not have been able to bring to a successful end his campaign against the Goths, had Zenobia not "kept guard over the eastern frontier of the Empire."

We have no record that Aurelian questioned Zenobia about her husband's assassination. This is interesting, because the charge that Pollio makes against Zenobia has never received any credit from other writers of the period, but is thought to have been the outgrowth of cruel, malicious gossip. Vopiscus says that Aurelian concentrated upon Zenobia's counselors and her secretary, Nicomachus. He accused them of having "advised her to begin and prepare and wage the war. . . ."

Vopiscus names only one counselor, Longinus. That other prominent men were being tried is certain, also that some of them were condemned to death, but since Aurelian reserved the "Palmyrene chiefs" for his triumphal procession into Rome, Zenobia's general Zabdas must have been among those who were to march with their Queen.

Longinus and Nicomachus were beheaded at Emesa. For their execution history has never acquitted either Aurelian or Zenobia. Nicomachus had done nothing except write the fatal letter that Zenobia dictated to him. (Aurelian seems to have been told that Nicomachus translated the letter into Greek and so readily believed those who attributed its uncompromising tone to him.)

Gibbon, who has tried Zenobia before the bar of history and has found her guilty, writes that Longinus calmly followed his executioner to the block. No complaint passed his lips. To the end he felt only pity for his one-time pupil who, according to Zosimus, betrayed Longinus by charging him with the full blame for her rebellion against Rome. Gibbon's comment is worth quoting in full: "But as female fortitude is commonly artificial, so it is seldom steady or consistent. The courage of Zenobia deserted her in the hour of trial; she trembled at the angry clamours of the soldiers, who called aloud for her immediate execution, forgot the generous despair of Cleopatra, which she had proposed as her model, and ignominiously purchased life by the sacrifice of her fame and her friends. . . . The fame of Longinus . . . will survive that of the queen who betrayed, or the tyrant who condemned him."

This is a harsh verdict, and one with which neither Pollio, Zonaras, nor Vopiscus would have agreed. Parker perhaps would; for he accuses Zenobia of "cowardly injustice" in singling out Longinus as the "arch-culprit." The evidence, it seems to me, supports neither Gibbon nor Parker. Zenobia's courage, according to Vopiscus, far from deserting her, when at her so-called trial Aurelian asked why she dared behave so insolently before an Emperor of Rome, led her to compare herself not only with Victoria but also with Aurelian. She felt herself the equal of the Emperor and said so frankly.

Ware, an ardent defender of Zenobia, rejects the entire accusation, based as it is upon the unsupported word of Zosimus, whom Gibbon himself characterizes as "credulous" and "partial." Why, asks Ware, when Pollio insinuates that Zenobia had some part in the murder of Odenath and Herodian, does he pass over in silence her betrayal of Longinus, if he thought she really did betray him?

Ware insists that Zenobia was never in any danger of death at Aurelian's hands, that his letter to the Roman Senate, which Vopiscus quotes, explains why he did not have her killed: she had performed valuable services for Rome by "protecting and saving the Empire in the East." Ware thinks that Aurelian really spared Zenobia because she was a woman, a "beautiful and . . . remarkable woman."

It would be helpful if we knew something about Zenobia's reaction to the execution of Longinus. It would also be helpful if we knew how the citizens of Emesa reacted. Longinus had been one of Emesa's most famous citizens. His uncle, the rhetorician Fronto, had been born in Emesa. About that there is no controversy, but there is about the birthplace of Longinus. Whether a native son or not, Longinus was a distinguished Syrian, and there must have been some reaction, unless in this crime-laden third century the minds of men had become so blunted that the beheading of even such a man as Longinus caused little stir.

But it is quite likely that, since Aurelian preferred for his own reasons to spare Zenobia, yet knew that he had to yield to his soldiers' demands or risk his own life, he was willing to sacrifice the second most important prisoner to satisfy the bloodthirsty desires of his soldiers.

Modern authorities are divided when it comes to deciding in which direction Longinus advised Zenobia to move. Some insist that he urged her to try to regain the complete independence that

Palmyra had once enjoyed. One historian feels that Longinus, "learned philosopher and man of the world that he was," must have tried to dissuade her from phrasing her letter to Aurelian in such arrogant terms. If we base our judgment of Longinus upon the authentic writings of his that have survived, moderation rather than excess would seem to have been one of his chief characteristics. And yet, as he looked back over the course of history, he must have realized that the Roman Empire under a series of dissolute Emperors was heading toward a fall, and that perhaps the time had come for the East to assert itself. Palmyra might lead the way back to sanity.

The decay of the Empire, Longinus might have known, had begun in the reign of Marcus Aurelius. Under the burden of heavy taxation, the independent farmer had been forced to become a *colonus* bound to the land, as Aurelian's father was. Unable to make a living, others drifted to the cities with their demoralizing influence; consequently food supplies diminished, purchasing power grew less and less, jobless men walked the city streets while their families subsisted on the dole.

Under Septimius Severus, army morale began to decline. Civil wars broke out. Within ninety years the Empire had eighty rulers. Few of them died a natural death. Everywhere anarchy, ignorance, and superstition undermined the morality of the past.

The anarchy was at its worst when Aurelian crossed the desert to drive Zenobia from her seat of power in the East. From today's vantage point, we can see that to dislodge a buffer state just when it was most needed, was a short-sighted move on Aurelian's part, and its later destruction, which occurred while Zenobia was on her way to Rome, may have given the first push toward the absolute monarchy which came into existence just ten years afterward and which under Diocletian became a military despotism. Then Palmyra suffered her final humiliation, for the Emperor Diocletian transformed part of Zenobia's beautiful city into a military camp, where heavy boots clumped through the colonnades so long accustomed to the soft tread of camels' feet.

We are now obliged to ask ourselves whether Zenobia was the product of her day. In other words, we wonder whether the collapse of morality had so affected Zenobia that she had lost whatever integrity she once may have had. The problem, as I see it, resolves itself into two parts: first, whether Zenobia really did name her advisers to Aurelian, and second, whether she accused Longinus of having inspired her "arrogant" letter. The problem is increased by the strange fact that no discussion of Zenobia's integrity has been handed down to us. Neither Pollio nor Vopiscus nor Zonaras, the three biographers, nor Zosimus, the historian, has concerned himself with what is, after all, more important than the inevitability of death. Longinus kept faith with himself and died; Zenobia remained alive, and would have had to live with herself, if we are to believe with Gibbon that she "ignominiously purchased life by the sacrifice of her fame and her friends." This we are at liberty to doubt, and by doubting, help to erase history's black mark from beside her name.

Baron pictures her as a distracted mother willing to lie to save herself for her children, through fear that her own death would seal the warrant for theirs. But we cannot be sure that she had any children left. We, who can look backward, know that, no matter what Aurelian wrote in his letter to the Senate, he could not have prophesied what the reaction of his soldiers would be, if he saved Zenobia. There is no question, I think, but that he chose to send Longinus to death to save both himself and Zenobia. Whether he believed Longinus guilty or not of urging Zenobia to rebel against Rome may not have mattered to him. In war, somebody has to die; Aurelian probably counted himself lucky not to be the victim.

Perhaps after Longinus was beheaded, Aurelian washed his hands, as Pilate did in Jerusalem.

Vopiscus sums up the whole sorry episode in one terse sentence: "But the woman he saved for his triumph." Aurelian's triumph was to take place in Rome, but his road to Rome lay through Antioch, where, according to the chronicler, Malalas, he made a public display of the captive Queen of Palmyra.

XVIII

The Queen of Palmyra
on Display

The sixth-century chronicler, Malalas of Antioch, who was well acquainted with local tradition, states that Aurelian displayed his prize captive, the defeated Queen of Palmyra, throughout the East. Malalas, however, names no place of display except Antioch. His description of the scene in the hippodrome, and of the cage in which Zenobia was afterward placed for a more extended public view, is as vivid as though Malalas had been an observer, instead of writing about a spectacle that occurred three hundred years earlier.

It is surprising that neither the biographers nor the historians mention the public humiliation of Zenobia, nor does Libanius. That Libanius does not include such a spectacle is understandable; he is glorifying his native city, and the show Aurelian put on for the people of Antioch would scarcely have fitted into his context. The biographers, it is obvious, were far more interested in the magnificent triumphal procession accorded Aurelian in Rome, in which Zenobia also had a part to play, and so they have ignored entirely the lesser affair in Antioch that, after all, added nothing to Aurelian's reputation.

We do not know just when Aurelian arrived in Antioch with his captives and the rest of his booty. A long cavalcade it must have been that made its way along the desert fringe northward from Emesa to Antioch: strings of loaded camels grunting and snarling, but moving steadily on behind the small donkey in the lead, oxcarts like Zenobia's but filled, unlike hers, with women and children picked up from small villages that had resisted the Emperor of Rome. Those in good health Aurelian probably sold along the way, the sick or maimed he left behind, then on and on the cavalcade would go, until one day it would pause outside the gates of Antioch.

Malalas disappoints us by not giving at least an inkling of Antioch's reaction to the arrival of Aurelian with the Queen of Palmyra in his baggage train. Perhaps Aurelian kept her concealed until the day of the exhibit; he may have held her under guard somewhere in the palace on the Orontes which adjoined the hippodrome; her chief officers, though, he would have kept elsewhere.

It seems to have been usual, on such occasions as a show in the hippodrome, for the ruling monarch to send out invitations. Probably Aurelian did not; he would surely have wanted the whole city present, if only to efface from their visual memories the impersonation of himself with which Zabdas so short a time before had tricked people into believing that he had captured the Emperor of Rome. Zabdas would now pay for that deception by being exhibited with his Queen in the hippodrome.

We do not know the date of the spectacle nor what other entertainment Aurelian offered the people. Nor do we know how the people reacted. Doubtless their reaction was as mixed as the population was. The Christians were, of course, still divided in their attitude toward the heretic Paul, whose residence Aurelian had assigned to the new bishop; some of them would have remained loyal to Zenobia, and some would not. The Jewish population, whom Zenobia is supposed to have favored, may also have been divided in their attitude, but for a different reason. Many of them may have feared another pogrom, in which they would lose, if not their lives, their hard-earned property, for they, too, may have heard of the gold Aurelian had promised his subjects in Rome.

197

Zenobia could not have been Aurelian's only exhibit, that day in the hippodrome. Like other Emperors, he would have had to precede it with wild beast fights, gladiatorial combats, perhaps provide a few executions of recalcitrant citizens, before he brought on his captives from Palmyra. For everywhere throughout the Empire, the public taste had become so jaded that only novel entertainments could rouse any enthusiasm. The chances are, therefore, that Aurelian reserved Zenobia and her chief officers for the end of the show.

Malalas does not mention the boy-king, Vaballath, or his young brothers, nor does he mention by name Zabdas or Vorodes among Aurelian's captives, yet the two officers must have been in the show, heavily manacled, and probably compelled to follow on foot behind Zenobia.

We may imagine, then, that after the preliminary shows had taken place, Aurelian's trumpeters would announce the entrance of Zenobia, once the conqueror of Antioch, now the prisoner of Rome. The golden eagles of Rome would be the first to appear, then Aurelian's colorguard followed by a detail of helmeted and armed legionaries, last of all a two-humped camel, a baggage-carrier, with Zenobia between the humps.

Malalas disposes of the whole scene by saying that Aurelian exhibited Zenobia in the hippodrome of Antioch, "riding on a camel." No eagles, no legionaries, just Zenobia on a camel. He does not even mention the captive "chiefs of Palmyra." We know they were still alive; Vopiscus tells us they were with Zenobia in Aurelian's Roman triumph. We can presume, therefore, that they were displayed with Zenobia in Antioch. Surely there would also have been legionaries, to protect the captives against any possible attempt either to rescue them or to kill them.

We must now try to imagine, since Malalas offers no help, what the spectators in the hippodrome saw when they looked at the Queen of Palmyra seated on a camel. Baron imagines her as having crawled through a disused water-channel. Then after riding at break-neck speed hour after hour on her dromedary, she is captured and dragged through sand. We cannot imagine a woman in Zenobia's situation packing a bag of clothes to take with her on that wild ride of hers to seek help at the Persian court. If she escaped from Palmyra clad in a thick Bedouin robe, which would not have torn easily, she would probably still be wearing it when she appeared on that camel in Antioch. For want of information to the contrary, we shall imagine that what the spectators in the hippodrome saw was a slight feminine figure in a soiled brown robe, its hood fallen back and disclosing the familiar features of the Queen of Palmyra.

To produce the desired effect upon the spectators, Aurelian would have chosen for Zenobia, not a swift dromedary, but an unkempt baggage camel led by a ragged Bedouin boy. On this ungainly beast Zenobia sat, her head high, a half smile on her lips. Malalas does not describe the effect upon the crowd, but surely instead of applause, there would have been a moment of stunned silence, then angry shouts.

When Zenobia reached the center of the hippodrome, her foot, accidentally it seemed, touched the camel's neck. But the creature, instead of hissing at her, jerked its rope loose from the Bedouin, and made directly for Aurelian's box. There it went down upon its knees and waited to be unloaded.

The crowd roared with joy; it was a desert trick which everyone, except perhaps Aurelian, understood. Zenobia did not move. Neither did Aurelian, but his face became mottled as the crowd, now in ecstasies, stood on their seats and yelled at him to unload his booty.

Zenobia, smiling, again touched her camel's neck. He rose and ambled back to his former place, his rope dragging behind him. The Bedouin boy, who had flung himself face down on the sand, grasped the rope and sprang to his feet.

Malalas supplies the sequel. Street loafers saw on the following day workmen erecting at a prominent place in the city what seemed to be a piece of stage setting. Soon they saw that it was a cage set on a platform, how high above the ground our chronicler does not say. In this cage Zenobia was placed and there she was kept, chained, for three days, exposed to view from all sides. Whether she had to stand or could sit on the floor, Malalas does not say. Nor does he say whether she was released at night.

To be exhibited to public view in an iron cage was not unknown to the later medieval world, and as every one knows, confinement in the stocks was often prescribed for minor offenses, especially among the early settlers in the United States. Malalas does not tell us whether any of Zenobia's visitors spat when they saw her; for in those days it was the custom to spit in the presence of evil, and some may have feared her.

The humiliation Zenobia was exposed to was little indeed, compared to the persecutions to which the Christians, both before and after these days, suffered at the hands of the Roman Emperors. A bishop was arrested and condemned to hard labor in the marble quarries; he lasted three years. Some Christians had their tongues cut out; others were roasted over slow fires, or eluded their captors by killing themselves. Zenobia was fortunate; Aurelian only wanted to break her spirit, not her body. He had uses for that.

If this humiliating episode occurred as Malalas relates it, we are led to wonder why our other sources have failed to mention it. Perhaps it was a tradition that only Antioch preserved. One is inclined, however, to doubt the veracity of our sixth-century chronicler, when he adds that Zenobia, after her three-day exposure, was taken out and beheaded. This contradicts the other well-authenticated tradition that Aurelian kept her a prisoner until after he had displayed her in Rome.

According to Malalas, Aurelian also showed his captive in other places. But if Aurelian had Zenobia beheaded in Antioch, then the "other places" were between Emesa and Antioch, and again Malalas is our only source.

Since no untoward news came to Aurelian from his deputy in Palmyra, he must have assumed that the defeated people had accepted a military government and that he could, without fear, start his overland journey from Antioch to Rome. Since after Antioch he would soon enter the pass through the Taurus Mountains, he may have shortened his caravan by selling some of the used women to the soldiers who would make them march alongside on their own feet. Their company would lighten the day's tedium, bring comfort at night, and perhaps lessen the men's grumbling over not having been allowed to revenge their dead comrades by killing Zenobia. Old Sword-in-Hand must be growing soft, they muttered. They had not even been allowed to loot Palmyra.

Exhausted though Zenobia must have been when she was finally released from her cage in Antioch, and taken back to the Imperial Palace, she was not broken. What thoughts went through her mind when she finally learned that Vaballath was not among the captives, we shall never know. For, if he had been brought to Antioch, he would surely have been exhibited with his mother. There is no evidence that Zenobia ever learned what happened to him. The chances are that whatever young princes there were, Aurelian would have had them put to death. All readers of the *Iliad* know that it was against reason to slay a father and leave his son alive to seek vengeance. Hector was killed; his son Astyanax, though an infant, had also to be destroyed. According to one tradition, the child was taken back to burning Troy and thrown from its walls. Zenobia would have known this.

Malalas says nothing about Zenobia's release from her cage. We assume that she was returned to the Palace. Twice she and Odenath had occupied the suite, and one of her attendants had always slept in the small chamber. She had recognized it when her guards had first carried her in, but she had been too tired to object. The second time she had fallen instantly asleep on the hard couch. When she wakened she was surprised to find herself lying on a bed of soft straw. Not until a jolt brought her fully awake did she realize that she was in a moving vehicle, closed on all sides with heavy leather curtains. Her hands were free; her feet were free. She felt refreshed and for the first time in weeks clean.

Some one had bathed her, had combed her hair, dressed her in a soft blue wool gown, and bound sandals on her feet. She turned over on her side and saw that she was not alone. One of her own slave girls sat on her haunches beside her. The girl touched her hand, then burst into tears. Zenobia smiled, turned back, and dropped again into sleep. The curtained wagon rolled on.

In some such way as this, Zenobia must have left her native land, never, if what we are told is true, to see it again. That chapter of her life was finished. The new chapter had started well; how it would end only we of today know.

The next time Zenobia awoke, it was to full consciousness. The past would have come flooding back: the blur of faces in the hippodrome, the blur of faces around her cage, faces everywhere. Unexpectedly one face stood out clearly, Aurelian's. It wavered, blurred, cleared, and wavered again. She put a hand up to her eyes; it came away wet. Surprised and horrified, Zenobia sat up, saw that she had frightened her slave girl, and reached for her hand.

A burst of laughter outside the wagon startled both mistress and slave. The laughter had come from the Roman soldiers marching beside the wagon; Zenobia could see them through an opening between the leather curtains. They began to talk in lowered voices; she caught a word, Taurus. She knew where she was. The air was fresher than it had been in Antioch. Soon they would have left Syria for Cilicia where Sarpedon's oracle had said she was a dove. She remembered her camel in the hippodrome and laughed.

The days slipped by. At regular intervals the wagon stopped; soldiers lifted out the captives, fed them, allowed them to attend to their private needs, returned them to the wagon, then off again, soldiers laughing and talking as they marched tirelessly on beside the wagon. Aurelian never appeared. Soon Zenobia began to wonder about him.

The food they ate came from the countryside through which the long cavalcade was passing. Zenobia knew what that meant; hungry children crying for the food their parents had had to give up to keep the Romans fed. She had taken food from them in the same way, when she had led her armies through, and had thought nothing of it. Now she saw angry faces and raised fists as her wagon passed.

On and on the cavalcade went, past Tyana, which Aurelian had not destroyed, past Ancyra, which he had, until they came to Nicaea, where Aurelian gave his men a chance to relax and rest for a few days. To enter Nicaea as a captive must have been a bitter blow to Zenobia. If her spy system had not failed her, she would have known the walls had been strengthened and have brought along her siege-engines.

We do not know whether Aurelian had a camp set up outside Nicaea or whether he quartered himself, his troops, and his prisoners in private houses, as he often did. Since Nicaea was a fairly large city for that day, Aurelian may have commandeered the governor's establishment for himself, his chief officers, and Zenobia, some private houses for his younger officers, and ordered tents set up in the public square for his men.

Vopiscus maintains that Aurelian, perhaps because of his lowly birth, never felt completely at home in the Imperial Palace of his predecessors on the throne. He preferred to live in the Gardens of Sallust on the northern slope of the Quirinal Hill. To the large villa there he had added a portico one thousand feet long which he used for exercising his horses and himself. Either place, the palace or the enlarged villa, would have been quite a change for the peasant boy from Sirmium. But Aurelian also owned a villa near Tibur where his wife and daughter seem to have spent their summers.

In neither Nicaea nor in Nicomedia, where Aurelian halted for a short time, did he exhibit Zenobia to the public. Both cities had, in past years, fought hard against invading Goths, barbaric savages with blond hair and frightening blue eyes, before whom the defenders of every city had at first fled in terror. Little by little the Romans had pushed them back and taken over the looted cities, put out the fires, and set to work to rebuild the fortifications. Now all was orderly, with Roman governors in command and Roman garrisons to call upon should the barbarians again descend upon them.

Chalcedon was the last stop in Asia; to Zenobia unknown ground, for Nicaea had blocked her way. In the busy harbor Roman ships rode at anchor, ready to transport the victorious army across to Byzantium on the European side of the Straits.

The crossing from East to West must have been attended by some disaster, because Zosimus states that Zenobia did not live to reach Rome. He thinks that she died on the way, either from disease or by committing suicide. It has been suggested that, since Zenobia's death at sea is mentioned nowhere else, Zosimus may have invented his story merely to heighten the similarity between Zenobia and Cleopatra.

Another report about the crossing is that a storm blew up and that the only survivors were Zenobia and Vaballath. There is no evidence to support any of these statements. Aurelian could not have been drowned; we know how and when he died. Zenobia could not have been lost, or Aurelian could not have held that expensive triumph of his which the grateful Roman Senate voted him and in which Zenobia was his most spectacular exhibit.

It seems more likely that Aurelian may have encountered one of those sudden storms that spring up in the Straits between Chalcedon and Byzantium and that he may have lost one or two ships. By the time the report reached Rome, the loss would have become a major disaster that caused many a family to besiege officials for recent news. News such as this has long been familiar to our modern world.

Since no one except Zosimus has mentioned that Aurelian suffered any mishap in the Straits, we are free to assume that he landed his prisoners and his booty on the European shore, relieved that he had brought them safely from the uncertain East to what Aurelian was now justified in considering the well-governed and secure West. He must have felt that soon he would be in his favorite residence on the Quirinal Hill, Zenobia within reach.

Never before, if our records are truthful, had Zenobia set foot on the European shore. She may have learned here that the princely Severi family had been closely associated with the early history of Byzantium. Septimius Severus had destroyed the city walls and put all its distinguished men to the sword. Here he had received the severed head of one of Syria's governors, sent to him that he might be certain his orders had been carried out.

These events had happened before Zenobia was born. But equally ruthless events had happened in her lifetime. For most of them, Roman Emperors had been responsible, usually in the name of law and order, but the result had almost always been that some weaker country lost its freedom. Though seldom defeated, Rome had met her match in Sapor I, who had shocked the whole Empire by resisting all appeals to free his captive, the Emperor Valerian.

Thinking of Valerian's dreadful fate must have brought home to Zenobia the humiliation she had so recently suffered at Aurelian's hands, and she must have wondered whether it could be only the preface to something worse. Sapor had flayed Valerian and stuffed his skin with straw, and she herself had rushed off to Ctesiphon to seek help from Sapor's son. For the first time Zenobia may have wondered whether Sapor might have instigated Odenath's assassination. She had no evidence except Sapor's unreasonable anger when Odenath had added gifts to his urgent request that the humiliated Emperor be freed.

Even if Sapor had only connived at Odenath's murder, what a mistake she had made in trying to obtain help for Palmyra from the Persian court. Help had come, though too late, and not through her. It was too hard a puzzle to try to solve.

How long Aurelian kept Zenobia and his other prisoners at Byzantium, neither biographers nor historians say. We know that he did finally set out, and that somewhere along the lower reaches of the Danube River he had to stop to crush another Gothic invasion from the North. While engaged in this operation, which seems to have consisted in following the usual Roman custom of settling those of the Goths, who survived, within the Roman frontiers (in this case, in northern Thrace), alarming news came to him from the East, specifically, from Alexandria and from Palmyra.

Both cities had rebelled against their governors, and in Palmyra the situation was serious.

XIX

The Fall of Palmyra

Vopiscus has included in his biography a letter that Aurelian is supposed to have written to a certain Ulpius in Rome. Though the letter is now considered a forgery, it may throw some light upon Aurelian's character. It purports to have been written after the revolt of the mint-workers, and in it Aurelian says that the gods have never granted him a victory "without some hardship." The hardship he refers to is the high cost of punishing the men his subordinate, Felicissimus, had urged to rebel. Aurelian had lost not only thousands of trained soldiers, but many auxiliary troops as well.

Aurelian might have made the same observation after he destroyed Palmyra. Felicissimus, whom Aurelian in his letter calls the "lowest of his slaves," not only betrayed the trust that Aurelian had placed in him but instigated and led the revolt. In Palmyra, after he had appointed Sandarion as governor, Aurelian had felt sure that the city would be in good hands and that the work of reconstruction and rehabilitation would proceed smoothly.

The news that came to Aurelian in Thrace may have caused him to doubt his ability to select the right men for important posts: Sandarion had not proved to be another Felicissimus, but he had been unable to withstand Antiochus, about whom a national liberation party had formed. Had it not been for the loyalty of a certain

Marcellinus, whom he had left to guard the Euphrates frontier, Aurelian would never have been able to claim the distinction of being the master of the East and the West.

The survivors of the war party in Palmyra, though they had lost their Queen and their chief officers, had quickly formed what we today would call an underground movement. They killed Sandarion and rallied around Antiochus. It would be interesting, indeed, if some day evidence were to turn up that would make the youthful Vaballath survive long enough to have become the heroic leader of that desperate movement to free Palmyra from Aurelian's clutches.

The revolt in Palmyra broke out, according to some historians, in the late summer of 272, when Aurelian, fully occupied in Europe, would be, supposedly, too busy and perhaps, with Zenobia as his captive, unable to believe that Palmyra would think of rebelling. If Vaballath, by some miracle, had escaped capture and death, he would have been an obvious rallying point for the loyal citizens of Palmyra.

The first move the rebels made was to get in touch with Marcellinus, the officer Aurelian had left behind to guard the Euphrates frontier against Persian attack. We do not know what the rebels promised Marcellinus if he would co-operate with them, probably an important post in the new government. Nor do we know whether the rebels contemplated an attempt to rescue Zenobia and reinstate her as their Queen.

Marcellinus, about whose loyalty to Aurelian there seems to have been no question, asked for time to consider what he must have known would entail great risk. If the movement failed, Aurelian would have no mercy on the conspirators, as he would regard them.

Marcellinus remained loyal. He managed to get word to Aurelian in Thrace that revolt was brewing in Palmyra. Meanwhile, the underground movement swelled to greater proportions. The first victim was the governor, Sandarion. The rebels had attacked and killed him, and with him the six hundred archers Aurelian had left as his bodyguard. According to one report, because Antiochus was a kinsman of Zenobia's, they set him up as King of Palmyra. In the fighting that swirled through the streets, we should like to think that it was here and now, not earlier, that Vaballath was killed; that he had survived to defend his city, and that only his death was the reason why the rebels chose Antiochus. This would be such a convenient way of solving the mystery which has surrounded Vaballath ever since his mother had those coins struck in Antioch and in Alexandria that brought Zenobia and Aurelian into open conflict.

Zenobia's first reaction to the news of the rebellion in Palmyra must have been a longing for her fleet-footed dromedary and her archers, that she might speed ahead of Aurelian, who had started off in haste as soon as he heard from Marcellinus, and lead her people to victory.

Unhampered by a baggage train, living off the country, Aurelian had driven his legionaries forward with such speed that even if Zenobia had had a fleet dromedary she could hardly have outdistanced them. She may have tried to send word to Palmyra to warn the city to put itself in readiness, or she may have been too closely guarded. Or she may have thought she would only make matters worse if she tried to help.

In Palmyra, Aurelian exacted a terrible revenge. He seems to have given his soldiers a free hand; they slaughtered hundreds of men, women, and children, so many that the streets are said to have run with enough blood to glut even the starving sheep dogs.

Nothing escaped Aurelian. A letter of his that Vopiscus has preserved says that the "eagle-bearers" of the Third Legion entered the temple of Bel and despoiled it. Other legionaries looted Zenobia's palace, carried away her household, her furniture, and, as one historian asserts "all her children." The loot included, according to Vopiscus, "those garments, encrusted with jewels which we now see in the Temple of the Sun, then, too, the Persian dragon-flags and head-dresses, and a species of purple, such as no nation ever afterward offered."

Without time to rebuild their shattered walls, without time to train men for adequate defense, without time to gather supplies for a siege; above all without the hoped-for assistance of Marcellinus and the garrison he commanded, Antiochus and his party had had no chance to succeed in their revolution. We do not know whether Aurelian himself participated in those terrible scenes of carnage that lasted for days in Palmyra, or whether he finally left everything in the hands of a certain Bassus, as a letter to him seems to indicate.

The letter orders Bassus to put an end to the senseless slaughter of the people, and to the looting and destruction of their houses. "The swords of the soldiers should not proceed further. . . . We have not spared the women, we have slain the children, we have butchered the old men, we have destroyed the peasants."

Some must be spared, Aurelian continues, to repopulate the city. He then orders the gold from "Zenobia's coffers," her royal jewels, and the "silver from the property of the Palmyrenes" to be used for restoring the temple of Bel to the "condition in which it formerly was." He adds that this will be a service pleasing to both himself and to the immortal gods. He will ask the Roman Senate to send out a "pontiff to dedicate the temple."

Aurelian's instructions to Bassus, Vopiscus comments, "show that the savagery of the hard-hearted prince had been glutted."

If Aurelian sent back to Thrace his fresh booty before he hurried to Alexandria to put down the revolt there, its arrival in the Thracian encampment where he had left Zenobia may have been her first knowledge that her Palmyra had ceased to exist. That Aurelian had spared Antiochus, or so we are told, would have been no consolation to Zenobia; her thoughts would have flown to Vaballath if she had believed he might have survived so long.

Alexandria has been called, without sufficient evidence, the seat of the revolt Aurelian had to put down after he had finished with Palmyra. Gibbon, for example, states that Firmus, an Egyptian merchant who claimed to be an ally of Odenath and Zenobia, inspired by the revolt of Palmyra, fired his fellows with the same desire for independence from Rome. At the head of an ill-trained militia, Firmus had entered Alexandria, assumed the purple, coined money (none has been found), and raised an army to defeat Aurelian.

That there was a revolt of some kind we learn from Zosimus, but, according to Vopiscus, Firmus seems to have made no claim to the Imperial power. He had tried to help the Palmyrenes living in Alexandria regain the supremacy which they had once held. When Aurelian appeared, as he seems to have done in an incredibly short time after the destruction of Palmyra, he arrested Firmus, tortured him, and put him to death. How many unlucky Palmyrenes suffered with their rash leader, we do not know. Another account is that Firmus was thrown into prison, where he committed suicide.

Vopiscus, who considers Firmus a minor Pretender, has some interesting things to relate about this wealthy Egyptian merchant whose various enterprises took him as far east as India. "He owned so many books," Vopiscus asserts, that he used often to say in public he could have supported an army on what his books had cost him in "paper and glue." Aurelian appears to have found among the dead man's effects two elephant tusks, each ten feet long. To these long tusks Aurelian intended to add two more and make out of them a throne worthy of Jupiter himself. On this throne Aurelian meant to place a statue of the god, made of gold and "decked with jewels" (Zenobia's perhaps), "and clad . . . in a bordered toga, to be set up in the Temple of the Sun."

The statue Vopiscus describes in such detail seems to be completely unknown. That it existed is of course possible. More interesting for the information it brings us about the life of Zenobia's century is the report that Firmus had set into the walls of his house "square panes of glass," which were held in place by pitch. This information allows us to think that Zenobia may also have had glass windows in her palace, not of course the kind of transparent glass we use today, since the process for making that had not yet been invented; but the opaque glass that vases were sometimes made of.

Though Alexandria's population did not suffer so much for its attempt to break away from Rome as Palmyra's did, Aurelian de-

stroyed many fine buildings and several of the libraries for which
the city was famous. He also razed the city walls and separated the
wealthy Greek quarter from the rest of the city.

Aurelian had now almost completed his self-imposed task of uni-
fying the Empire. He had crushed all attempts at independence
throughout the East; he had reduced Lower Egypt to its former
status as a Roman province, and no fresh trouble had broken out
along the Danube. Well content, he returned to Thrace and found
everything as he had left it. So far as we know, he neither summoned Zenobia, nor did he seek her out. She had no city; therefore
she no longer had the right to call herself the Queen of Palmyra.
Though he still had to face the Senate, his plan for Zenobia was
now clear in his mind.

A small part of Aurelian's task remained to be attended to: he
had to dispose, once and for all, of the incapable Tetricus. Though
Tetricus had betrayed his own soldiers, Aurelian had allowed him
to remain as the governor of Gaul. Now Tetricus was again in
trouble. A tribe of Germans had attacked him; his soldiers, not
relying on him to protect the country, had deserted to the governor
of a nearby province. We are not told how Aurelian got rid of the
Germans, but since we shall soon have the opportunity of seeing
Tetricus himself walking in Aurelian's parade in Rome, we assume
that the disturbance was quickly settled and that Aurelian had the
satisfaction of reporting to the Senate that East and West were now
firmly in his hands.

No record has come down to us of Aurelian's homeward march
from Gaul. Nor do we hear whether he paused in Sirmium, where
both he and Claudius had been born and where with almost his
last breath Claudius had designated Aurelian as his successor.

Modern novelists interested in the drama of Zenobia and Aurelian would have been gratified if the Roman Senate had been able
to look ahead and suggest to Aurelian that he should pause at Sirmium on his return journey to Rome. The Senate could then have
filled Aurelian's cup, not of happiness, for he could not have been
a happy man, but of deep satisfaction, by greeting him there with

the announcement that the Senators had voted him the highest honor in their power to grant: a triumphal entry through the gates of Rome.

A triumph meant that Aurelian, gorgeously appareled, would drive in his war chariot the length of the Sacred Way. His entire army, or as much of it as he should decide, would accompany him and share his glory. His prisoners and his booty would also be in the long line of march, that the whole city might be able to judge his exploits in the field.

Aurelian deserved this mark of recognition. By his recovery of the eastern provinces, by his victory over the Gauls, and by his conquest of Palmyra and of Alexandria he had not only unified the Empire; he had so increased the Imperial treasury that he was enabled to balance his budget, a feat no predecessor had for years been able to accomplish.

One of Aurelian's first acts was to advise the Senate that he wished *oraria* (handkerchiefs) to be given to the people, "to be waved in showing approval." This was an innovation, Vopiscus explains.

To Zenobia, jogging along in her ox-cart with the leather curtains that kept her safe from prying eyes, but let her hear the soldiers' talk as they marched along on either side, the news that Aurelian had been accorded a triumphal entry into Rome could not have been a surprise. The Roman Senate had voted Odenath a like honor, she knew. But she also knew that Aurelian's would outdo any other procession Rome had ever witnessed. The long train of captives and of booty would have told her that, aside from the fact that she, the Queen of Palmyra, was also a captive and almost certain to be displayed as Aurelian's chief prize. He would not show her in Rome as he had shown her in Antioch. She would probably ride in her beautiful silver chariot; her slave girl had seen it swung off the ship when they landed in Byzantium.

Huntress and warrior though she had been the greater part of her life, Zenobia was also a woman and, as the great jewel she was accustomed to wear indicates, she was not averse to adornments.

And so we shall not go amiss if we assume that Zenobia began to think of her appearance, and to wonder where in his baggage train Aurelian had stowed those possessions of hers he had stolen and sent back to Thrace.

She probably did not know that Aurelian had instructed his deputy, Bassus, to take "three hundred pounds of gold," from her treasury, all her jewels, and the "eighteen hundred pounds of silver" that had been realized from the sale of property belonging to the citizens, and use the whole of it to restore the devastated temple of Bel. If she had, she would have mourned the loss of the *cochlis* she had worn on her forehead. She probably felt as undressed without it as today many women do without their earrings.

Though the humiliation Zenobia had suffered at Antioch must have been uppermost in her mind, and though she must have brooded over it all the way from Thrace to the gates of Rome, she began to realize that methods other emperors had employed to humiliate their prisoners during a triumphant passage along the Sacred Way could not be used by a man who had risen from the ranks, as Aurelian had. He could not afford to risk public criticism. His treatment of his prisoners and his distribution of booty must meet with the approval of the populace and especially of the powerful legionaries.

Details of her trial at Emesa took on a new significance. Aurelian had never intended to turn her over to his clamoring soldiers who would have torn her limb from limb. And he had not asked her a single question about Odenath's death. Instead, he had asked endless questions about her relationship with Longinus, and in Antioch he had acted strangely whenever Paul's name had been mentioned.

Probing still deeper into her recollections, Zenobia came up with what she seemed not to have noticed at Emesa, a look in Aurelian's eyes. She had seen it in other men's eyes. Yet he had not violated her when he had had the opportunity, those nights in his palace at Antioch. If her instincts were right, she had nothing to fear; he would not humiliate the Queen of Palmyra before the critical eyes of the matrons of Rome. She smoothed the folds of the blue woolen dress and laughed. It may have been a rather shaky laugh, but creditable. After all, she was still young and beautiful, and she knew her power.

Zenobia must also have known what was common knowledge, that the slightest of mistakes on an emperor's part could cause a quick shifting of loyalty. One day an Emperor would be the darling of his people; the next day or the next, off with his head, and a new Emperor on the throne. But Aurelian's soldiers adored him, perhaps more than ever since he had allowed them to indulge in such a mad orgy of destruction that in Palmyra even he had been forced to call a halt. At this point Zenobia must have remembered the promise Aurelian had made, to give each person in Rome two pounds of gold after his conquest of Palmyra. To be sure of that, every man, woman, and child would be out on the streets to wave those handkerchiefs Aurelian had ordered for them.

Yet, however wildly the spectators waved those gift handkerchiefs, their eyes would not be focused on Aurelian, but on her, Zenobia, the captured Queen of a city that had once been the center of the world's caravan trade, and had now become the victim of Imperial greed.

XX

Chains of Gold

The custom was centuries-old and surely could have permitted no deviation, or Vopiscus would have mentioned it in his description of Aurelian's triumphal procession. It was a wise provision and, one would think, even a prime necessity in this turbulent third century when no man knew whether he would be alive on the morrow. The custom was that no conquering hero, with victorious troops at his back, should be allowed to pass through the gates of Rome until formal permission had been granted.

To this custom Aurelian, Emperor of the whole vast and intricate Roman Empire, must have had to conform. Indeed, the more successful an Emperor, the more essential was it for the city to insist that he be made to realize that he was not an absolute monarch, but that he ruled with the consent of the Senate. Those who could read the signs that pointed toward the future must have feared that the power of the Senate would soon vanish and autocracy take its place, but in Aurelian's day the Senate still held the reins.

It appears to have been late summer when Aurelian finally stood before the closed gates of Rome, an Italian summer with the sun beating impartially down upon the acknowledged master of the whole civilized world and upon Zenobia, who was, to her way of thinking, still the Queen of Palmyra. Conqueror though he was, with his long array of cavalry, infantry, prisoners, camels, horses, and ox-carts to prove his claim, he had to wait patiently outside the gates until the proper official should arrive to announce that the Senate was pleased to grant him permission to enter the city with his victorious troops and proceed along the Sacred Way to the Capitol.

The immense throng at Aurelian's back would not have been milling about in disorderly fashion; each section would have been assigned its proper place. Orders had probably been issued beforehand that the rank and file of the legionaries were to wear their new tunics with the embroidered bands, their new gold tunic clasps instead of their battle-worn and tarnished silver ones—these were the tunics and clasps Vopiscus says Aurelian had recently presented to his men. Helmets, shields, arm-bands, finger-rings, and all other metal gear were to be brightly polished, and if a man needed new sandals, they were to be issued, free of charge.

The centurions no doubt always added, when they transmitted Aurelian's orders, that Old-Sword-in-Hand would punish severely any man whose appearance or conduct displeased him.

Orders must also have been given to Zenobia's slave girl rather than directly to Zenobia herself, since Aurelian could not have been sure that she would have obeyed them. There is no evidence that any such orders were issued to a slave girl, but as Vopiscus describes Zenobia's appearance in the procession, some one had to be responsible; she could not have arrayed herself as Aurelian intended to present her to the Roman populace.

If the girl's fingers trembled when she carefully draped her royal mistress in the long ceremonial robe of heavy purple silk Aurelian had ordered her to wear, Zenobia would not have noticed it; she was searching wildly about for Zabdas and Vorodes. She had not seen them since they had been shown with her at Antioch. Even her helmet and her purple fillet edged with precious gems and in its center the cochlis she had thought never to wear again did not distract her. She wondered a little when her neck, arms, wrists, and hands were left bare. But she soon saw the reason for that. Two officers came; they pushed her slave girl aside, put a light gold collar around her neck, bound her arms close to her body with chains, also of gold, wound the chains round and round her, and fettered her feet so close together that she could barely walk. The gold collar she understood; Aurelian thought her his slave. But surely she was not to walk on fettered feet; she must be going to ride, with Aurelian or in her own chariot.

She took a tentative step, trying to put one sandalled foot before the other. She could not move. Quickly one of the Roman officers bent and loosened her chains. Suddenly the sight of the chained animals sculptured on the tariff list near her palace in Palmyra returned to mock her. She had not heeded the oracles; the animals were trying to tell her something; she had not heeded them either. She looked around again for her officers, and wondered if they were chained, too. But though she searched for them until the procession started to move through the gates, she did not see them anywhere.

Her helmet, her purple robe probably much too long for her, and her gold shackles must have soon brought her mind back to her own predicament. She began to fear she could not endure their weight if she had to walk. As the morning advanced, and Aurelian did not appear to lead the procession, she became worried.

Soon all sounds were stilled; Aurelian arrived. He was splendidly dressed in a white tunic embroidered with palm trees and a short purple cloak swinging from his shoulders. A crested helmet sat low on his head. But it was not so much Aurelian himself that attracted the attention of the waiting crowd; it was his chariot and the creatures that drew it. The chariot, emblazoned with gold, had once belonged to the King of the Goths whom Aurelian had killed with his bare hands. Four stags, each with branching antlers, were harnessed to the chariot, and Aurelian himself held the reins. Looking neither to the right nor to the left, Aurelian drove his stags to a space obviously reserved for him in front of the closed gates.

On the wall to Aurelian's right appeared a trumpeter, flanked by a civil magistrate on either side. The trumpet blared. Somewhere a child whimpered. A second blare, and silence spread over the crowd. One of the magistrates unrolled a parchment and began to read:

The Roman Senate had graciously accorded to Lucius Marcus Aurelianus, the Emperor of Rome, permission to bring his army, his captives, and other booty within the walls of the city. Long life to the Emperor Aurelian, the restorer of the East and the West, the unifier of the Empire!

So much of the formal Latin pronouncement Zenobia could have easily understood. She probably did not listen to the long string of Aurelian's titles that followed; they could have held no interest for her. Not at that time, surely, if ever.

The great iron-studded gates creaked open.

"It is not without advantage to know what manner of triumph Aurelian had," Vopiscus writes, "for it was a most brilliant spectacle."

Then he describes, with many an embellishment and many a digression, Aurelian's booty: the costly chariots, once the proud possessions of royalty, the prisoners of war both noble and common, the wild beasts, tigers, leopards, elephants, and the gladiators who will fight them. The all-powerful army is there, too, cavalry and infantry, Romans and provincials. They follow the eagles of Rome, each legion identified by its proud standard-bearer who thrusts his pennant high into the air.

According to Vopiscus, the procession was so long that the ninth hour of the day had already rung out over the excited city before the eagles reached the steps of the magnificent temple on the Capitoline Hill. Here the Emperor must pause to offer sacrifice on the altar and dedicate part of his spoils to the Sun-god.

The news that the notorious Zenobia, the Queen of Palmyra, was not dead, as had been rumored, but had been captured and kept alive must have spread days beforehand through the fine houses of Rome, through the streets, the slums, and the back alleys, wherever people congregated. And when the final report came that Zenobia in person, with those of her chiefs who had not yet been killed, would grace Aurelian's triumph, the excitement rose to an unprecedented pitch of anticipation. Aurelian deserved his plaudits, and all Rome was going to be on hand to see that he got his deserts.

No record exists to tell us how many people rushed from wherever they were when they heard the first trumpet blare. But in an incredibly short time every available place along the line of march was taken. Then, as now, people crowded their housetops, climbed trees, hung precariously from windows, and waved those new flags, as many must have thought Aurelian's handkerchiefs were. And still in the whole of Rome there was probably not space enough for all who were determined to see the Emperor with his captured stags and his captured Queen.

Vopiscus tells us that each group in the procession was made known to the spectators by a placard held high in the air "displaying the names of the nations" that composed the group. Apparently Aurelian had no placard, but no one could have mistaken his identity, since his chariot with the stags must have been the first through the gates. He was preceded, however, by a huge blond man with a red beard and little else. The placard the huge man carried stated that Aurelian had not only destroyed the Gothic King and seized his chariot and stags, but that he had killed five thousand of the King's best soldiers. Closely behind the chariot of their slain King came ten Gothic women, each in male fighting-gear. Their placard announced that they were "of the race of the Amazons."

Vopiscus adds, somewhat as an afterthought, that Aurelian had vowed to sacrifice his stags on the altar before Jupiter's temple, but we are not told whether the sacrifice was consummated.

Another chariot appeared, profusely decorated "with silver and gold and jewels." The placard told the spectators that the chariot had been the property of Zenobia's murdered husband, Odenath, who had tried to persuade Sapor to release the Emperor Valerian. Failing in that, he and Zenobia had gone to war together against the recalcitrant Persian. This recollection may have softened a little Rome's resentful fear of Zenobia.

Vopiscus wastes no words upon the third chariot. He contents himself with the laconic statement that it also was "wrought with similar care." The placard stated that the King of the Persians had presented the chariot to Aurelian. Vopiscus does not say whether the donor was Sapor or another Persian monarch.

The crowds were doubtless beginning to tire of chariots when what they had been waiting for appeared, Zenobia's own chariot. Vopiscus says Zenobia had "hoped in it to visit the city of Rome." If the people had expected to see Zenobia in her chariot, they were disappointed. Except for a Roman soldier holding the reins, the chariot was empty. Many may have thought that what they had first heard was the truth, that Zenobia had died crossing the Straits.

Actually, no one really knows what became of Zenobia after she was captured at the Euphrates River. The best informed sources, though, agree that she lived and that she walked in Aurelian's triumph. Not directly behind her chariot, however, if Vopiscus is to be believed. A modern novelist has fitted her in there. This, of course, he has every right to do, since the order of march we read in Vopiscus has little dramatic value.

The disappointment of the spectators may have lifted somewhat when the wild animals came into view. First lumbered twenty huge elephants, the wrinkled end of each beast's trunk clasping the tail of the one in front. On each huge head a trainer perched.

After the elephants came two hundred "tamed beasts." These Aurelian afterward presented to individual private citizens, that the government might not be "burdened with the cost of their food." Tamed beasts would of course be useless, since they could not be fought in the arena, as wild beasts could be. Next came tigers, giraffes, elks, and "other wild animals," also eight hundred pairs of gladiators (ten thousand, according to one account). The sight of the gladiators would have helped to quiet the crowd's impatient cries for Zenobia, who had not yet appeared.

Long lines of captives followed, mostly women and children, all with their hands tied behind them. "There also advanced among them certain men of Palmyra, who had survived its fall, the foremost of the State, and Egyptians, too, because of their rebellion." Sixteen conquered nations were represented, according to Vopiscus, who adds that all were "bearing gifts." Yet he also tells us that all were "captive, with their hands bound fast."

A large placard now identified a distinguished looking man, dressed in "scarlet cloak, a yellow tunic, and Gallic *bracis*" (trousers) as C. Pius Esuvius Tetricus Augustus, formerly a Roman senator, but now in disgrace. Those of the spectators, who knew the story of his betrayal of his soldiers, may have greeted him with jeers and insults. With him walked his son, Tetricus the Younger. Vopiscus states that afterward "Aurelian . . . exceedingly stern though he was, overcome by a sense of shame, made Tetricus . . . supervisor over the whole of Italy."

No one, so far as I know, except Ware, has satisfactorily compared Tetricus and Zenobia. Tetricus not only finally accepted the title of Augustus, but, according to Pollio, also conferred the same title upon his son. Both acts were treasonable. In battle, he not only betrayed his troops to Aurelian, but he escaped from the field, taking with him a few loyal friends.

Zenobia was young, inexperienced, though she learned fast, and ambitious, some say for herself, others for her son, who had no one else to protect his right to follow his father on the throne. History has not yet decided whether Zenobia actually intended to become head of state herself and a rival of Rome or whether she was acting solely in the interests of Vaballath.

But now Zenobia herself has at last appeared in the procession. She is on foot, walking alone behind Tetricus, a short space between them. Taller than most Oriental women, slender, with dark, flashing eyes, an imperial carriage, she must have struck every one as a woman worthy to be a Queen. Perhaps at first they did not even notice her chains, so proudly did she bear herself.

Vopiscus disposes of Zenobia in a few brief words: "And there came Zenobia, too, decked with jewels and in golden chains, the weight of which was borne by others."

It is easy to imagine the buzz of talk that must have broken out soon after Zenobia appeared, especially if Aurelian's wife and daughter were present among the spectators, as they must have been, probably seated in an Imperial box erected for the occasion. Beautiful as Zenobia was (indeed partly because of her beauty), many a person may have been ready to believe her guilty of all she had been charged with: the murder of her husband and stepson, the attempt to set up a rival state, and her dastardly betrayal of her chief adviser, the distinguished Longinus.

Pollio describes her more fully. "She was adorned with gems so huge that she laboured under the weight of her ornaments; for it is said that this woman, courageous though she was, halted very frequently, saying that she could not endure the load of her gems. Furthermore, her feet were bound with shackles of gold and her hands with golden fetters, and even on her neck she wore a chain of gold, the weight of which was borne by a Persian buffoon."

Vopiscus does not mention a "Persian buffoon." Nor does he identify the "others," who in his account supported the weight of Zenobia's golden chains. Certainly they were not Roman soldiers; they could not have so lowered themselves. Let us hope that the "others" were eunuchs from her own household in Palmyra, and not a Persian buffoon.

No further details about Zenobia's part in Aurelian's triumph have come down to us. But when we recall that his decision to sacrifice Longinus and satisfy his soldiers had not met with complete approval in Rome, and that he was also criticized for warring against a woman, Zenobia's beauty, her loneliness, and her plight must have affected differently at least some of the volatile Roman public. Her pride would have kept her head erect and her shoulders from sagging beneath the weight of her golden chains, even had they not been supported.

Zenobia may have looked fragile, but she could not have been fragile. She had long been inured to physical hardship, marching on foot, hunting with her dogs, and riding either horseback or camel-back. She would not have broken. If Pollio is right in saying that she halted frequently, she probably did so not because her gems were so heavy, or to call attention to herself, but because her shackled feet prevented her from walking as she was accustomed to.

Compassion was not one of the virtues of the pre-Christian world, as we know, and the new religion had not yet succeeded in entirely changing the ingrained habits of antiquity. It is refreshing then to find that there was in Rome at that time some criticism of Aurelian's treatment of the dethroned Queen.

The criticism levelled at Aurelian may not have been dictated by compassion, though that may well have been dormant in some people's minds, but as Pollio expresses it, by a feeling that, in giving Zenobia a place in his triumphal procession, Aurelian had honored her as if she were a conquered general. If this were the real objection, it should also have applied to the ten Gothic women in military uniform. They were being "honored" in the same way.

Aurelian, according to Vopiscus, defended himself. He wrote a letter to the "senate and the Roman people." The letter is a remarkable document. "Men are reproaching me for having performed an unmanly deed in leading Zenobia in triumph," the letter states. To our surprise, the rest of the letter is really a eulogy of Zenobia, so much so that one begins to think that Aurelian's real feeling toward Zenobia was that of unbounded admiration, and, dare one add, perhaps of love, since love and hatred might easily fulfill the Socratic definition of pleasure and pain that spring from one head.

"Therefore let those whom nothing pleases keep the venom of their own tongues to themselves," Aurelian adds in a letter in which Pollio represents him as justifying himself for not having put Zenobia to death, as his angered soldiers had demanded at Emesa. At the close of his letter Aurelian praises Zenobia for her "great service to the Roman state when she preserved the Imperial power in the East for herself; or for her children." (Pollio persists in believing that Zenobia had several children with her.)

For some of the spectators who lined the Sacred Way in Rome, the rest of the procession that came along after Zenobia had passed by may have been an anticlimax; for others, less sensitive perhaps, it may have proved more exciting than the sight of a woman in chains who probably deserved whatever fate held in store for her.

A veritable forest of great golden crowns followed Zenobia, each preceded by its placard announcing the name of the city whose pleasure it was to send a gift to the Emperor of Rome. More placards followed; they identified for the onlookers the guilds of the tradespeople, the military camps, and the "wealth of Kings." Last of all came the "entire army," and the full Roman Senate, each member in his white toga with its purple stripe. Some of them were saddened, Vopiscus adds, when they saw their former member, Tetricus, among Aurelian's captives.

Vopiscus does not say whether the four stags that had drawn Aurelian's chariot were sacrificed when they reached the temple of Jupiter. If the stags were really sacrificed, we should like to know whether Aurelian's war horses were then attached in their places. It is inconceivable that Aurelian would have climbed the Palatine Hill on foot to reach his palace. That would have reduced him to Zenobia's level, except that his feet would have been free.

So far as we know, there was no further exhibition of Zenobia in Rome. Nor do we hear anything more about the chief men of Palmyra who walked in the procession. Since the next few days were devoted to amusing the people, as was the custom, perhaps Zenobia and her chiefs were required to attend the various celebrations. Aurelian and Zenobia, seated together in the Imperial box at the theater, or at the circus, would have made a handsome couple. For, according to Vopiscus, there were "plays in the theatres, races in the circus, wild-beast hunts, gladiatorial fights and also a naval battle."

Such games, bloody as they were and in some ways as artistic and all-absorbing as a Spanish bullfight, would not have troubled Zenobia. She belonged to her day. She might even, for a few moments, have forgotten her troubles in the excitement of the arena. She was an active person, and the blood ran quick in her veins. And perhaps, if Aurelian had required her presence, he might have had the grace to have left only a token chain around her neck.

Zenobia's later history is somewhat confused. Now and then a

CHAINS OF GOLD

guide at Tivoli, where the celebrated villa of the Emperor Hadrian
has now been almost entirely excavated, will tell his party that
Queen Zenobia once lived in the villa. Though there is no evidence to connect Zenobia with Hadrian's villa, Pollio tells us that
she lived "not far away" in a villa that belonged to the Emperor
Aurelian.

XXI

The Villa Near Tibur

Tibur's modern descendant, Tivoli, has become so well known to enthusiastic tourists that its fame has almost entirely eclipsed the reputation of its equally distinguished progenitor. Built upon the extensive terraces of an ancient temple of Hercules, Tivoli lies some eight hundred feet above sea level and about sixteen miles northeast of Rome.

Today the road winds slowly upward through cypresses—said to be the tallest in Italy—groves of gnarled olive trees, and acres of vineyards. From the Belvedere at the summit you can look down upon the wide Campagna that stretches between the present-day village and the blue Tyrrhenian Sea. On clear days you can see Rome in the distance. When the wind is in the right direction, you can smell the sulphur baths five miles to the west.

Visitors who come to Tivoli expecting to find the ancient Tibur which the lyrical verses of Horace and other poets have made famous will find little to remind them of the past. The Renaissance Villa d'Este and its beautiful gardens, laid out for Cardinal Ippolito d'Este, captivate the eye and help to soften any disappointment the visitors may feel. Waterfalls and cascading fountains that would have astounded Tibur—channels had to be cut through the rocks to bring in the water from the Anio River—artificial lakes

226

and streams; nothing like this existed in the third century when Aurelian, at the close of his costly triumph in Rome, brought Zenobia to live the rest of her days in a villa somewhere near Tibur, for it was not until the eighth century that the name was changed to Tivoli.

Long before Zenobia's arrival, Tibur had become a favorite summer resort for wealthy Romans, who built here and there in the Sabine hills villas that were often more luxurious than their mansions in the city. Today the most famous—and a *must* for all who visit present-day Tivoli—is the well-known villa of the Emperor Hadrian. Though the villa has not yet been altogether excavated, its entire area is thought to have been about seven square miles.

"Her life was granted her by Aurelian," Pollio writes, "and they say that thereafter she lived with her children in the manner of a Roman matron on an estate that had been presented to her at Tibur, which even to this day is called Zenobia, not far from the palace of Hadrian or from that place which bears the name of Concha."

Though Pollio is irritatingly vague, he is generally thought to have meant that Aurelian settled Zenobia there in a villa that belonged to him. Perhaps, though we hope not, he may have removed his family from what had been their country home in order to install his beautiful captive Queen in a villa of her own. Here she lived and left her name behind her for posterity to wonder about.

A modern commentator upon the passage has substituted for Pollio's drab statement that Zenobia lived the life of a Roman matron one that paints for us a picture more in keeping with her previous place in the world's history. Zenobia lived in her villa, he writes, not as a Roman matron, but with all the "pomp that befitted an eastern princess."

For Zenobia's life in Italy, Aurelian could not have selected a better place. Hadrian's name was one that every citizen of Palmyra respected and admired. More than any other Roman ruler, Hadrian had taken such a deep interest in Palmyra that he was remembered with affection as almost a second founder of the city. Though Hadrian had long since taken his place among the Immortals, his spirit and his memory would have lived on for Zenobia in the exquisitely beautiful villa near her alien home.

Pollio does not mention the sulphur baths west of Concha, but they were doubtless as well known in the third century as they were centuries before and as they still are today. How familiar the smell of sulphur must have been to Zenobia needs no comment.

On topographical maps of Tivoli the region known to Pollio as Concha is marked *Le Fosse*, the quarries that are said to have provided building material for St. Peter's in Rome. The name Zenobia does not occur on the map.

Attempts have been made to find Zenobia's villa. It could not have been as large as Hadrian's, or surely some trace of it would have been discovered. Perhaps some future archaeologist will stumble upon it and relieve our curiosity. One investigator believed he had located the villa near a small church of the Madonna Michele, built in 1694 by the Jesuit Michele Sardelli, whose name was then used to distinguish the Madonna. We do not know upon what evidence this investigator based his identification of the villa.

The supposed proximity of Zenobia's villa to the seventeenth-century church may have given rise to a statement by a certain Bishop Terzi in *Storia Sacra* that Zenobia, while living in her villa *with* her daughter (*colla figlia nella villa di Tivoli*) embraced Christianity.

These are surprising statements. So far as I know, there is no corroborative evidence to support either claim, yet neither one is impossible. Zenobia's strong support of the so-called heretic Paul in Antioch may have been interpreted in church history to mean an ardent interest in Christianity, when her point seems to have been that Paul had a right to uphold his own belief.

It may not be too far-fetched to suggest that possibly the fearful persecutions which occurred in Zenobia's girlhood might have led her to study the tenets of the new faith and later to become, as so many aristocratic Roman women of her century did, a convert.

It is interesting at this point to note that the Ecumenical Council, led by Pope Paul, has gone on record to affirm that a person has the right to believe as he chooses. In ancient Palmyra we hear of no persecutions but neither do we hear of any Christians. Philip, the Arab, whose short reign took place in Zenobia's girlhood, is said to have been the first Christian Emperor, and Zenobia may have had some contact with him. But of this we have no evidence.

The implacable Decius followed Philip. Convinced that the new sect was a threat to the state religion which derived its authority from the custom of deifying and worshipping the Emperor, Decius bathed his empire in blood. He tried to revive the dying state religion by issuing a decree to which every Roman subject had to conform. Those who refused were severely punished.

The decree required every person suspected of being a Christian to appear before a local committee and make a "sacrifice to the gods of Rome." This meant recognizing the Emperor's divinity. To satisfy the committee, the suspect often had merely to throw a little incense upon an altar. Those who complied were issued a certificate; those who refused were arrested and imprisoned. "The apostates, of whom there were many, were released; the stout-hearted, among them the Bishops of Antioch and of Jerusalem, died in prison; and in Rome Pope Fabian was put to death."

Aware of the persecutions that Decius and then Valerian had set on foot, and that Emperor-worship was still obligatory, Zenobia, if Bishop Terzi is right in saying that she had become a Christian, would have had one of two courses open to her: to recant or take the consequences. The bishop's remark about Zenobia's daughter also needs to be clarified. If his statement can be relied upon and if our biographers are equally reliable in their statements that Zenobia had three sons (Zonaras, we recall, mentions daughters, all of whom Aurelian disposed of), then this hitherto unknown girl might have sprung from a liaison between Aurelian and Zenobia, which is not at all unlikely.

At this point we might also recall how Pollio stresses Zenobia's conjugal relations with Odenath, perhaps one of the earliest comments upon birth-control that we have. Aurelian, according to Vopiscus, left only a daughter, whose descendants, he reports, were still living in Rome while he was engaged in his research in the Ulpian Library. This daughter is the one Aurelian is presumed to have killed. Whether that report is true or false is not, however, our present concern, since those descendants are not Zenobia's. And it is to Zenobia, not to Aurelian, that many noble Roman families are said to have traced their descent.

Bishop Terzi does not mention the "children" Pollio says were with Zenobia in her exile, possibly because he had never heard of them. They could hardly have been Zenobia's by Aurelian, since the first authentic meeting between the two occurred after Zenobia's capture in the summer of 273, when Aurelian brought her to trial at Emesa. And since Aurelian was assassinated early in 275, their last meeting must have taken place before then.

Vopiscus tells us that Aurelian was a good family man, that he disliked living in his palace and preferred lesser establishments, such as his villa at Tibur, perhaps. He would not permit wealthy men to have free-born women as concubines. Of mistresses who were given their own establishments he says nothing, nor does he mention Aurelian in that connection. He does say that Aurelian was noted for his generosity to his friends.

Every year at the gay Saturnalia, which, though not a religious festival, was somewhat comparable to our Christmas, Aurelian, Vopiscus says, gave presents to his wife and daughter: little terra-cotta figurines supposed to bring good luck. His legitimate family may never have heard that Aurelian's present to Zenobia was far handsomer, a villa near Tibur. Here Aurelian may have found relief from the burden of public affairs, and here Zenobia, if she had a child to replace those she had lost, may have been content to live, as Pollio has told us, in the "manner of a Roman matron."

To round out his characterization of Aurelian, Vopiscus shows us another side of the Emperor which perhaps his wife saw, but which he surely did not exhibit to the Queen of Palmyra. Aurelian, claims Vopiscus, often invited a glutton of his acquaintance to dine at his own table, just for the pleasure of watching him eat. Once in the course of a single day the glutton devoured an "entire wild boar, one hundred loaves of bread, a sheep and a pig and, putting a funnel to his mouth, drank more than a caskful." Aurelian, too, was fond of wine, especially red wine, but he confined himself to smaller amounts.

A document that Vopiscus includes, but which is thought to have been a forgery, illustrates how little it may have cost Aurelian to provide so lavishly for his glutton, also how easily he could have supported a second household. Once when he returned from a successful military expedition, the city prefect was ordered to supply him with a daily allowance of "sixteen loaves of soldiers' bread of the finest quality used in camp, forty pints of table wine, half a swine, two fowl, thirty pounds of pork, forty pounds of beef, one pint of oil . . . one pint of fish-pickle, one pint of salt, and greens and vegetables as much as shall be sufficient."

The idyll of the Emperor and the Queen, if idyll it was, did not last long. Aurelian spent the greater part of the year 274 attending to long-neglected duties and doubtless refreshing himself by frequent visits out of town. Toward the end of the year he had to go to Lugdunum (Lyons) to quell some sort of disturbance there and then repel another barbarian invasion of the Empire by the Germans. He returned briefly to Rome, but early in the summer of 275 trouble broke out in Mesopotamia. Aided by the Sassanid Persians, Mesopotamia had thrown off the Roman yoke and proclaimed her independence.

Aurelian with his legionaries set out once more, this time for the Straits. He was within fifty miles of Byzantium when he was assassinated, apparently because he incurred the hatred of an underling by threatening to punish him for some misdeed or other. Fearing for his life, the man decided that the only way to save himself would be to implicate Aurelian in a plot against his own officers. He drew up a list of names, including his own to avoid suspicion, and read it to each officer. To each one he declared that Aurelian had made "arrangements to have them all put to death," and that the only way to save themselves was to kill the Emperor.

Vopiscus says the officers agreed, the guilty "moved by fear, the

. . . innocent by sorrow" that Aurelian was showing himself ungrateful for their loyalty to him. And so one day, in October or November, they attacked and killed their Emperor, thus adding one more name to the long list of assassinated monarchs.

"A piece of senseless intrigue," comments Parker, "robbed Rome of one of the greatest of her Emperors." Vopiscus does not put Aurelian upon quite so high a pedestal; he calls him a "prince who was necessary rather than good."

Though the Senate had long feared Aurelian because of his increasing power, the people, we are told, "loved him." Month after month the army refused to name a successor. Finally the Senate issued a decree that declared Aurelian a god, and the army, mollified, agreed to accept a new Emperor. But for six months there was no ruler.

Another report of Aurelian's death, which Vopiscus has preserved, is that certain provincial officers resented the Emperor's sternness in punishing them for the extortion practices they had been guilty of and conspired to murder him. Vopiscus adds to his first account that when the officers discovered that the underling had duped them, they gave Aurelian a "mighty tomb and a temple." Afterward they tied the informer to a stake and set wild beasts upon him.

Aurelian's widow, Severina, outlived her husband. The Roman Senate, when they were unable to find a successor for the throne acceptable to the army, acknowledged Severina as Empress and had coins struck for her in Alexandria. At the end of the six months' interregnum the Senate and the army agreed upon a Senator whose name was Tacitus.

The fact that Severina outlived Aurelian throws some light upon our matrimonial tangle. She must have been alive when Aurelian, so we are told, married a daughter of Zenobia's. Ware obviously accepts the report of the marriage because at the close of his novel he represents Piso as delighted to hear that Aurelian has married Livia, the youngest, according to Ware, of Zenobia's *three* daughters.

Since we assume that Vaballath was born in 256 and since we know that Odenath was assassinated in 267/268, we have a stretch of eleven, possibly twelve, years for two more boys and three girls to be borne by a mother who was actively engaged in warfare most of that time. The figures, I think, speak for themselves.

We must also remember Aurelian's law that forbade a man to keep a free-born woman in his house as a concubine. Aurelian could not, therefore, have taken Livia into his house (whatever her age), without breaking his own law. Nothing prevented him, of course, from setting up Zenobia in a separate establishment. Ware, though he accepts as a fact (in his novel) Aurelian's marriage to Livia, states in his notes that Aurelian would never have married a daughter of Zenobia's had he believed her mother guilty of having betrayed Longinus.

Neither the biographers nor the historians have left us with any idea of Zenobia's reaction to Aurelian's death. His successor Tacitus in a fulsome speech he made in the Senate—before he himself was elevated to the throne—said that the gods should make "good emperors invulnerable to steel," that they might not come into the power of those who "contrive abominable murder." Then Tacitus added that he could justly bring charges against the gods, "were it not that perchance they preferred to have him [Aurelian] among themselves." The speaker then proposed that Aurelian should be deified.

Since no women were allowed in the Senate House, some one, no doubt, informed Zenobia of the proposal to deify Aurelian. If, as Bishop Terzi suggests, Zenobia became a Christian, whether before or after the Senate proclaimed Aurelian a god, she would really be in serious trouble. To live forever in the realm of the immortal gods, either in the kingdom of the Sun or elsewhere, would not have been a new idea to her, but that a group of men could proclaim one of their number a god and order people to worship him would have clashed with her new faith.

The Emperor Gallienus had not been deified, as Zenobia must have known; Trajan, Hadrian, and Claudius had been, and now

Aurelian; and that classed him among the good Emperors. Vopiscus notes that in the time of Claudius a jester on the stage said that the "names and the portraits of the good emperors could be engraved on a single ring."

Nothing could be harder, as Zenobia must have been aware from her own experience, than to rule well. If she could have known that even history would be at a loss in judging Aurelian, she would probably have agreed with what many others have thought: that Aurelian, as Vopiscus reports, belongs among neither the "good nor the evil emperors . . . that he lacked the quality of mercy," the first necessity of a ruler.

Vopiscus enumerates some of the material benefits Aurelian conferred upon Rome: glass, paper, linen from Egypt; a one-ounce increase in the weight of bread; free oil, pork, and bread—he had planned to give free wine to everyone—clothing and money to the needy. His plans for the future were many and various: he had intended to buy up vast tracts of land and settle them with war-captives who were to plant vines and produce wine for Rome; he intended to "restore to the matrons their senate," apparently an organization of priestesses. Other things he forbade: purple or white boots for men, though women could wear them; commoners could not own eunuchs; a single piece of silver tableware could not weigh more than thirty pounds; unruly slaves were to be punished according to law, though once Aurelian had a slave of his put to death in his presence.

All this and much more we read in the pages of Vopiscus. Zenobia, though she spent only a few years with Aurelian, must have heard him talk often of his plans. But whether these material benefits qualified Aurelian for deification she might have felt unable to judge. Nor can we.

Parker suggests that two main causes had operated together to destroy the integrity of both Emperor and Empire, and, he seems to think, also Zenobia's integrity. These causes had been insidiously at work since the days of Septimius Severus, the Emperor with whose dynasty Odenath's family had been so closely associated.

The first cause of the disintegration in the third century was the inadequacy of the Empire's military resources. The second cause was economic, to which the personal extravagances of the Emperors and their wars contributed their full share. Aurelian's triumph, voted him by the Senate, was, as we have seen, an excellent example of unnecessary and wasteful expense. For this every man, woman, and child throughout the great Empire had to suffer.

By the middle of the century irretrievable damage to the Empire had already taken place. Emperors had risen and had fallen, cities had risen and had fallen, and everywhere lawlessness was rampant. This was the unsettled state of affairs that Zenobia had inherited from Odenath and that history accuses her of attempting to turn to her own advantage.

The situation did not improve after Aurelian's death. Ten years later the Emperor Diocletian took his seat upon the Imperial throne. During the interval five Emperors had sat briefly upon that throne. Few mourned them when they fell. Diocletian was elevated to the purple by a group of his fellow-generals who saw in him some hope for the future. But the future they visualized was not what Diocletian had in mind.

To Zenobia in her villa near Tibur, the accession of the Emperor Diocletian could have meant only one thing, the complete loss of Palmyra. For Diocletian built a great military camp in the midst of the ruined city she had loved and had fought to retain for her son.

It is tantalizing to know so much and still so little about Zenobia's life both before and after she was captured and brought to Rome. We should like to know definitely whether she had a daughter by Odenath (the odds are against it), whether she was a party to his murder, whether she was guilty of having betrayed Longinus to whom she owed so much, and finally, after all Aurelian had made her suffer, whether she fell in love with him and he with her. If so, perhaps she had a few months of happiness with him before she lost him as she had lost Odenath and her sons. And if Bishop Terzi was correctly informed about that daughter he mentions, whose father may well have been Aurelian, Zenobia would have had something left to live for.

This assumption, even if unsupported by evidence, need not contradict the tradition, which Ware follows, that Zenobia married a Roman senator, for this could easily have occurred after Aurelian's death. Those noble Roman families who, according to Pollio, traced their descent from Zenobia may, then, choose as an ancestress the offspring of a senator or the love-child of Aurelian and Zenobia.

Among the poets who thronged the Villa d'Este in the days of its splendor, there was a certain Fulvio Testi, whose political activities involved him in trouble with the authorities. Testi was born at Ferrara in 1593; he died in prison in 1646. While living at the Villa d'Este he began to write a drama about Zenobia; its purpose was to celebrate her *virtù*. As with much else in the story of Zenobia of Palmyra, his drama remains unfinished.

Author's Note

Palmyra is still being excavated. Perhaps some day more inscriptions will appear. Then we may be able to finish Zenobia's story. Meanwhile, the following books and articles may prove helpful to those who would like to read further.

Augustan Histories: Flavius Vopiscus, *Aurelian;* Trebellius Pollio, *Zenobia,* Loeb, Vol. 3, 1924.

Baron, A., (Historical Novel), *Queen of the East,* New York, 1956.

Barton, G. A., *The Archaeology of the Bible,* Philadelphia, 1937.

Bounni, A., *Les Annales Archèologues de Syrie,* Vol. 15, 1965.

Breasted, J., *Ancient Times,* New York, 1944.

Cambridge Ancient History, Vol. 12.

Dawkins, H. and Wood, R., *The Ruins of Palmyra, or Tadmor in the Desert,* 1st Ed., London, 1753.

Downey, G., *Ancient Antioch,* Princeton, 1963.

Eusebius, *Ecclesiastical History,* Loeb, New York, 1932.

Gibbon, E., *The Decline and Fall of the Roman Empire,* (The Modern Library Edition), Vol. I.

Huxley, J., *From an Antique Land,* London, 1961.

Kennedy, Sir Alexander, *Petra,* London, 1925.

Parker, H. M. D., *A History of the Roman World*, London, 1935.

Rostovtzeff, M. I., *Caravan Cities*, Oxford, 1932.

Seyrig, A. S., *Les Annales Archèologues de Syrie*, Vol. 13, 1963.

Starcky, J., *Palmyre*, Paris, 1952.

Ware, W., (Historical Novel), *Zenobia, or The Fall of Palmyra*, Boston, 1885.

Wright, W., *An Account of Palmyra and Zenobia*, New York, 1895.

Index

241